UNDER THE INFLUENCE

Pitt Series in Russian and East European Studies

Jonathan Harris, *Editor*

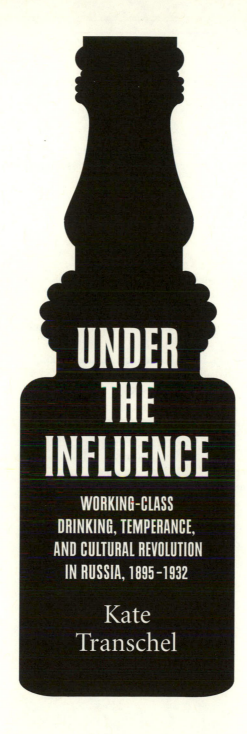

UNDER THE INFLUENCE

WORKING-CLASS
DRINKING, TEMPERANCE,
AND CULTURAL REVOLUTION
IN RUSSIA, 1895–1932

Kate
Transchel

UNIVERSITY OF PITTSBURGH PRESS

Published by the University of Pittsburgh Press, Pittsburgh, Pa., 15260
Copyright © 2006, University of Pittsburgh Press
Manufactured in the United States of America
Printed on acid-free paper
10 9 8 7 6 5 4 3 2 1

Library of Congress Cataloging-in-Publication Data

Transchel, Kate.
  Under the influence : working-class drinking, temperance, and cultural
revolution in Russia, 1895–1932 / Kate Transchel.
    p. cm. — (Pitt series in Russian and East European studies)
  Includes bibliographical references and index.
  ISBN 0-8229-4278-x (cloth : alk. paper)
    1. Alcoholism—Russia. 2. Alcoholism—Soviet Union. 3. Social
problems—Russia. 4. Social problems—Soviet Union. 5. Working class
—Russia. 6. Working class—Soviet Union. 7. Soviet Union—History
—Revolution, 1917-1921—Social aspects.   I. Title. II. Series.
  HV5513.T72 2006
  362.2920947'09041—dc22

                                          2005027954

To Donald J. Raleigh,

my mentor and friend.

Without his steady support and encouragement

my life would not be nearly as rich.

CONTENTS

ACKNOWLEDGMENTS

I would like to express my gratitude for the institutions that so generously supported the many years of work that went into this project. I received long-term travel and research grants from the International Research and Exchange Board (IREX) and the National Council for Eurasian and East European Research (NCEEER). I also received travel grants from the National Endowment for the Humanities, California State University Foundation Grants, University of North Carolina Off-Campus Research Grant, Department of Education Title VI FLAS Fellowship, and the University of North Carolina Mowry Award. None of these organizations are responsible for the opinions contained in this book.

I am also deeply grateful for the help, patience, and expert advice I received from the staffs of numerous archives and libraries in Russia and Ukraine. In Moscow, I worked in the State Archive of the Russian Federation, Russian State Archive of the Economy, Russian Center for the Preservation and Study of Documents on Recent History, Central State Archive RSFSR, Moscow Oblast Center for the Documentation of Recent History, Central State Archive of Moscow Oblast, Central State Archive of the October Revolution, and Socialist Construction of the City of Moscow. In Saratov, the staffs at the State Archive of Saratov Oblast and Saratov Oblast Center for the Documentation of Recent History aided me greatly. In Tomsk, I received invaluable advice from the director and staffs of the State Archive of Tomsk Oblast and Tomsk Oblast Center for the Documentation of Recent History. I am especially grateful to the staff at Tomsk University Scientific Library, whose expertise and kindness made my time there a joy. I also profited greatly from the insights, questions, and suggestions offered me by the History Department faculty at Tomsk State University. The staffs at the State Archive of Kharkov Oblast and Kharkov Oblast Center for the Documentation of Recent History were also quite generous with their time and support. I am especially grateful for the assistance and friendship so freely given to me by the directors and staff of the Korolenko Library in Kharkov.

I am very happy for the opportunity to express thanks to the many colleagues and friends who proffered encouragement and assistance. Don Reid, Jerry Surh, and Vlad Treml helped shape the work in its early stages. I am especially grateful to Paula Michaels and two unidentified readers who took great care in reading and commenting on the manuscript. I profited greatly from their suggestions and remarks. I thank Fran Bernstein, Greta Bucher, Bill Husband, Caroline Marks, Ed Roslov, and Tricia Starks for their camaraderie and help and for making long hours in cold archives not so dreary. My dear friend Heather Schlaff read the entire manuscript and made useful comments. Ingenious, efficient, and irretrievably optimistic, Don Raleigh offered hearty support and incisive suggestions from beginning to end.

I am forever indebted to a number of close friends in Russia. With grace and wit Lubov Obratszova aided me with difficult translations and helped me accomplish the impossible in Moscow. Her friendship and support are invaluable. Sasha Emelianenko provided unfailing support and friendship, for which I am deeply grateful. I am also grateful to Bolshaia Marina and to all of Bill Wilson's friends in Moscow, Kharkov, Kiev, and Tomsk who helped me keep trudging the road to happy destiny in all corners of Russia.

Last, but certainly not least, I owe a debt of gratitude to three very special people. Noa Price and Drew Pawlak supported me through good times and bad and gave me the courage and discipline to accomplish my goals. Without them my life would be very different. And finally, I wish to thank my husband, Dee Randolph, who suffered my trips to Russia and long hours at the computer with patience and great kindness. He also read and commented on parts of the manuscript, discussed interpretations, and pointed out errors. But best of all, he has always been my soft place to land.

UNDER THE INFLUENCE

"Drinking . . . We Cannot Do without It"

RUSSIA'S FIRST VODKA MUSEUM OPENED IN ST. PETERSBURG on May 27, 2001, in anticipation of the 500th anniversary of vodka. Situated prominently between two of the city's most popular tourist attractions—the Bronze Horseman statue and St. Isaac's Cathedral—the museum rightly takes its place among Russia's historical icons. It is no accident that it has become one of the most visited places in the city: Russians have an almost mystical relationship to drink in general and vodka in particular. Legend has it that a thousand years ago, when Grand Prince Vladimir (r. 980–1015) pondered over which faith to adopt, he rejected Islam because it imposed restrictions on the consumption of hard liquor. Whether or not Grand Prince Vladimir actually said, "Drinking is the joy of Rus' we cannot do without it," it is significant that these words are still attributed to him more than a thousand years later. Vladimir's proclamation highlights the reverence with which Russians regard alcohol and underscores the importance of drink to the Russian state and society. In the words of one commentator, "God, bread, water, and vodka were the mainstays of Russia."[1]

Indeed, alcohol has been central to the social, cultural, and economic life of the country from the first written accounts. As early as the fifteenth century, monasteries began producing grain alcohol. In the sixteenth century, the

1

first state-owned taverns (*kabaks*) were opened and became so profitable that by the seventeenth century the state established a monopoly over all commercial distilling. The Law Code (*Ulozhenie*) of 1649 made it illegal to buy or sell vodka except through government-owned taverns, and all revenues from the sale of alcohol were by law a part of the royal purse. By the beginning of the twentieth century, alcohol revenues made up a third of all state revenues. Despite vodka's fiscal importance to the state, the tsarist government instituted prohibition in 1914 as part of the mobilization of men and resources for World War I. The loss of such an important source of revenue during the war exacerbated Russia's economic crises and ultimately helped spark a revolution. After the October Revolution of 1917, the state reestablished a monopoly on alcohol production, and vodka once again became the single most important source of revenue. Because of social problems related to widespread drunkenness and moral issues surrounding government production and sale of alcohol, nowhere has the problem of alcoholism been more politicized.

This book examines one highly significant chapter in the history of the Russian state and society both before and after the revolution: how those in power in Russia have understood and represented drinking and the impact that has had on state policy and on Russia's working classes between 1895 and 1932. From the 1890s, Russia experienced a growth in industry and with it the expansion of dirty, overcrowded industrial neighborhoods, where decrepit housing overflowed with peasants newly emigrated from the countryside. The squalor and stench of these dismal districts, accompanied by a sharp increase in prostitution and the ubiquitous drunks swearing and brawling in the streets, produced among observers a perception of deep social problems. In the 1920s, when the new Soviet leadership launched a program of rapid industrialization, these problems intensified. Most social reformers before and after 1917 tied these problems to the issue of alcoholism.

Alcoholism and Social Control

A Swedish researcher, Magnus Huss, first used the term "alcoholism" in 1849 to describe a wide variety of symptoms associated with drunkenness.[2] He classified alcoholism as a physical illness and hence a medical problem rather than as a form of insanity or moral failing. Throughout the 1860s, Russian physicians, pharmacologists, physiologists, and psychiatrists built on Huss's theories and drew from concepts of alcoholism developed in French and

German universities. They sought physiological explanations for excessive drinking and adopted the term "alcoholism" (*alkogolizm*) as opposed to "drunkenness" (*p'ianstvo*) to connote the phenomenon of disease. Later, Soviet physicians also made this distinction.

Yet the professionals who aspired to enlighten and counsel reformers on the means of preventing or curing alcoholism could not reach a consensus on its causes or cures. Experts agreed on the danger of this disease, but what exactly it was, what caused it, why it seemed to be prevalent among certain groups, especially urban workers, and how to cure it were topics of heated debate. Consequently, various groups in Russia sought to define the causes of and cures for alcoholism. At the heart of this quest was a bid for political power and social control through the establishment of norms that would assert upper-class cultural authority over the lower classes.

The first sustained attack on working-class drinking and the state's liquor monopoly had its roots in the reforms of the mid-nineteenth century. The Great Reforms of the 1860s lessened censorship constraints and created the rudiments of a modern civic order. This relaxation of censorship opened a field of public discourse and within it the expression of an emerging civic establishment made up of members of the professions.[3] These professional strata, under the influence of Western liberalism (even when they rejected it), constructed alcoholism as a social and medical problem in their battle against the old order. They all agreed that drunkenness was one of the most pressing problems facing Russian society. However, they differed in their prescriptions on how to cure this problem. The different ideas about drunkenness advanced by members of the professions and others attempting to shape civic and popular culture expressed tensions between ideas imported from the West and countervailing cultural assumptions in Russia. Whether it was members of the clergy defining alcoholism as a moral failing, medical professionals declaring it a medical problem, liberals tying it to the failures of autocracy, or socialists decrying bourgeois exploitation, they all sought cultural hegemony over the working classes. Their subjective, emotional, and value-laden definitions of alcoholism reflect class and cultural conflicts in the chaos of the revolutionary era and underscore the struggle of the upper classes to establish power, authority, and legitimacy.

Focused attention on working-class drinking intensified in the chaotic years of fin de siècle Russia and reached a peak in the first decades of the twentieth century as revolutionary leaders tried to create a new socialist society.

Both before and after 1917, reformers tried to control the drinking behavior—and hence the social identities and cultural values—of the lower classes with little success. Moreover, important aspects of prerevolutionary bourgeois social reform influenced postrevolutionary construction of socialist culture. Yet traditional drinking practices firmly embedded in Russian popular culture thwarted temperance activists' best efforts. Just as authorities devised strategies to reform working-class culture, so, too, the working classes devised strategies to maintain their traditional cultural practices—most notably drinking.

The prerevolutionary struggle for hegemony over definitions of alcoholism and its treatment came to an end with the tsarist government's formal institution of prohibition in 1914. Nonetheless, the population found ways to distill illicit alcohol. In the disorders of World War I, the revolutions of 1917, and the resulting civil war (1918–1921), drunkenness among the lower classes reached epidemic proportions. The problem took on more urgency after 1920, as the Bolsheviks believed that the success of the revolution depended on the transformation of traditional Russian values in general and drinking practices in particular.

Toward a New Way of Life

Under new political conditions, Soviet leaders and health care practitioners revived the struggle for authority and professional legitimacy during the late 1920s over the issue of alcoholism. The so-called Stalin Revolution that coincided with the First Five-Year Plan (1928–1932) aimed at speeding up industrialization while modernizing the country. As with nearly all industrializing nations, modernization in the Soviet Union included changing people's thinking and behavior. It necessitated inculcating new cultural norms and values that would make daily life for the general population orderly and productive. Efficiency, literacy, cleanliness, and above all sobriety gained attention from Soviet officials and public professionals. In these endeavors, Russians were not unique. Throughout Europe, social reformers launched nationwide campaigns to "civilize" the masses through literacy campaigns, sanitation drives, temperance movements, and the like.[4]

"Civilizing" the masses in Russia, however, was made all the more complicated by the legacies of war, revolution, and civil war, as well as the Bolsheviks' insistence on subsuming all endeavors into a single ideology. As collectivization in the Russian countryside destroyed traditional communities and structures, peasants migrated to Soviet cities in droves. Bringing their culture and traditions with them, the masses of peasant migrants transformed the urban Soviet workforce into a social unit comprising elements of both urban and rural culture. The simultaneous existence of different cultural modes, including different modes of drinking and sobriety indigenous to the working class, became fraught with profound political significance as Bolshevik leaders sought to eliminate "anti-Soviet elements" from the population. By the late 1920s Communist Party leaders initiated extensive political and cultural programs to transform recalcitrant peasants into loyal (sober) socialist workers. One of the more active and highly publicized campaigns was a nationwide temperance campaign that borrowed heavily from its bourgeois predecessors.

Yet the millions of peasants who entered Soviet industry, as well as the older hereditary workers, resisted official ideology and drew upon their preindustrial culture and traditions to structure social identities and relationships. Primary among these were drinking practices and rituals. At the same time, party visionaries and theorists constructed ideological edifices to extend their moral authority and to create a new socialist society with acceptable cultural values. Foremost among these was sobriety. Implicit in the conflict of cultures and traditions were the negotiation and struggle between the working class and Soviet officialdom, which helped shape important aspects of the emerging Soviet order. These aspects included establishing the parameters of public behavior, defining the spheres of public and private, creating social divisions within the working class, and interpreting forms of political expression and activity. In all of these, drinking and sobriety played a vital role.

Cultural Revolution

Clearly, the critical issue facing the Bolsheviks was not simply the seizure of power. They sought as well to establish cultural hegemony through, in their words, a cultural revolution.[5] Over the last two decades, a number of histories have illuminated various aspects of the Soviet Union's cultural revolution and are essential for an understanding of it.[6] Many of these, however, do not place cultural transformation in the center of the Bolshevik project. Rather, they treat it as a fascinating, but secondary, goal of the revolution. The cultural dimension of Bolshevik state building, however, was of utmost importance to V. I. Lenin and other revolutionary leaders. At its core, Bolshevism intended to transform the values of the Russian population and ultimately transform human nature.[7]

Recently, a few notable histories have taken great strides toward deepening our understanding of the centrality of cultural transformation to the Bolshevik project.[8] They highlight some of the more important institutional and organizational devices used by the nascent state to effect a cultural revolution. Yet even these studies deal only tangentially, if at all, with one of the most troublesome and intractable aspects of what the Bolsheviks saw as prerevolutionary working-class culture—drunkenness.

Despite the centrality of drink and temperance to understanding Russia's industrial modernization and working-class culture both before and after the revolution, scholarship on the topic is remarkably thin. A few studies by Russian historians focus on the Soviet anti-alcohol campaign but do not place it within the context of cultural revolution or discuss its impact on workers' lives.[9] Operating from the premise that drinking is problematic, most Western studies generally focus on prerevolutionary temperance and do not analyze the place of alcohol in the daily lives of Russians.[10] One notable exception is a recent book by Laura Phillips that examines drink and working-class culture in St. Petersburg.[11] Treating alcohol consumption as a normal component of working-class life, Phillips has taken the first steps toward understanding the social utility of alcohol among workers. My study, however, challenges Phillips's argument that drinking behaviors among workers changed in important ways after the October Revolution. Since St. Petersburg was the heart of the revolutionary movement, Philips's narrow focus on workers in St. Petersburg limits the importance of her study. As Philips herself notes, workers in St. Petersburg initiated the revolution and were steeped in revolutionary culture more than anywhere else in the country.[12] As such, working-class life in St. Petersburg cannot be viewed as representative of workers in general. On the contrary, my study reveals that prerevolutionary culture, including drinking practices, continued to structure lower-class identities and socialization well after the revolution.

Filling in Some "Blank Spots"

In light of the substantial lacunae in the existing scholarship, the first goal of this book is to explore how those in power in Russia, both before and after the revolution, defined working-class drinking as problematic and how they sought cultural modernization through addressing Russia's "drink problem." In this sense, then, I approach cultural revolution as a process tied to Russia's modernization that began before 1917. In doing so, two questions immediately arise: First, to what extent did prerevolutionary culture, society, and politics determine the nature of Bolshevism? Second, did the revolution ultimately fail because instead of inculcating the working class with new values and a new culture, the revolutionaries were overwhelmed by "traditional" values of drunkenness, suspicion of authorities, and passive forms of resistance? While no single study can claim a definitive assessment of these issues, examining them through the prism of drinking and temperance illuminates important aspects of how the revolutionary regime sought to establish power.

In addressing these two questions, the first chapters of the book deal with the prerevolutionary period. Here I revisit territory that others have already covered but with a different purpose and perspective. In tracing the evolution of Russian drinking culture as the country industrialized in the late nineteenth century, my work complements the earlier work of David Christian in his pathbreaking history of vodka.[13] My study highlights the importance of alcohol in the daily lives of both workers and peasants as well as its tremendous fiscal importance to the state. Further, by recalling the place of drinking among Russia's lower classes, the book's first chapters underscore the tenacity of prerevolutionary practices despite the attempted imposition of revolutionary culture by state and party authorities after 1917.

A second theme I trace in the prerevolutionary period is the construction of alcoholism as a social problem from the 1860s to 1914 in order to examine the tensions between different conceptions of alcoholism: as an individual failing, as a social disease, and as a by-product of the social and cultural environment. The definition and treatment of alcohol became highly politicized in this period, as various professional groups sought to claim the moral authority to cure Russia's ills. The most recent histories of temperance organizations in Russia inform this discussion. Tracing some of the political implications of temperance, Patricia Herlihy covers a bit of the same ground.[14] Her focus, however, remains narrowly fixed on problematic drinking and temperance and does not address the larger social and political processes occurring after the 1860s. My study reflects upon the larger struggle within the upper classes to appropriate and to redefine political power embedded in social relations, public institutions, and intellectual authority.

This book's second goal is to highlight the Bolshevik approach to social modernization and cultural revolution. It seeks to do so through an examination of the institutional, organizational, and propagandistic devices used in the 1920s and early 1930s by state and party officials to inculcate the working class with Bolshevik-defined socialist values—in this case, sobriety. Under the auspices of the voluntary Society for the Struggle with Alcoholism (Obshchestvo po bor'be s alkogolizmom, OBSA), the leadership launched a nationwide temperance campaign that was quite representative of other mobilization campaigns in the early Soviet years. Here we must remember that throughout the 1920s, the fledgling revolutionary state was not the powerful dictatorship it became under high Stalinism (1937–1941). While the leadership assumed it had the moral authority and political legitimacy to transform society, mass political support for the new regime never materialized, and class antagonisms stubbornly persisted.

More important, despite the fact that the historical context changed from tsarist to Soviet times, the lower classes clung to their traditional cultural expressions. The typical worker altered his or her drinking patterns little, if at all, when he or she became part of the "workers' state." Indeed, individual workers and the party had very different ideas about what it meant to be a worker in the workers' state. While party theorists imagined the creation of a socialist society made up of sober, disciplined citizens, workers refused to abandon their traditional modes of drunken camaraderie on the shop floor, in taverns, and in working-class neighborhoods. In many respects, the socialists who in 1917 claimed to be liberators of the workers and peasants became alien oppressors of the working class by the 1930s. Just as prerevolutionary liberal professionals and social reformers had enlisted temperance in their struggles for power, Soviet reformers enlisted temperance in their struggle for moral authority, cultural hegemony, and legitimacy in the 1920s. An examination of the Soviet temperance campaign reveals how the party conceptualized these problems and highlights two conflicting impulses in Bolshevik policy: revolutionary ideology and political expediency.

Finally, this project attempts to reveal and explain the various strategies used by members of the working class to cope with new realities. In doing so, it casts attention on various strategies the party employed in symbiosis with the working class to transform traditional cultural values. As Phillips notes, some workers did indeed adopt Soviet values or adapted them to serve their particular interests. More commonly, however, workers reacted to Bolshevik initiatives and class hierarchies with defiance, circumvention, and numerous passive strategies of resistance.

In an attempt to find a broad foundation for investigating the interplay between working-class realities and state social policy, I focus on four cities: Moscow, Kharkov, Saratov, and Tomsk. As the nation's capital for most of the period under consideration and the largest industrial center, Moscow is a logical choice. A city rich in institutions and traditions that predated Soviet industrialization, it continued to influence and shape events and behaviors during the period of rapid industrialization and cultural revolution. Huge new plants were constructed in Moscow, and existing factories doubled or tripled in size, attracting tremendous numbers of peasant migrants.[15] Moreover, the most active Soviet temperance efforts were centered in Moscow, and sources from this region are quite rich. I chose Kharkov for many of the same reasons. At the time, it was the capital of the Ukrainian republic and the largest industrial center in Ukraine. Patterns of industrial development and the consequent in-migration of peasant laborers were similar to those of Moscow.

I included Saratov, a provincial capital far removed from the center, because in many respects it is more representative of urban Russia than either Kharkov or Moscow.[16] Located at the tip of the black earth region, Saratov stood at the crossroads of industry and agriculture. It acquired large, urban-based industrial enterprises during the state-sponsored industrialization program of the 1890s, yet the local economy remained tied to agriculture. The working class, therefore, was predominately urban-based with ties to the countryside, a situation that was typical of much of provincial Russia.

The fourth city under study is Tomsk, in the Kuzbass industrial region of western Siberia. The Kuzbass formed the eastern anchor of the new Soviet Siberian industrial fortress and, like the well-known western anchor, Magnitigorsk, was the site of some of the most intense industrial construction throughout the 1920s. Tens of thousands of Soviet citizens and foreign Communists migrated to Tomsk to participate in huge construction projects.

This concentration on four geographical locations provides a broader picture of the process of cultural revolution. Because of the vagaries of Russian sources, however, this study cannot claim to be a true comparative history. The collections of various types of data are quite uneven and differ from region to region. Moreover, a tremendous number of archives were destroyed during World War II or subsequently lost owing to poor storage facilities, because of mismanagement, or in the chaos of restructuring following the collapse of the Soviet Union in 1992. For example, OBSA's archives in Moscow were lost during World War II. Fearing the destruction of valuable documents if Moscow were invaded, archivists at the Semashko Institute (where OBSA's archives were housed) loaded the archives on a ship to be sent down the Moscow River. The ship, unfortunately, sank and all the documents were lost. Additionally, the archives of the local branch of OBSA in Kharkov were among thousands of archival documents burned by the Nazis during their occupation of Ukraine. In Moscow, some of the archives from the Institute of Sanitary Culture simply disappeared when the archive was being reorganized in 1993. Despite these problems, enough overlapping materials exist to allow for generalizations about a broad spectrum of the working classes and the state's efforts to control them.

This study privileges male workers in heavy industry because that is what the Soviet regime did. Since it was precisely construction and heavy industry that were the focus of the Soviet industrialization drive during the First Five-Year Plan, both expanded greatly.[17] Drinking among rural peasants, the intelligentsia, and the middle strata of white-collar workers does not factor into this study because these groups figured differently from industrial workers in the regime's plans for cultural revolution. Because of the focus on heavy industry, discussion of drinking centers on male workers, largely because few women were employed in this type of work. In fact, the shift to a more modern drinking culture in the nineteenth century excluded women from taverns as well as from the drunken camaraderie on the shop floor.

Specific statistical information regarding drinking behaviors of women does not exist, perhaps because female drinking was not thought pervasive enough to warrant special study. None of the sources suggest that drinking among female workers was problematic—women generally were not suspended from work for drunkenness, nor were they arrested or forced into treatment centers. This does not mean that women did not drink. Indeed, the paucity of evidence may indicate that cultural injunctions against women drinking were so strong that authorities did not see their drinking as problematic.[18] Women, however, were the main producers and purveyors of illegal alcohol. In the 1920s untold thousands of women were arrested or fined for making moonshine.

The revolutionary state's construction of alcoholism as a petit bourgeois holdover from the tsarist past highlights problems the Bolsheviks encountered in trying to bring about a Marxist revolution in an overwhelmingly peasant society. By examining the context in which drinking became a problem before and after 1917, this study traces the state's failure to establish cultural hegemony as it sought to inculcate social controls through legislative action, coercion, and voluntary societies. Having found themselves helpless to curb the flow of illegal alcohol, unable to generate acceptable forms of revenue to replace alcohol revenues, and utterly incapable of changing traditional drinking habits, the Bolsheviks attempted to school workers on correct drinking practices through propaganda. Yet the demise of the temperance campaign illustrates how workers' resistance forced party leaders to seek ideological retreats and accommodations. Whether in the form of a toast or as the subject of a temperance poster, alcohol has defined not only a stereotype of Russian culture but also a nexus of early-twentieth-century reform movements. This book seeks to uncover the various forms of control that crisscrossed Russian society and politics—control that *can* be found at the bottom of a glass.

C　H　A　P　T　E　R　　2

Swimming in a Drunken Sea

I N 986 GRAND PRINCE VLADIMIR ADOPTED CHRISTIANITY AS the official religion of Kievan Rus', in part because it offered no prohibition against strong drink. He reasoned that Russians would not tolerate a religion that banned alcohol consumption. Nearly a thousand years later, a speaker at the All-Russian Congress on the Struggle against Alcoholism observed:

> When the Russian is born, when he marries or dies, when he goes to court or is reconciled, when he makes a new acquaintance or parts from an old friend, when he negotiates a purchase or sale, realizes a profit or suffers a loss—every activity is copiously baptized with vodka. . . . The Russian spends his entire life from cradle to grave, bathing and swimming in this drunken sea.[1]

However hyperbolic these assessments might be, no one can deny that drinking is an integral part of Russian life. Indeed, Russians' consumption of alcohol is legendary. Since the sixteenth century, foreign travelers have commented on the drinking habits of the peasants, as well as those of the court. Some of the earliest written accounts by foreign visitors detail the Russians' great propensity for drink. In the late 1400s the Venetian ambassador Ambrogio Contarini noted with some disdain that the Russians, taking great pride in being drunkards, hated abstainers. According to Contarini, they "spend all morning in the bazaars until about midday, when they set off to the taverns to eat and drink; it is impossible to get them to do anything afterwards."[2]

Similarly, Giles Fletcher, whose sixteenth-century travel account of Russia is considered the most detailed of its kind, discussed the pervasiveness of drunkenness among the working masses.[3] But the lower classes were not the only group that drank. In the seventeenth century Adam Olearius, a member of the Holstein embassy to Moscow, wrote at length about Russian drinking practices. He was shocked to find that high-ranking nobles and royal ambassadors drank with impunity, more often than not drinking themselves into a stupor. In his words, "The vice of drunkenness is prevalent among this people in all classes, both secular and ecclesiastical, high and low, men and women, young and old. To see them lying here and there in the streets, wallowing in the filth, is so common that no notice is taken of it."[4]

In trying to explain the phenomenon, observers have attributed Russian drinking to climate, lack of safe drinking water, and myriad other causes.[5] Whatever the reason, alcoholic beverages have been the lifeblood of nearly all domestic, religious, political, and economic rituals, marking every important transition and passage in the lives of ordinary Russians.

Because alcohol, and especially vodka, was a central feature of ceremonial and social life in both village and town, it has also held a place of unparalleled importance in the Russian economy. (The word "vodka" historically referred to all common drinks based on spirits. In nineteenth-century Russian usage, the word "*vino*" was more common than "vodka" but still meant grain alcohol).[6] In the middle of the seventeenth century the government established a monopoly over all commercial distilling, providing the state with a large and reliable income.[7] By the nineteenth century, trade in spirits was the single largest source of revenue for the state, comprising on average 30 percent of all ordinary revenues, sometimes reaching as high as 46 percent.[8]

Economic and demographic changes during the nineteenth and early twentieth centuries altered the country's social and political landscape and reshaped traditional identities and cultures. This metamorphosis had a cultural component that found expression in drinking practices. Playing a central role in village rituals and celebrations, traditional vodka consumption among peasants was episodic and intense, usually linked to church holidays and seasonal events. With the revolutionary transformations of Russia in the latter half of the nineteenth century—industrialization, urbanization, and increased population pressures—peasants flocked to the towns, bringing with them their customs and drinking habits and acquiring new ones. This new influx, combined with the growth of a cash economy and wage-labor, gave rise to more regular patterns of consumption and set the foundation for the widespread use of alcohol as a permanent feature of working-class life. Moreover, as peasants left the countryside for temporary or permanent work in the towns, the lines between classes and social groups became blurred, as did the behaviors associated with these groups. Nonetheless, distinctions in drinking patterns did exist, and they serve as a lens through which we can view the larger processes taking place within Russian society at the turn of the century.

Tracing the evolution of drinking cultures from traditional rural practices to more modern urban practices, this chapter highlights social and cultural shifts as Russia began to modernize and emphasizes the importance of drink in the daily lives of the toiling masses. It also examines the interplay between economic, social, and political factors influencing Russian drinking cultures to reveal that these factors simultaneously reinforced some and altered other drinking behaviors. Ultimately, this chapter underscores the tenacity of traditional cultural practices that remained firmly embedded in working-class life and survived both tsarist and Soviet moral reformers' best efforts to separate Russian workers from their passion for vodka.

Traditional (Rural) Drinking Culture

According to recent scholarship, two drinking cultures existed among the Russian lower classes by the nineteenth century: one with roots in the traditional life of the peasant community, the other associated with urbanization and the evolution of a cash economy.[9] Both patterns of lower-class drinking were part of centuries-old traditional Russian popular culture and shared common characteristics. Primary among these was the choice of beverage. The upper classes and the intelligentsia tended to drink fortified wines and imported liqueurs while peasants and urban workers in Great Russia mainly consumed vodka, followed by beer and kvass. Kvass, a mildly alcoholic fermented drink, is usually made from flour, bread, malt, and water.[10] A peasant saying offers a clear ranking order for these drinks: "No vodka, then drink a little beer, no beer, then drink a little kvass, no kvass, then drink a little water from a small spoon."[11]

For Russian peasants and workers, drinking consistently remained the most important form of recreation and release. Many upper-class observers lamented that more civilized forms of entertainment, such as balls, concerts, and literature, were not open to Russia's working masses who overindulged in vodka to escape the burdens of their dreary lives.[12] While such observations usually were not wholly disinterested, they do point to specific patterns of excessiveness in consumption. Lower-class Russians usually drank heavily and concentrated on getting drunk.[13] Often lasting several days, drinking binges were common around religious holidays or community events such as weddings or funerals. For the urban worker, in addition to these occasions, the arrival of the weekend or receiving a paycheck was sufficient cause for celebration, and Monday was often viewed as an extension of Sunday's debauch.

Despite these similarities, by the end of the nineteenth century there were discernable differences between traditional and urban drinking cultures. Traditional drinking in the village was generally collective and expressed in "ceremonial" binge drinking associated with church festivals, rites of passage, family celebrations, and any special occasions in the life of the rural community. Numerous studies using thousands of questionnaires circulated by the zemstvos (organs of local self-government set up in the 1860s) throughout rural Russia were conducted between 1890 and 1909. Compiling the results of these studies, S. A. Pervushin confirmed that rural drinking took the form of communal binges intimately linked to village events.[14] In the words of a peasant, "We drink the damned vodka at weddings and christenings, at funerals and church holidays, when receiving guests, at every purchase and sale, on going to the market and at meetings . . . at every occasion."[15]

Because the labor of an individual peasant family on its plot of land was typically solitary, rural family life was often closed, and households were economically isolated. At the same time, poverty and the precariousness of rural life dictated the need for peasant families to come together as a community and establish stable social and economic relationships.[16] In an environment of isolated work, recreational activities took on great significance. Therefore, the whole village participated in church holidays and festivals, usually with everyone in the parish getting—and staying—drunk. In most villages, women drank as earnestly as the men, and even children were often invited to drink at these festivities. In a good harvest year the celebratory drinking would last a week, but even in lean years the village managed to stay drunk for at least three days.[17] Upon finding an entire village in a collective binge following a religious holiday, one upper-class observer noted that the peasants believed that the mother of God commanded the three-day debauch because of the peasants' passion for drink.[18]

There were twelve principal church holidays during which peasants heavily imbibed. These holidays, which were seasonal and typically lasted three to five days, had their roots in the pagan traditions of the ancient Slavs and coincided with the fall harvest, Christmas, Shrovetide, and Easter. The exact dates varied from region to region, but the "joyful season" generally began in mid-September and lasted until the beginning of March. In addition, there were local festivals, usually associated with the saints' days of local churches, and special feast days in the summer for each village.

Overlapping conveniently so that each village could help in the celebrations of its neighbors, local festivals brought the entire community together and provided an opportunity to extend social networks outside the village on "visiting holidays" (s"ezzhii prazdnik). Each village selected the holiday to be celebrated at its convenience. These holidays rarely had any religious purpose.[19] The celebrations usually began in one parish at the end of the church service with the whole village sharing drinks and food. Over the course of the next few days the villagers gradually spread out to neighboring villages. Peasants from outlying villages most often traveled to more central villages, where they would be the guests of relatives and friends. After much drinking, they would slowly migrate back to their home villages, inviting all who had hosted them to come be their guests.[20] The wide diversity of people attending these visiting holidays promoted an active exchange of information, knowledge, and rumors. Lasting anywhere from three to eight days, such celebrations not only gave peasants a reprieve from the drudgery of village life but also were crucial in maintaining the peasants' sense of community and reinforcing the reciprocity of social relationships within peasant society.

At the same time, these celebrations could quickly turn into violent brawls between "them" and "us." Nonvillagers who attended these celebrations had to conform to village norms or fights would ensue. In the spirit of reciprocity upon which village customs hinged, host villages invited "outsiders" with the expectation that the favor would be returned. Insults and fists would fly if reciprocity were not forthcoming or if uninvited guests showed up without the requisite offerings. If uninvited guests did not assuage their hosts' anger by treating them to vodka, the hosts beat up the guests. Often, a young male tough would seek retribution by rounding up some buddies from his village; they would bolster their courage with shots of vodka and descend in battle on the young men from the opposing village. The losers had to provide the winners with vodka at future celebrations.[21]

The social nature of ceremonial drinking meant that it was as much an obligation as it was a pleasure. Tradition and custom demanded drunkenness on certain occasions, and those failing to respond "dishonored" themselves in the eyes the community. In order to avoid this stigma, families often spent their last kopeck and even sold their property to purchase enough vodka for the upcoming festival or event.[22] As one survey in 1916 noted, "The greater the drunkenness [at a wedding] . . . the more honored will be the marriage and the couple's happiness. . . . [Such celebrations] are remembered for years."[23] Indeed, a marriage could not be agreed upon, a funeral arranged, a wedding conducted, or a bargain sealed without the required amount of vodka. To be binding, every type of transaction or agreement had to conclude with all parties "wetting the bargain"—sharing a drink of vodka. Custom established firm norms on the amount of vodka that should be provided, below which a peasant family could not go without being shamed.[24] Varying according to regional traditions, a household's wealth, and the type of event, these norms in most villages were as compulsory as taxes. According to one study conducted in 1912 in Penza province, an average peasant household of six spent no less than 10 percent of the family budget on alcohol and often much more.[25]

Weddings demanded the most vodka. Regional norms in Penza determined that a wedding celebration must continue two days after the wedding for average families and that rich peasants must provide for at least four to five days of merrymaking. Local custom required a minimum of ten *vedros* (one *vedro* is 3.25 gallons, or 12.30 liters) of vodka, up to five *vedros* of beer, and one-half *vedro* of grape wine.[26] In a society where nearly all food and clothes were produced in the home, obligatory purchases of vodka were one of the main uses of cash and an important expenditure in the peasant household budget. Unfortunately, since figures on peasants' household budgets for this period are scattered and fragmentary, it is impossible to be specific about the percent of cash outlays on vodka in household budgets. Nonetheless, there is sufficient evidence to conclude that expenditures on vodka were an important part of the family budget.[27] Large outlays on vodka for weddings and other celebrations, therefore, served as a form of redistribution of wealth, with the buyer obtaining "symbolic capital"—respect, status, and personal leverage within the village.

Not only could families use vodka to raise their status within the village, but individuals also found vodka important in maintaining networks of patronage and manipulating village politics. Typically, meetings of village elders took place inside the village tavern, and decisions concerning the levying of taxes, election of officials, or punishment of offenders were often influenced by who bought whom how much vodka.[28]

In village elections and assemblies, wealthy peasants commonly dispensed vodka as bribes and devices for controlling the outcomes. One Russian historian recounts a fairly typical village election: Several days prior to a commune meeting for the appointment of the coveted post of commune head, peasants wishing to secure an appointment toured the village with barrels of vodka. In order to elicit villagers' support, candidates dispensed drinks while deriding the previous commune head and making promises about what they would do if appointed. On the day of the meeting, the villagers gathered without any sort of order or division into parties, ostensibly to vote, but in fact to drink. After three of four hours of drinking, brawling, and general rowdiness, people drifted away, and the "election" was over. The village assessor along with a few other peasants then quite arbitrarily wrote "minutes" of the election and decided who was to be appointed, primarily based on who provided the most vodka.[29]

Vodka also influenced communal justice. Commonly known as "softening up the judge," a defendant or petitioner could ply elders with vodka to ensure a favorable decision or lighter punishment for a crime. As one peasant complained, "With some vodka and money, any judge can be persuaded to declare the guilty party to be in the right."[30] Once an offender had been found guilty, vodka played a crucial role in reconciling the community to those who had been punished. A. N. Engelgardt, a prominent St. Petersburg chemist who had been exiled to his estate in Smolensk province, recounts a case in 1872 in which a man, having seriously beaten his married lover, had to compensate the woman's husband and buy the commune a *vedro* of vodka, which they drank on the spot.[31] In treating the commune to vodka, the perpetrator offered a symbolic gesture of reconciliation and won forgiveness and readmittance into the community. Often the victim also treated the commune to vodka, thereby affirming his or her acceptance of the punishment.[32]

At times the political and economic uses of vodka were both linked in the important village institution of work parties, which existed throughout European Russia. Known as *pomochi* (from the word *pomoshch'*, to help), these work parties consumed the second greatest amounts of vodka, after weddings.[33] Essentially, *pomochi* were to gather as many people as possible to get an urgent task done, such as building a road or harvesting crops. In return for their labor, the host would supply the workers with food and, most important, vodka. As one local parish priest lamented, "*Pomoch'* is inconceivable without vodka. The work begins with vodka, continues with vodka, and ends with vodka. . . . If you do not give the peasant plenty to drink, he will work poorly out of annoyance; if you do, he will work poorly because he is so drunk."[34]

Here, too, local custom determined the amount of vodka required for the task. Moreover, once the task was completed, the host had to invite everyone back the next day for a celebratory debauch for a job well done.[35] Generally, all who participated in the shared labor drank—from vigorous young men to old grandmothers. Those who did not drink were not expected to participate in the work but rather looked after the families of those who did. One source noted that since women tended to drink less than men, in addition to food and drink women were often presented with small gifts, such as scarves, for their labor.[36]

From the peasants' perspective, by offering vodka the host showed respect for the peasants, and they reciprocated by working "for respect." Peasants did not view their labor as a commercial commodity requiring payment in cash, preferring instead informal systems of mutual aid and compensation.[37] Indeed, one source noted that it was impossible to get anyone to work for cash payment—villagers much preferred strong drink and good food.[38] Peasants would offer labor as a deposit against their potential future needs (with the understanding that today's host would be tomorrow's worker). Vodka was the reward for their labor, but in addition, it was a symbol of the mutuality of the exchange, reinforcing the network of interdependent relationships in the community.[39]

Pomochi were also an essential means for adolescent village boys to mark their separation from the domestic sphere of their mothers and transition to the man's world of work and drink. As with all work parties, a man in the village would summon a group of young men to work for him in exchange for food and vodka. After the job was done, everyone would drink together, ostensibly to relax at the end of a hard day. However, such binge drinking initiated the young men into the adult world of responsibility and sociability.[40] At these events, a young man learned how to hold his drink, and sometimes outdo his peers, as he built bonds for future village networks.

Despite the frequency and intensity of drinking occasions, isolated individual drinking was rare in traditional peasant culture, and noncommunal drunkenness was disdained. A peasant saying declared, "A fiddle and a horn lost the whole house," while another warned, "Drink to the bottom and you will not know good times."[41] According to one contemporary observer, peasants "drink when everyone agrees to, everyone together."[42]

In an attempt to analyze the magnitude of alcoholism in the countryside, a 1913 survey of 20,000 peasants found that only 20 consumed alcohol daily in small doses "for health" or "to improve appetite." Almost as rare were "problem drinkers" whose frequent nonritualistic drinking was excessive. The survey found forty of these problem drinkers who, deviating from accepted behavioral norms, were condemned by their neighbors.[43] Residents in a small Siberian village also condemned three of the villagers who caroused and drank on workdays. They lamented, "Vasilisko Konovalov's wife, Avdot'ia, in the absence of her husband lived in an unseemly way, was often drunk, and did not exert herself in work."[44] In a system where all peasants shared responsibility for taxes, a household head who was a drunkard was a great liability.

At the same time, the community viewed a refusal to drink when custom or ceremony called for it as a deviation not to be tolerated. Excessive isolated drinking or refusals to drink were met with ridicule, public shaming, and the implied threat of social isolation, which could have devastating economic repercussions if members of the village refused to help the offender with harvesting or other critical tasks. Even priests were not exempt from the obligations of ceremonial drinking, as a parish priest, I. S. Belliustin, complained:

> Say it is a holiday like Easter, and the priest conducts an icon procession. Each house offers hospitality, that is, vodka and something to eat. The prayer sung, they ask the priest to "pay his respects" to the master of the house: that is to drink vodka. If the priest refuses, everyone in the family falls to his knees and will not rise until the priest has had a drink. This too does not work: the priest implores his hosts to rise and leaves without drinking. The host is terribly offended, of course, fuming with indignation. . . . Afterward, if the priest should dare approach the peasant about some need, it would evoke a rude refusal: "You didn't pay respects to me, and well, I'm not your servant." . . . If the priest accepts the vodka, by the time he has gone through the whole village even the most cautious, sturdiest soul hardly has the strength to perform his duty.[45]

Traditional, ceremonial drinking was a cohesive force in village life, well integrated into the life of the community. Shared drinking experiences reinforced social, political, and economic networks in village society and helped maintain informal systems of patronage and mutual aid. In the village, therefore, drinking was not centered around a specific site, and it did not separate people by age, gender, or income to the extent more modern drinking did.

The Role of the Tavern

The locus of the evolution of traditional rural drinking culture was the tavern, although the existence of a local tavern did not necessarily signify a shift to more modern drinking behaviors.[46] The first state-owned taverns, called *kabaks,* were introduced into Russian life in the 1550s. Impressed by the Tatar *kabaks* he had seen during the siege of Kazan, Tsar Ivan IV (r. 1533–1584) began to establish his own taverns.[47] The records lack detailed information on the spread of taverns prior to the nineteenth century, but evidence suggests that initially only in towns or on royal, religious, or noble estates were there sufficient numbers of cash-paying customers to support a *kabak.* Instead, numerous other types of retail liquor outlets made vodka available to lower-class Russians. These sold vodka in larger quantities (the smallest being half a *vedro,* approximately 1.65 gallons), which the lower classes bought in bulk for ceremonial drinking.[48]

Once a tavern was established in a locale, the local population began to drink on days that were not part of traditional ceremonial drinking occasions, especially in areas where local industries provided cash wages. An account written in 1824 explains:

> I remember the days of my youth. Back then it was only on main annual festivals that the peasants celebrated and got drunk, either on homemade beer or on vodka bought in towns. Now, everyday is a festival, and you find everywhere helpful "servants" under the Imperial Eagle ready to relieve peasants of their money, their mind, and their health. Rare is the village that doesn't have a tavern.[49]

Beginning in the 1700s, all state taverns had the Russian national symbol, the double-headed eagle, placed above the door. This functioned as an "official license" and was an effort to mark the legality of the establishment.

With the increase of wage labor and the spread of local taverns, drinking began to lose its links with the traditional patterns of rural life. While the lower classes still drank according to custom and convention, increasingly drinking also became a matter of choice, inclination, or habit. The recreational aspects of drinking started to eclipse the ceremonial. This trend accelerated after the Great Reforms of the 1860s, as the development of a cash economy, an all-national market, and urbanization altered economic conditions in the village.[50] The prerevolutionary Marxist student of vodka consumption V. K. Dmitriev, in trying to distinguish between "peasant" and "proletarian" drinking, claimed that the different ways of drinking reflected the different worlds of "Mr. Harvest" and "Mr. Capital." He argued that the rise of regular, as opposed to sporadic, drinking reflected an increase in the cash component in working-class budgets, which in turn reflected the rise in the amount of wage work and the size of the urban and rural proletariat.[51]

There is evidence to support Dmitriev's thesis of a correlation between consumption levels, wage earning, and capricious or spontaneous drinking. In 1852 the Ministry of Finance observed that in any given area, the amount of vodka consumed by the local population depended on the amount of cash available.[52] Noting the same phenomenon, Vasilii Kokorev, a local tax farmer, declared, "It is not the stomach that drinks, but the pocket."[53] As David Christian has shown, the spread of a cash economy and the growing number of taverns at the very least provided more opportunities for getting drunk without any ceremonial occasion.[54]

Literary images of the time reflect the impact of a cash economy, elements of modernization, and the incursion of the outside world on peasant culture. The themes of the dangers of money and the vulnerability of the muzhik (peasant) are most closely associated with the writings of G. I. Uspenskii. In *The Power of the Earth,* Uspenskii develops the image of the "ruined" peasant through the central character, Ivan Bosykh. Making money through occasional work at the railroad station, Bosykh promptly spent it on drink at the local tavern. His drunkenness, and hence his moral deterioration, resulted from the freedoms granted by the emancipation of the serfs in 1861. Freed from the constraints of village traditions and able to make easy cash, Bosykh fell prey to the evil influence of the tavern.[55]

Yet Bosykh, like his real-life counterparts, never was fully emancipated from village norms. Economic changes stemming from the Great Reforms forced peasants in the late nineteenth century more and more into migrant labor, and as a result they began relying more on a cash economy and the national market. Despite the fact that many peasants increasingly entered the urban world of work and leisure and were probably attracted by the trappings of urban life, they still retained their village mores, worldview, social relationships, and institutions. One example of this was the custom of "wetting the bargain," which peasant migrants adapted for use in the hiring market. In the village, sharing a drink signified that an equitable economic transaction had been negotiated. In the hiring market, migrants forced potential employers to "wet the bargain" before they would agree to the terms of employment. The toast was a type of social leveling, symbolizing the migrant's equality and forcing employers to respect (at least symbolically) the peasant's dignity and humanity.

Modern Drinking Culture

While the bulk of the population remained steeped in the traditional culture of rural life, economic changes in the second half of the nineteenth century slowly altered Russia's cultural terrain. The growth and persistence of a large number of peasant households based simultaneously on the farm and on urban wage work generated a "third" culture—neither fully traditional nor fully modernized or urbanized.[56] In the mid-1800s, therefore, lower-class culture as it centered around the tavern was a mixture of both the traditional and the modern. Traditional attitudes about drinking coexisted with modern drinking practices, and elements of both cultures met, intertwined, and diverged in the tavern as drinking became more of a leisure activity.

One source paints a vivid illustration of both cultures at play in the local tavern in Bogorodsk, a leather-working town about forty kilometers from Nizhnii Novgorod, in 1859. The author describes the tavern as a refuge for men to gather and discuss their state of affairs, gossip, or curse fate over a glass of vodka. Finding no such camaraderie at home, often men drank up their last kopeck with friends at the tavern. On holidays, however, the entire village—young, old, male, and female—celebrated in the tavern.[57] Singing, swearing, and fighting accompanied the communal holiday trek to the tavern. Women, however, only went to the tavern on these holiday celebrations or on those occasions when they had to come to collect their drunken husbands. During the holiday, the trek to the tavern was a community event, fitting the ceremonial and collective drinking behavior of traditional culture. At the same time, the tavern was predominantly a male refuge where a man spent his leisure time, a more modern use of public space and drinking that excluded women and needed no ceremonial excuse.

Another account, written nearly twenty years later in 1876 in a village in Smolensk province, describes the tavern as exclusively male territory serving as the hub of social, political, and economic networks. In this account, the reasons for drinking were no longer tied to community rituals. The tavern— an old, tumbledown, half-rotten hut—provided a sanctuary for men to meet and satisfy the need for companionship and news and to fill leisure time. Despite the fact that inside it was dirty, dark, and filled with pipe smoke, and the liquor was ordinary green "excise" vodka, lower than official strength, men always crowded into this particular tavern.[58] It was the source of the very latest political news, even though there were no newspapers present in the tavern, and the main meeting place for transacting business. Obviously, the patrons were not drawn there for its homey atmosphere or its good drink. The dwelling itself was not inviting, and neither was the vodka. Patrons frequented the tavern for individual reasons and not as part of a community event.

As peasant migrants moved into urban areas, it is not surprising they sought out taverns in which to spend their leisure time and establish social networks. With the industrialization and urbanization of the 1890s, an increasing number of peasants swelled the ranks of the urban workers. While it is difficult to determine with precision the total number of *otkhodniki* (peasants who left their villages for wage work), most estimates agree on a figure for the 1890s of two million (more than one-third of the total rural population of adult males) for the nine provinces in the Central Industrial Region and more than six million for all of European Russia.[59] Many of these moved into workers' settlements (*rabochie poselki*) in St. Petersburg and Moscow. For example, between 1890 and 1900 an average of 40,000 migrants arrived in St. Petersburg each year, expanding the city's industrial workers' settlements by 30.7 percent.[60] The bulk of these were men aged between sixteen and thirty-five years old.[61]

As these settlements grew, so did the number of taverns and liquor outlets around them. As early as 1865 St. Petersburg had 1,840 taverns, 562 inns, 399 alcoholic beverage stores, and 299 wine cellars.[62] Throughout the empire, taverns sprang up near any working-class settlement or industrial complex. In a new Donbass-Dnepr Bend industrial enterprise, for example, the taverns opened for business the day the first construction workers were hired.[63] In

Kamenskoe, sixteen taverns catered to steelworkers within fifty meters of their barracks.[64]

As men flocked into the cities and into workers' settlements in industrial regions, taverns played a greater function in workers' lives, leading to more regular or habitual patterns of consumption. Especially for workers living in company barracks, the tavern served as an informal social center, club, and friendly refuge beyond the meddling of bosses that provided a temporary escape from their dreary lives. Compared to the conviviality, women, and gambling that taverns offered, hanging out in a bleak barracks held little appeal. When asked in a questionnaire to discuss the causes of drinking, workers gave some of the following responses: "There are 40,000 people living in my settlement and we have only two libraries, which are usually closed. We have no workers' club or theater. In short, there is nowhere for us to study or spend our leisure time." Another respondent noted the lack of teahouses, even in Moscow, so workers went to the taverns: "When we get there, we don't really plan to get drunk. We just want to talk and rest. But if we sit there we must drink or get out." Some respondents complained that an alternative to the tavern would be going to the theater, but workers "can't go because we don't have the right clothes."[65] Workers also emphasized poor living conditions as the main reason they spent time in the taverns. As one respondent stated, "Imagine an apartment in which fifteen to twenty people live in a comparatively small space. It is stuffy and damp, water seeps from the walls, bedbugs swarm like ants—whether you want to or not, you run to the tavern."[66] On any payday the taverns would be filled to overflowing while prostitutes strolled by and a few anxious wives waited to repossess their husbands before they drank the entire paycheck.

Whatever the individual reason, the tavern became the center of social activity and the exclusive preserve of male workers, stratifying and segregating society. Whereas in traditional drinking cultures the entire family (and often the entire village) engaged in alcohol consumption, in modern drinking culture the tavern became primarily a male institution and its patrons drawn there through individual choice. Further, tavern customers bought drinks "by the glass" for cash at higher prices than pails of vodka peasants bought or traded for on ceremonial occasions. This meant that modern drinking not only had its own distinctive purchasing patterns based on a cash economy but also that those who were not wage-earners were excluded from tavern society, becoming the "others" of the lower classes.

The Social Utility of Alcohol

It was not only exclusion from taverns that widened the wedge between wage-earning "workers" and "others." Various drinking practices also served as important mechanisms for distinguishing workers from nonworkers and establishing a working-class hierarchy. As one worker who recently arrived in the city from the village recalled: "I left half of my earnings in the tavern but I was proud: now I was a 'real' worker."[67] Even though women were also wage-earning workers, they fell into the category of "other," or "nonworker." Like male workers, women who entered the industrial labor force in the nineteenth century adapted traditional drinking practices to fit the urban environment. Moreover, like men, as they had access to more cash wages, they drank more frequently than in the village.[68] Yet they were excluded from the category of worker: "real" workers drank in taverns; women did not.[69]

Practices centered on the intake of alcohol at the workplace also fortified social relations among some workers and excluded others. At most establishments, pay packets were distributed on Saturday, and Sunday was a day of rest. Rare was the worker who did not immediately begin serious drinking upon quitting time at 2 P.M. on Saturday. This often meant that workers started drinking while on the street, and it was not uncommon to see a small group of workers huddled around a bottle in alleyways and on side streets. Binge drinking would continue on Sundays, and on Mondays workers often skipped work in order to nurse their hangovers.[70] Some workers had long histories of rarely making it to work on Monday.

"Blue Monday" became a widespread custom among male workers in artisanal shops, commercial firms, and factory enterprises. Arriving at their jobs hung over from weekend drinking, they used Monday as an occasion for more drinking. As one observer wrote, "Blue Monday is a regular ritual. Even the owner himself is prone to alcoholic binges."[71] In mining and metallurgy, as Charters Wynn notes, nearly the entire workforce participated in weekend and holiday debauchery, with extreme consequences. At some mines in the Donbass-Dnepr Bend, mass drunkenness following paydays reached such a scale that absenteeism on Mondays would force the mines to close down, and they sometimes remained closed for up to three days.[72]

Further, each new male worker who entered a shop or enterprise underwent an initiation rite, which typically centered on buying and drinking vodka.[73] In some factories, "the new worker will not even be addressed by name [by other workers] but will be called 'Taras'" until he provided drinks for the whole shop. "Taras" was a derogatory term, probably stemming from the noun *tarasun*. In poorer regions, rather than discarding the dregs from distilling vodka from grain, these dregs would be distilled a second time, producing weak, bitter vodka known as *tarasun*, also called "milk vodka" (*molochnaia vodka*), meaning baby's vodka.

The appointment of a new shop foreman was accompanied by a ritual ceremony in which the workers expressed homage and the foreman reciprocated by buying drinks for them all.[74] Treating with vodka strengthened shop solidarities, reinforced hierarchies among workers, and symbolized a type of rite of passage into the world of "real" workers. As in taverns where male sociability centered on drinking and largely excluded women, drink also imbued the culture of the factory with masculine significance.

Since purchasing vodka had traditionally been one of the main uses of cash, and drinking it one of the main uses of leisure time, as more cash became available through wage work, workers spent more on vodka. Once a peasant man moved to the city and bought a jacket and a watch, one observer noted, he did not know how to spend his money on anything but drinking.[75] More available cash led to the development of more capricious alcohol consumption among workers, especially unskilled blue-collar workers and artisans. Preserving some of the patterns of the traditional drinking culture, urban workers consumed large amounts of vodka during religious holidays, but they also drank on ordinary Sundays and in their free time.[76]

Several studies on workers' drinking at the turn of the century note this practice of binging on the weekends, demonstrating very different consumption patterns among urban workers than among village residents. For example, a survey of 470 craftsmen in St. Petersburg showed that 130 drank daily; 120 always drank on holidays and Sundays; 104 drank periodically (several times a month); and the remaining 116 drank only occasionally, but 51 of these drank to absolute drunkenness when they imbibed.[77] In another survey of 2,000 workers, 1,300 reported that they drank excessively on holidays and weekends.[78] Moreover, a study of St. Petersburg workers detained in detoxification shelters (*vytrezvitely*) in 1907 shows the same pattern: on Sunday, 11,345 were detained and on Monday, 10,015, whereas during the rest of the week the numbers ranged from 6,838 to 7,766.[79]

The statistics in these surveys need to be viewed with caution. Actual consumption figures in these studies varied greatly depending on geographical location, the level of industrialization, and many other factors. Moreover, the figures are suspect because all published studies of alcohol consumption were designed for a political purpose: either by temperance advocates trying to discredit the state liquor trade or by the Ministry of Finance trying to defend its interests. The investigators or observers carried the context of educated society's expectations into the settlements and approached worker culture with intellectual predispositions that led them to see only what they were looking for—either drunken, oppressed worker-peasants or self-controlled, disciplined workers.

Despite the bias inherent in these studies, there is enough evidence to conclude that, freed from communal restraints, workers in the cities drank more frequently and spontaneously, suggesting a shift in drinking cultures to accommodate changes in the urban environment. Centered on the tavern, this culture segregated and stratified the lower classes according to gender, income, and social status. Workers forged and maintained social relationships in the tavern, adapting old customs to fit their new environment.

In many ways the tavern replaced some of the functions of the village commune (mir). From time immemorial, Russian peasants have resided in village communes. Most comprised small villages of four to eighty households engaged in agriculture. The commune defined a peasant's entire existence from birth to death and provided for or determined everything that concerned the community, including supervising religious observances, allocating taxes, solving domestic feuds, allocating work assignments, and overseeing births, deaths, and marriages. In short, the commune negotiated all contacts between the peasant and the external world and its authorities. Since the collective took precedence over the individual, the peasant commune fostered a homogeneous, cohesive society based on common interests and values. As the nineteenth century wore on and modern drinking culture altered traditional social structures, the tavern took on some of the characteristics of the commune.

Alcohol and the State

In addition to its social and cultural functions, the tavern became the primary contact point where the consumers' thirst for vodka, the retailers' thirst for profits, and the state's thirst for revenue converged and at times collided. Taverns were not the only retail outlets for alcohol, but they were without question the most significant. In 1859, according to figures compiled by the

Ministry of Finance, 64,000 of the total 121,788 liquor outlets in the Russian empire, or 53 percent, were taverns. Other types of liquor outlets included bottle shops (3,800), kiosks (8,500), vodka stores (1,088), and a miscellaneous category that included warehouses, cellars, and so forth (44,400).[80] Since taverns were the most permanent structures of all the liquor outlets, they were the most easily regulated and the focal point of the conflict between the state's need for liquor revenues and its role as defender of public morals and order. As a well-known temperance activist wrote in 1909:

> Drinking here in Russia poses an extremely important and also a peculiar problem. On the one hand, alcohol is a social evil of tremendous proportions, which is still increasing, thanks to the deterioration of the villages and the growth of capitalism. Of course, we must fight this evil at all costs. On the other hand, alcohol is the major source of income for the state budget, without which, under the present circumstances, we could hardly manage in the very near future.[81]

The government exercised a considerable degree of political and fiscal control over the liquor trade since the first appearance of distilled drinks in Muscovy in the sixteenth century. Initially, state involvement took the form of owning and regulating taverns and inns, which distilled and sold liquor. In the mid-sixteenth century the state began farming out the rights to collect taxes on vodka. By 1767 it extended tax farming to all the Russian provinces. Surviving as the primary means of extracting revenue from the liquor trade, tax farming thrived until the state published a complex law of 279 articles entitled "Statute on Liquor Taxes" in 1861 and put it into practice in 1863.[82]

Tax farms were commercial enterprises, generally funded by an individual entrepreneur, often with backing from others, which contracted with the government to collect taxes in return for the right to make profits from monopolies granted by governments. Particularly common in seventeenth- and eighteenth-century Europe, tax farming was a critical feature of the early modern state. The best known of an important and influential group of merchants in eighteenth-century Europe were the French tax farmers. Viewed as one of the most deeply entrenched features of France's ancien régime, revolutionaries targeted the tax farm as one of the first institutions to be overthrown during the French Revolution.[83]

The history and details of liquor tax farming in Russia are quite complex and beyond the scope of this project.[84] Basically, the government granted exclusive rights to distil grain alcohol to the nobility. From these gentry distillers the government received vodka, which it stored in cellars and warehouses before transferring it to tax farmers. Every four years the state auctioned the rights to administer the trade in vodka within a specified area to tax farmers for an agreed-upon sum of money. Based on how much vodka the government anticipated it would sell in the region over a four-year period, the contract was paid for by the tax farmer, who also collected "excise articles"— a miscellaneous assortment of excises and license fees on different types of manufacturers or retailers. After paying the government for the alcohol and for taxes levied on the sale of the alcohol (which was, in essence, the amount bid at the tax farm auction), the tax farmer could pocket the profits. It was in the farmers' best interests, therefore, to sell vodka at the highest possible price and to water it down to increase volume.

The structure of this system posed obvious problems. In its concern to protect its own revenues, the state traditionally issued regulations that left little opportunity for the tax farmers to make legitimate profits, so they craftily found numerous ways to profit illegitimately. Dependent on the revenues raised by tax farmers, the state disregarded a certain amount of corruption and ignored violations of its own regulations so that tax farmers would continue to take tax farm leases. By the time it reached the lips of tavern patrons, vodka, which was supposed to contain 40 to 50 percent pure alcohol by volume, had usually been watered down two or three times; contained additives such as jimsonweed (durman), oils, soap, copper, and other harmful substances; and carried inflated prices.[85] In order to get drunk, peasants and workers had to consume large amounts of this "excise liquor" for which they had numerous nicknames: French fourteenth class; thinner than water; orphan's tears; tongue-untier; don't ask for purity; liquor's auntie; oh to be drunk; scalds the mouth but leaves you sober.[86] The combination of poor quality and high prices had an enormous economic impact on the lower classes' household budgets. Since vodka was not a luxury item but a necessity for the lower classes, they therefore paid the greatest price for corruption in the vodka trade. Normally this would not attract much attention from the ruling elite, but in 1859 peasants protested high liquor prices, and liquor riots swept through European Russia.

The 1863 reform abolished the tax farm and set up an excise system, largely as an attempt to end officially sanctioned corruption and increase the government's share of the revenues. Under the provisions of the excise system, the state allowed relatively free manufacture and sale of alcoholic beverages with the payment of a tax. Distillers had to pay the excise, and retailers had to pay license fees.[87] Local authorities and organs of self-government granted rights to retail vodka either by the bottle or by the glass, yet the production of alcohol was still reserved for landowners and other members of the gentry class.

Between 1865 and 1885, the excise system appears to have increased state revenues from 126.7 million to 239.0 million rubles by circumventing the tax farmers' share of the profits and curtailing the corruption that system fostered.[88] However, it did not take long for distillers and retailers to find other forms of corruption, fraud, and bribery at the expense of state revenues. Government regulation became more difficult, resulting in a marked increase in smuggling illegal spirits and the spread of illegal retail outlets.[89] Since the state taxed vodka at the point of production, distillers became adept at hiding the amount of liquor produced.

Because of the nearly institutionalized practice of undermeasuring and watering down vodka, as well as the vagaries of Russian statistics, it is nearly impossible to estimate actual consumption of alcohol. What is important is that by the end of the century, upper-class commentators began expressing both concern and condemnation of widespread drunkenness. Playing a greater role in Russian national life, such public concerns began to generate debate over the government's role in promoting drunkenness and the state's moral obligations to the people. Whether drunkenness was actually on the rise is difficult to discern. Various "official" figures show a steady rise in per capita consumption from the 1880s on, but these figures for the most part are meaningless in reflecting real consumption levels. Nonetheless, the intelligentsia used them to wage battle against the state for profiting from the misery of the *narod* (common people) and contributing to the oppression and decay of society.

Under fire from the intelligentsia and under pressure from more conservative circles to end corruption in the liquor trade through the establishment of a state monopoly, the administration of Tsar Alexander III (r. 1881–1894) implemented a reform of the state's alcohol policies. In 1892 Minister of Finance Sergei Witte introduced the reform that he declared "must be directed first of all toward increasing popular sobriety, and only then can it concern itself with the treasury."[90] The basic provisions of the reform created a new

monopolistic system and left vodka distilleries in the hands of private owners, who now had to purchase raw materials from the state. Under the new
law, the Ministry of Finance set the prices and standards of quality for alcohol and granted permission to open new distilleries. The treasury held exclusive rights for the sale of alcoholic beverages, which could only be sold in
warehouses owned by the state or from private establishments supplied with
alcohol by the state. Stores and warehouses could sell vodka only in sealed
bottles to take away; on-premise consumption was prohibited. Taverns could
sell liquor at set prices in sealed bottles only for off-premise consumption,
unless local authorities granted specific institutions permission for on-premise
consumption.

This new monopoly gave the state far more control over the liquor trade
but not over the private drinking behaviors of workers and peasants. Consequently, the reform had a few unintended results. Despite government claims
that the reform was aimed at fostering popular sobriety, state revenues
jumped dramatically—from 230 million rubles in 1895 to 576 million rubles
in 1904.[91] State regulation of the liquor trade resulted in a greater volume of
vodka being produced and sold at lower prices and higher quality. For the
working classes, this meant that more, better, and cheaper vodka was available. It is logical to assume that they drank it in greater quantities.[92]

Street drunkenness increased following the reform. Although the evidence is thin, there were reports that the new laws resulted in the closure of
many establishments selling vodka for on-premise consumption. Moreover,
for a brief time the Ministry of Finance curtailed opening new establishments.[93] Not having public enterprises within which to drink, working-class
drinkers simply moved into the streets. Street drunkenness became especially concentrated around state stores where entrepreneurial *stakanshchiki* (people who would, for a fee, provide drinking glasses) set up stands, providing
glasses for those who had just bought a bottle in the store.[94] Upper-class
observers complained that, contrary to the goals of the reform, popular
drinking did not abate but merely moved from the tavern into the streets.[95] In
the words of one of these, "The pre-reform *kabak* [tavern] disappeared . . . but
the Russian people still rushed after vodka in a frenzy and yielded to unre-
strained drunkenness in taverns and in the streets."[96] The ministry rapidly
reversed its policy against opening new taverns, and from 1902 the number of
public drinking houses steadily increased, especially in urban working-class
districts. This trend continued until prohibition in 1914.[97]

Alcohol, Revolts, and Revolutions

Because drinking was a critical feature of lower-class social and cultural life, the spread of taverns and of a cash economy in the late nineteenth century altered traditional drinking practices and created new drinking problems. At the same time, the state's dependence on liquor revenues made it vulnerable to corruption within the liquor trade and made liquor outlets an appropriate target for political discontent, giving the political meaning of drink greater significance than anywhere else in Europe. From the 1890s until the government's imposition of prohibition in 1914, social critics of every persuasion spoke out against drunkenness, implicitly or explicitly criticizing the government for its involvement in the liquor trade. Newspaper and magazine articles, books, speeches in the Russian Duma (national legislature), and special congresses and conferences addressed the problem of widespread alcoholism among workers and peasants and its devastating implications for Russian social and moral order.

The upper classes expressed genuine concern about the moral decay of society and the spread of drunkenness, especially as drinking became more habitual and drunkenness became more visible. But these concerns were usually expressions of a broader political agenda—the appropriation and redefinition of political power and authority (discussed in chapter 3). Physicians, psychiatrists, and sociologists began to try to define alcoholism and determine its causes. Moral reformers founded a host of temperance societies.

Lower-class Russians lent substance to upper-class fears of chaos and anarchy resulting from drunkenness. The romantic images of the happy-go-lucky muzhik began to fade in the last decades of the nineteenth century as migrant workers flocked to squalid and overcrowded settlements and as the working classes began to resemble the more ominous unwashed masses of industrial Europe—criminal, drunk, and debauched. Further, the state's dependence on liquor revenues left it vulnerable to workers and peasants who could, and did, make tremendous political statements by refraining from drink, challenging the power, authority, and, more poignantly, the purse of the ruling elite. Violence unleashed against taverns as state institutions became part of a protest pattern directed against the entire tsarist political order. Social crises experienced by the lower classes often exploded into all-out liquor riots or boycotts, especially in times of popular political unrest.

The first, most widespread, and perhaps most significant boycotts occurred in 1859 on the eve of the emancipation of the serfs. As peasant protests against serfdom turned into violent uprisings against landowners, a series of widespread liquor riots also shook the country. Of 938 separate reports of massive peasant insubordination, 636, or 68 percent, involved boycotts of vodka sales or attacks on taverns.[98] Soviet historians, not surprisingly, tried to link these liquor boycotts to what Lenin called the "revolutionary situation" in Russia.[99] David Christian has demonstrated, however, that these first boycotts and subsequent riots were more complex and were linked to what the peasants perceived as violations of their traditional rights.[100]

The rising prices and falling quality of vodka in the 1840s and 1850s greatly affected the living standards of the lower classes, for whom vodka was a necessity. By law, 40 percent vodka was to sell at three rubles for one *vedro*. Yet because of the rising bids on tax farms and increasing corruption, by 1858 watered-down vodka retailed at ten rubles a *vedro*.[101] Angry peasants took oaths of sobriety and boycotted alcohol as a form of political protest. According to one report, state peasants organized to protest universal drunkenness. However, it very quickly turned into a protest against the church and the entire state administration. Taking solemn vows of sobriety, a large number of peasants went so far as to break all ties with the Orthodox Church and join secret temperance societies.[102] There is little evidence to suggest these peasants actually intended to reject drunkenness, since they would in effect be protesting against cultural practices that were fundamental to village life.

Unfortunately, upper-class observers wrote most of the accounts of the liquor riots and boycotts. Consequently, they tell us more about upper-class fears than about the motivations of the protesters. Considering the important role vodka played in the villages, a more reasonable explanation is that they were protesting the violation of what they saw as their rights, in this instance the right to buy good quality vodka at a reasonable price. In February 1859 in Balashov, a town in Saratov province, citizens decided to boycott vodka until the tax farmer agreed to sell it at one ruble a *vedro* and "at the strength at which it is sold from the state's cellars."[103] Other than alarmist accounts by upper-class observers, there is no evidence that the protesters wanted a disruption of the old order but rather a restoration of their rights within it.

These liquor boycotts highlight the fact that the lower classes considered vodka a basic necessity and right. When vodka became difficult to obtain, members of the working classes became willing to take collective political action, a rare occurrence among Russian peasantry. Indeed, Russian serfs resorted to protest only when they believed their collective rights were being violated.[104] That peasants banded together to bring down vodka prices suggests they were aware of the power they could wield by boycotting an item so crucial to the state's finances. Rising vodka prices hurt all working people, but the peasantry perceived high prices as an assault on traditional rights and living standards, one that had to be resisted.

Such vodka boycotts created an embarrassing dilemma for the government, which could not openly attack the movement's expressed goals—sobriety and morality. At the same time, the boycotts provided a menacing display of independent political action on the part of the peasantry, one that threatened the fiscal system of tsarist Russia and frightened the upper classes. This dilemma was not resolved until it erupted in violent liquor riots that swept through fifteen provinces in 1859, resulting in over 220 taverns being damaged and 780 people arrested.[105]

The liquor riots of 1859 were the first of what became a pattern of targeting the state's liquor outlets in times of social upheaval. As widespread political unrest and strikes rocked the country during the Revolution of 1905, and again as economic and political strains in 1913–1914 made working-class life untenable, large groups of workers boycotted vodka, avoided taverns en masse, and destroyed state taverns and liquor outlets. The goals of these boycotts are not entirely clear. Nonetheless, since taxes on drink provided the government with nearly a third of its revenue, one can assume that collective boycotts advocated and engaged in by activist workers consciously altering their normal drinking patterns (especially in times of political unrest) were expressions of political protest and attacks against the state. Yet these organized and disciplined workers were only a fragment of the working masses, and it would be wrong to conclude that all attacks against taverns were a form of nascent labor protest. Rather, by the turn of the century the drink trade had become so politicized that, in an environment of revolutionary ferment and violence, taverns became symbols of government authority—targets against which crowds of workers could vent their rage.

For example, on Sunday, January 9, 1905, a large gathering of workers from various parts of St. Petersburg marched on the Winter Palace to petition the tsar for better working conditions, political reforms, and an end to the Russo-Japanese War. Bearing icons and singing hymns, the marchers—men, women, and children—clearly intended no violence. Yet when they disregarded orders to halt, the tsar's troops opened fire on the unarmed crowd, slaughtering hundreds of them. Known as Bloody Sunday, this event triggered wide-spread revolutionary street violence that ebbed and flowed for two years. The revolution was a prolonged episode of violence and social disorganization.[106] Sensational incidents of violence accounted for many thousands of deaths in terrorist assassinations, peasant revolts, and street battles during armed upris-ings. At the same time, an unprecedented rise in crime and criminal violence, street disorders, and public violence accompanied politically oriented vio-lence.[107] Bloody Sunday also marked the beginning of the 1905–1906 liquor boycotts, when "the streets and taverns became deserted."[108] Politically active workers abstained from drinking vodka and boycotted state shops and tav-erns in an effort to strike at the purse of the government.[109] During the spring and summer of 1905, neighborhood taverns were often the scenes of much violence and destruction. For example, in June, on three separate occasions, fights in working-class neighborhoods turned into riots that demolished gov-ernment liquor stores.[110] In August several fights involving hundreds of peo-ple broke out in taverns throughout St. Petersburg, resulting in the total destruction of those buildings.[111]

The 1905–1906 liquor boycotts and attacks on public drinking houses did not last long. Concurrent with the lull in the revolutionary movement in the aftermath of the Revolution of 1905, workers resumed their normal drinking behaviors. In the intervening years, strikes were relatively few, until a massacre of striking workers in the British-owned Lena Goldfields in April 1912 trig-gered riots that engulfed the empire until the outbreak of World War I. Once again, workers directed their rage against the government by attacking drink-ing establishments. Beginning on July 7, 1914, groups of workers in St. Peters-burg initiated a systematic movement to close alcohol outlets. The *Gazeta Kopeika* (Penny Gazette) carried daily stories chronicling the movement to shut down drink shops throughout the city. Within two days all the taverns in the city were closed, and by the end of the week workers began smashing tav-ern windows and looting government liquor stores.[112]

Although the evidence is sketchy, the initial impetus for these boycotts most probably was an effort on the part of activist workers to attack the gov-ernment where it hurt the most—in the purse. Moreover, it is likely that, for many, the state-owned liquor outlet had become a symbol of government intervention into the most privileged and private area of a worker's life. By destroying drink shops in their own neighborhoods, workers asserted their authority over these places and vented the rage of people with no other means of expression.

The Importance of Alcohol

For over 500 years, the drink of choice for most Russians has been vodka. Having powerful associations with health, happiness, and even national character, vodka evolved into a symbol of mythic proportions since its introduction into Muscovy. Since that time, alcohol consumption has become an everyday occurrence for ordinary Russians—as a regular accompaniment to food and present at even the most mundane social occasions, including business transactions of every sort.

Until the nineteenth century, the ritual nature of traditional drinking acted as an informal social control and limited the regular consumption of vodka by village populations. In traditional society, drinking was an obligation as well as a pleasure. The communal nature of traditional drinking both established and strengthened social, political, and economic relationships within village society, reinforcing peasants' sense of community and maintaining village hierarchies. The community perceived any deviation from local norms as an offense. Violating drinking traditions, whether it be abstaining from drinking when custom required it or consuming excessive amounts as a matter of individual preference, could result in social and economic isolation.

Toward the end of the nineteenth century, the availability of cheap alcohol and the shift to a cash economy as the country industrialized eroded this control, leading to at least the appearance of excessive alcohol consumption among the working masses. Moreover, economic developments in nineteenth-century Russia deepened and solidified drinking practices to the extent that drink became a fundamental factor in the social and cultural lives of peasants and workers. With industrialization and urbanization, the lower classes adapted traditional drinking patterns to fit a more modern milieu, and drinking became more a matter of personal choice. With the spread of taverns, the leisure aspects of drinking functioned to structure that milieu by segregating and stratifying segments of the population according to gender, profession, and social status. Both in taverns and in factories, male camaraderie centered on drinking rituals that became exclusionary and delineated the "other"—nonworker, woman, or peasant.

Nonetheless, throughout the nineteenth and early twentieth centuries, drink retained its centrality to the daily lives of lower-class Russians. And throughout the nineteenth and early twentieth centuries, vodka remained the most lucrative source of revenue for the state. Because the state had a pro-

found degree of influence over the basic structure of the liquor industry, changes in government policy had a profound effect on the social and economic lives of peasants and workers. As a result, drinking in Russia was politicized to a degree unmatched in Western countries. Attacks by the upper classes against the state liquor monopoly were often thinly veiled attacks against the tsarist order as a whole. Further, at times of political unrest, the working classes destroyed liquor outlets or boycotted alcohol as a form of protest against the state.

Because of alcohol's social and cultural importance to the lower classes and its economic importance to the state, upper-class reformers began to focus attention on "the drink question." Exponents of theories of social control argue that the development of a modern, industrialized society has increased attempts to control social behavior through the creation of institutions and organizations for legal and moral reform. Toward the end of the nineteenth century, various reform movements and institutions concerned with alcoholism emerged and spread throughout Europe. The next chapter considers these organizations in Russia and how they reflected the larger issue of social control and the establishment of power and legitimacy in fin de siècle Russia.

Tippling and Temperance: Constructing the Drink Problem in Russia

DESPITE THE CENTRALITY OF ALCOHOL TO RUSSIAN SOCIAL, political, and economic life, Russia did not have a "drink problem" until lower-class drinking caught the attention of the upper classes in the late nineteenth century. The emergence of a drink problem in any country or context cannot be explained merely by measuring the extent of alcohol abuse— what constitutes abuse and the standards of measurement themselves are established by those who are engaged in defining the problem. Moreover, the problems and solutions associated with drinking and temperance register the currents, pressures, and tensions at work in the society that created them.

In her monograph on French temperance movements, Patricia E. Prestwich concludes that in France, the anti-alcohol movement attracted public support only when it became a "symbol of some deeper crisis."[1] Similarly, Edwin Chadwick (1800–1890) focused public attention on working-class drunkenness in Great Britain when he connected it with poverty. When presenting evidence to a committee of the House of Commons in 1833, he spoke in favor of restricting the sale of hard liquor and for the provision of healthy recreations for the people. The same appears to be true in Russia. Following shifts in the social and cultural environment resulting from the Great Reforms of the 1860s came the rapid surge of industrialization in the 1890s.

Together, these intensified the forces that drew public attention toward public drunkenness and laid the groundwork for one of the future Soviet state's
top priorities—fostering popular temperance.

At the turn of the twentieth century, the expansion of dirty industrial
neighborhoods, overcrowded housing bursting with newly migrated peasants, the sharp increase in prostitution, and the ever-present drunks in the
streets produced among social critics alarm at what they perceived to be deep
social problems. Consequently, various groups in Russia sought to define the
causes of and cures for alcoholism. At the heart of this quest was a bid for
political power and social control through the establishment of norms that
would assert upper-class cultural authority over the lower classes.

In fewer than fifty years following the Great Reforms, the Russian autocracy collapsed, with the abdication of Tsar Nicholas II (r. 1894–1917) in 1917.
The inefficacy of the Provisional Government ultimately resulted in a second
revolution five months later that swept the Bolsheviks into power. The October Revolution brought the establishment of a Soviet regime and the begin-
nings of immense social upheaval as the Bolsheviks sought to create a sober
socialist society. At the heart of this quest was a bid for cultural hegemony and
social control through the establishment of norms that would assert Bolshevik moral authority over the working class. In short, the Soviet temperance
movement differed little in tone and method from that of the late nineteenth
century. Therefore, an examination of prerevolutionary temperance is critical
in order to uncover the roots of the Bolsheviks' social experimentation.

As early as the 1850s, members of the upper class launched protests against
the liquor tax farm. In the main, these were thinly veiled attacks by liberals
against the archaic and recalcitrant tsarist system. Within a decade, the radical changes brought on by the Great Reforms helped establish the rudiments
of a modern civic order within the confines of an unmodified political frame-
work that deliberately exempted the institutions of absolute rule. Social
groups liberated from antiquated constraints but not yet in possession of
political power, authority, or legitimacy became increasingly self-conscious
and discontented and sought public forums through which to challenge the
regime.[2] Within a widening field of public discourse and an emerging civic
establishment made up primarily of members of the professions influenced
by Western liberalism, the Russian professional strata concerned with issues
of alcoholism and temperance enlisted education and social reform in the
battle against the old order. At the same time, the Orthodox Church, alarmed

by its declining authority and threatened by the rise of secular groups, took up the issue of temperance in an attempt to assert its moral authority and to draw people back into its fold.[3] Throughout the second half of the nineteenth century, groups of physicians, psychiatrists, politicians, business leaders, socialists, liberals, clergy, and even state bureaucrats put forth definitions of and cures for alcoholism. They all agreed that drunkenness was one of the most pressing problems facing Russian society. However, they differed in their prescriptions on how to cure this problem. These different notions about drunkenness expressed tensions between ideas imported from the West and countervailing cultural assumptions in Russia.[4] This chapter aims to highlight these tensions as one aspect of the larger struggle within the upper classes to appropriate and to redefine political power embedded in social relations, public institutions, and intellectual authority. This struggle would be replicated in the 1920s as the Bolsheviks sought to establish power and legitimacy (discussed in chapter 5). In this sense, the Bolshevik project of cultural revolution in the 1920s and 1930s must be seen as part of a process that began well before the revolutions of 1917.

The Tippling Theory

The first sustained public discussions about drunkenness and temperance took place in the 1840s and were grounded in criticisms of the tax farm and, later, the excise tax system. As such, they are not central to this study. They are, however, worth mentioning because they raised the issue of popular drunkenness as a moral and social problem and set the stage for future debates. That is not to say that no one in previous centuries had noticed the vast amounts of alcohol consumed by the Russian population: priests railed against it, foreigners commented on it, and writers satirized it. Sporadic efforts were made to promote sobriety, usually by the church, but these ran afoul of both the customs of the country and the needs of the treasury.[5]

As we have seen, the problem of drink primarily remained the concern of bureaucrats and ecclesiastics until the 1850s, when popular protests against the rising price and falling quality of government vodka led to widespread boycotts and riots.[6] The scale and violence of these boycotts stimulated criticisms of the tax farm and brought the issue of drunkenness into the public arena. For the most part, attacks against the vodka trade were carried out in the press by progressive landowners and economists who spoke out against the economic problems of tax farming and in favor a free-market system.[7] Within these debates, drunkenness had to be addressed in order to counter claims that free trade would result in increased alcohol abuse.

Supporters of free trade in vodka devised an ingenious "tippling" theory, which played a considerable role in future debates over tax farming. They argued that drunkenness had little to do with the amount of vodka consumed but rather was a function of *how* it was consumed. According to this theory, peasants, unaccustomed to regular consumption of vodka because of its high price, drank to excess whenever they had access to alcohol. It followed that the solution to drunkenness consisted of educating peasants to drink more regularly but in moderation; the state could then allow freer trade in vodka at lower prices.[8]

A temperance pamphlet from the 1840s entitled "Drink but Do Not Drink to Recover from a Hangover; Drink but Do Not Become a Drunkard" outlined the positive effects of regular drinking. It claimed that Russians need to drink because of the climate but warned that excessive drinking would lead to spiritual ruin.[9] This pamphlet echoes a miracle tale where the mother of God is supposed to have admonished, "Know, child that it is not evil to drink wine, but it is evil to drink to drunkenness, outside the proper time."[10] This view was also consistent with the position of the church, which had historically been quite accommodating toward drinking. Most clergy, supported by select biblical texts, held to the view that drinking was not harmful and actually had healthful benefits.

The issue of drunkenness had always been a problem for Russian authorities wanting to profit from alcohol revenues without paying the social consequences. The nineteenth century was no exception. Since the church was under the tutelage of the state, the issue of temperance put hierarchs in an uncomfortable position—as arbiters of popular morality, they denounced drunkenness, yet they had to do so in a way that would not discourage drinking entirely, thereby threatening state revenues.

It is not clear where the tippling theory originated, but throughout the late 1800s it gained currency with members of the upper classes concerned with drink, especially those who stood to profit from the liquor trade.[11] It also had merit with the clergy, who themselves often engaged in drinking, sometimes to excess. The Orthodox Church had a deep-seated suspicion of sobriety owing to the fact that almost all sectarians, and a huge contingent of Old Believers, totally abstained from drinking alcohol. These religious sects, under siege from the dominant church, chose abstemiousness as a strict community marker to differentiate themselves from the Orthodox Church, which had no injunctions against strong drink.[12] As Arthur McKee notes, with sobriety so closely associated with sectarianism, many clergymen were hostile even to the church's own temperance movement in the late nineteenth century.[13]

Reflecting the drinking patterns of the upper classes, the tippling theory promised increased consumption, and hence revenues, while decreasing drunkenness. It became the dominant paradigm for discussing the causes of and cures for drunkenness for nearly forty years. The assumptions about drinking and drinkers inherent in this theory reveal some prevailing cultural assumptions of the prereform period. In general, the upper classes viewed drunkenness as a continually annoying and occasionally dangerous problem but a fairly simple matter to be dealt with by the police. Naturally they decried drunkenness, especially when associated with crime, but they did not perceive it as a disorder that threatened public morals or social order. Once peasants gained access to a fairly steady supply of alcohol and were educated on how to consume it, the problem would disappear.

This definition assumed the peasantry to be fairly passive, simple, and pliable, and it discounted the strength and importance of local custom.[14] In both the city and the village, the lower classes were not viewed as objects of punishment or reform but were seen as curiosities, even subjects of celebration. Populist writers of the period described lower-class settlement patterns and the colorful street life in the cities, including pleasantly drunk workers, as representative of the Russian character and traditions.[15]

The tippling theory demonstrated the confidence of the upper classes in their ability to control and regulate lower-class behavior. Beginning in the 1860s, modes of thought changed, facilitating a shift in the public's ideas about temperance. Temperance came to be seen as a solution to the social problem of alcoholism, as opposed to "tippling," which was designed to lessen drunkenness and protect state and gentry alcohol profits. Between 1890 and 1914 the significant increase in the number of public and private temperance societies concerned directly or indirectly with the drink problem and its broader implications traces this evolution. These societies, and the solutions they proposed, reflect structural changes in late Imperial Russia that took place after Tsar Alexander II (r. 1855–1881) and his enlightened bureaucrats set the stage for modernization. Traditional ritualized drinking acted as an informal social control and limited regular consumption among the populace.

However, the migration of peasants to the cities, along with the increased availability of cheap vodka and the evolution of a money economy, began to erode this control in the second half of the nineteenth century and led to at least the appearance of excessive consumption.

The Politicization of Temperance

The Great Reforms of the 1860s liberated the serfs, reconstituted the judicial system, laid the basis for local self-government, and, perhaps most important for our purposes, alleviated censorship restraints. This widened the field of public discourse and within it the expression of an emerging civic establishment.[16] These transformations created an amorphous public domain and launched a struggle for public power and cultural influence between the old regime and the new social forces unleashed by the state's own program of modernization. The question of alcoholism and temperance was one aspect of that contest as the state came under increasing attacks from all sectors for its role in promoting drunkenness. Most notably, from the mid-nineteenth century, middle- and upper-class moral reformers as well as the Orthodox Church began to take an increasingly firm and vocal stand in favor of temperance.[17]

Over the next several decades, and especially after the Revolution of 1905, the nature of class relations shifted, opening a new political arena in which educated society was more free to act yet more threatened by action from the lower ranks. The working class, once regarded by the upper class as fragmented and undeveloped, began to resemble the dangerous, dark, ignorant masses of Europe.[18] In the aftermath of the revolution, Russia acquired a semblance of institutionalized political life in the form of an elected state Duma, accompanied by other guarantees of civic freedom created by the October Manifesto of 1905. At the same time, Nicholas II granted freedom of conscience, breaking the formal monopoly Orthodoxy had over religious life while maintaining the church's subordinate status to the state. As a result, upper-class social reformers who saw themselves as guardians of moral order and cultural hierarchy gained access to institutionalized power, while the church's position as the primary arbiter of public morality was challenged. Consequently, newly enfranchised and emboldened groups began publicly debating the politicized issues of culture, morality, and civic values.

The question of alcoholism and temperance was an important aspect of these debates. Popular drunkenness, which seemed to intensify with urbanization and which upper-class observers blamed for the waves of street violence during the 1905 revolution, was the perfect symbol of the bankruptcy of the old cultural and political order. As it became apparent that the state was not willing to compromise its lucrative liquor monopoly and the lower classes were not interested in "going on the wagon," social and moral reformers jumped on the bandwagon of temperance. Drunkenness became a major issue in Russian public life.[19] The progressive forces responsible for undermining the rigid institutional structures of the old order set in motion revolutionary social and cultural changes that were played out over the issue of alcoholism. As the autocracy clung to its traditional principles, cultural assumptions were breaking down, particularly in the cities and among the educated population, and the question of alcoholism became embedded in the larger question of Russia's future path.

The educated elite, which included members of the state bureaucracy, exhibited great ideological diversity despite belonging to a sociologically defined class. In postemancipation Russia, members of both the bureaucracy and educated society responded to the changes taking place by formulating various ideologies that redefined their self-identity, their social role, and the criteria for determining social status. Ensuing ideological conflicts helped produce societal cohesion and fragmentation in the last prerevolutionary decades. This fragmentation can be seen in the way different groups within the educated upper classes addressed the problem of alcoholism, its causes and cures, and how each group claimed to be particularly suited to solve this problem.[20]

At the risk of oversimplifying some very complex material, it is possible to identify three main ideological orientations in the development of temperance societies and professional discourse on alcoholism between the 1890s and 1914: liberalism, professionalism, and socialism. By liberalism I do not mean the ideas and endeavors of political activists in a narrow sense but a system of attitudes and values dispersed among different social groups and in various cultural locations.[21] In late Imperial Russia, liberalism was expressed most acutely in social activism and reform-mindedness, as connoted by the Russian term "*obshchestvennost*,"[22] which relates in some basic ways to the English term "public." *Obshchestvennost*' signifies the public sphere; a sense of public duty and civic spirit, increasingly in an urban context; and the groups that possessed these values. Liberal intellectuals—educated men and women who were not devoted to politics as a profession but who lived and thought politics in the course of their professional and civic lives—embodied the principles of *obshchestvennost'*. When the Great Reforms broke officialdom's monopoly on public life, nongovernmental institutions such as the zemstvo began to play a greater public role. Consequently, the reforms imbued liberalism with an expressed yearning for social duty and a commitment among Russian professionals to make society function better by applying their expertise to perceived social ills.

Though still operating from old bases—the academy, the professions, the zemstvo, and the press—this liberal stratum of society expanded steadily with the growth of the professional classes and acquired dozens of organizational outlets for opinions and activities, such as private associations, unions, and professional congresses. Temperance societies and congresses were some of the bodies that gave structure to liberal opinion. Liberalism, as expressed through the issue of temperance, greatly influenced the professionalization, and hence the medicalization, of the drink problem. There were, however, significant differences between the medical professionals' approach to alcoholism and that of the liberal social reformers. Those differences most clearly highlight the struggle for intellectual authority and political or social legitimacy and power.

Russian liberalism embraced the values of personal autonomy, individual equality, and the rule of law as opposed to the traditional patriarchal order and its dependence on police rule and human servitude. These newer values influenced how liberal social reformers concerned with temperance constructed the problem and proposed solutions to alcoholism. Naturally, liberal reformers' assumptions and attitudes about alcoholism began with moral judgments about human nature in general and the character of the lower classes they hoped to reform in particular. Although structural causes of alcoholism were increasingly recognized in Russia—specifically poverty and poor living and working conditions—the liberal reformers' enchantment with the idea of the individual, as opposed to the communal, led them to emphasize alcoholism as an individual moral failing.

Moreover, the postreform economic order created and perpetuated glaring inequalities and injustices that could not be resolved by liberals lacking institutional or political power. This, too, caused them to stress the importance of individual rather than social change. At the same time, Russia's expanding urban-based industries drew an unprecedented number of unskilled laborers into the cities. The middle and upper classes characterized these migrant workers who inhabited overcrowded and filthy settlements as unruly, vagrant, weak willed, and potentially dangerous. As such, they threatened the liberal vision of a reformed, responsible, and self-reliant Russia.[23] Not surprisingly, temperance advocates and the societies they founded concentrated on reforming the morals of the urban poor and emphasized morality (*nravstvennost'*), thrift (*berezhlivost'*), and moderation (*umerennost'*) as instruments of self-help by which downtrodden alcoholics could lift themselves up. Liberals believed the civilizing influence of a more disciplined, organized, and rational culture and value system could reform the habits and vices of the common people.

Between 1895 and 1914 literally thousands of local and national, professional and private, Orthodox and lay societies and associations concerned with the issue of temperance emerged in Russia. The spread of temperance societies was part of a pan-European trend. In 1835 Joseph Livesey founded the British Association for the Promotion of Temperance. Within a few years, hundreds of temperance societies emerged throughout Britain, including the National Temperance Federation, the Irish Temperance League, and numerous societies sponsored by the Quakers and the Salvation Army. In 1837 Vicar Peter Wieselgren established Sweden's first temperance society, giving birth to several nationwide temperance campaigns. Throughout the nineteenth century, countries such as France, Finland, Germany, and Belgium had temperance movements. Even the United States, Australia, and New Zealand caught "temperance fever" from their European cousins and sponsored numerous campaigns aimed at fostering popular temperance.

Boris Segal claims that by 1912, there were 8,000 temperance societies with a total of 500,000 members throughout the Russian Empire.[24] These societies deserve further attention, but for purposes of this study it is sufficient to discuss only two examples. The two largest and most visible lay societies, the First Moscow Temperance Society (Pervoe Moskovskoe Obshchestvo Trezvosti) and the national Guardianships of Popular Temperance (Popechitel'stva o Narodnoi Trezvosti), were strongly influenced by liberalism and serve as examples of liberal social reform. At no time did either society mention drinking among the middle or upper classes as problematic. For them, alcoholism afflicted only the lower classes, especially the urban poor. Both these societies viewed alcoholism as basically an individual moral failing resulting from faulty upbringing, a lack of resistance to vice, grim social conditions, or inherent character weaknesses. Their solutions were to provide the lower classes with "rational" amusements and educational and inspirational literature.[25]

Funded by the state treasury out of the proceeds of the liquor monopoly, the Guardianships, founded in 1895, operated a wide network of libraries, teahouses, and public readings before 1917. Membership was comprised of representatives of the state, church, and local governmental bureaucracies, in addition to nonvoting members, primarily landowners, clerics, and military officials, who donated their time but did not participate in policy matters. Functioning at the provincial and district levels, the Guardianships sought to divert the lower classes from drink, especially in taverns, and to improve their morals by raising their cultural level and cultivating spiritual interests.[26] The Guardianships' strategy was to organize the lives and culture of the urban poor in two ways: to create an inviting diversion in the teahouses and to disseminate literature that would educate and spiritually uplift the lower classes. The Guardianships' representative in the Ministry of Finance stipulated that the teahouses should "not only serve as buffets, but must be popular clubs . . . housed in light and spacious places. Every teahouse must provide newspapers and journals. . . . [V]isitors must be able to find entertainment, gymnastics facilities, and the opportunity to listen to music."[27] The Guardianships' recommended reading lists included, for the most part, religious and patriotic propaganda and works by well-known Russian writers such as L. N. Tolstoy and A. P. Chekhov.[28]

Operating in much the same vein, the First Moscow Temperance Society tried to substitute rational or useful amusements for the "perverse influence of the tavern."[29] The attitude of the society can be summed up in the words of one of its members, A. R. Lednitskii, "It is not enough to give the stomach food or the hands work: one must give spiritual food, establish mental hygiene, freshen the sensations of man's soul with noble amusements and moral books."[30] Founded in 1896, the society operated two teahouses and libraries in workers' districts, sponsored concerts and public readings, ran a literacy school on Sunday evenings, published books and temperance materials, and even had a "Sober Choir" that performed occasionally in local churches.[31] Nearly half of their funds came from the Guardianships, 25 percent from teahouse profits and literature sales, and the rest from private contributions and membership dues. The society's board of directors, which included doctors, merchants, priests, shopkeepers, a factory inspector, and a peasant, decided policy matters. Only 11 of the 235 full members were women. Twenty listed themselves as nondrinkers, and 158 claimed to drink heavily and often.[32]

Judging from the occupations of the Guardianships' members, and especially those of the Moscow Temperance Society's members, these organizations attracted people who fell between the highly educated or noble elite and the barely literate poor. They worked for a living, but in commercial enterprises or government offices, not with their hands. At the turn of the twentieth century, this emerging middle class was differentiated by occupation and stratified economically yet was fused by a common sense of being set apart from the masses below and aspiring to the wealth and values of those above.[33]

In cultural terms, this middle class existed as a group that was poised uncomfortably between the less-educated common people and the educated old intelligentsia. They wanted their tastes to be recognized as legitimate, and they sought to be included in the cultural life dominated traditionally by intelligentsia.[34] Class and cultural self-consciousness made it important for this new middle class to make manifestly clear that they had risen above the "uncultured" masses. They therefore adopted values and conventions that would mark their arrival into "civilized" society: hard work, responsibility, and ambition; self-discipline and restraint in emotional and sexual expression; and an abhorrence (at least in public) of activities considered vices—smoking, gambling, and especially drinking. In short, the combination of Victorian and liberal values they embraced set them apart from the lower classes and signaled a demand for equal status for their tastes and values from the classes above.[35]

The rather Victorian temperance societies attracted members of the nascent middle class who clung tenaciously to this vision of civilization largely because they had only recently acquired the right to consider themselves civilized. In an effort to confirm their new status in society, members of temperance societies defined alcoholism as a moral failing coming from the cultural, economic, and moral poverty of the lower classes. They emphasized the virtues of "cultured" amusements, such as reading literature, drinking tea, and listening to music, to replace drinking. There is no evidence to suggest that members of these societies tempered their own drinking—in fact, over half the members of the Moscow Temperance Society drank heavily and often. Also, at no time did middle- or upper-class drinking enter into their discussions of alcoholism. It seems, therefore, that the manner in which they sought to reform and order lower-class culture was ultimately to protect the outward symbols of their own privilege and cultural attainment. By asserting a certain amount of control over the social environment, members of the middle class could validate their cultural values, thereby claiming their place in society.

At least one portion of this emerging middle stratum did not aspire to the values of the elite but sought to advance and legitimize its own practical "modern" values.[36] This group consisted of Russian professionals whose values also found expression in temperance, most notably among physicians and psychiatrists. As members of the emerging middle class, they had a sense of isolation from the rest of society and embraced common middle-class liberal values such as personal autonomy and the rights of the individual. They also had a commitment to social activism, adopting the mantle of social and moral reform. However, one factor that differentiated professionals from other members of the middle stratum was their identification with an international community of specialists. The programs advocated by many Russian reformers from the professional stratum, especially medical and psychiatric professionals, borrowed heavily from European models.[37]

In western Europe, the professions grew with relatively little guidance from the state. Rooted in medieval guilds, they had a history of self-government, enjoyed special privileges, and were regarded with respect.[38] Russian professionals hoped to emulate their Western counterparts. This urge to develop autonomous professional organizations led to another characteristic that distinguished them from liberal moral reformers: an expressed desire for their own special place in society where they could live and work without government interference and be free to make their own independent contribution to Russian life. Russian professionals did not aspire to the nobility or the bureaucracy; instead, they hoped to create a new sphere of activity outside the government.[39]

Beginning in the 1860s, Russian professionals voiced a desire to establish autonomous professional organizations and scientific societies, but the government closely monitored and at times prohibited such groups.[40] Restrained from activities open to professionals in the West, Russian professionals channeled their efforts into the one area in which they could be effective—public welfare. Many professionals believed that both society and the state would eventually acknowledge their efforts to improve and modernize Russia—that the important contributions they could make as autonomous professionals to public welfare would overcome the government's suspicion of independent groups.[41]

Virtually every profession contained a faction that argued its program was essential to Russia's salvation. Individuals could, and did, engage in informal group activity, and certain professional groups obtained government permission to hold national or international congresses.[42] These congresses, therefore, became one of most important forums for the development of professional groups. Those that succeeded in convening meetings often provided an umbrella under which other nascent professions could meet and organize.[43]

Medicine and public health were two such areas of professional endeavor that enjoyed a modicum of autonomy, secured permission to convene congresses, and, owing to the efforts of some activists, generated increased attention in the public sphere for issues of public welfare. Professionals from within these fields strove to define alcoholism in terms of a medical and public health problem, attempting to make alcoholism the domain of doctors and not moral reformers. According to their arguments, the danger was chronic alcoholism, not occasional drunkenness, and the issue was public health, not public order. In this way they could claim authority over the private behaviors of the lower classes. Safeguarding public health by combating alcoholism would not only create a public role for health care professionals, but in the process it would also confer legitimacy and authority on their social activism. Ultimately, their aims were political: to effect a shift to modernity and a new social order by redefining the status of the individual in relation to the state and by regulating private behaviors for the physical welfare of the community.

Russian medical practitioners sought physiological explanations for excessive drinking and adopted the term "alcoholism" (*alkogolizm*) as opposed to "drunkenness" (*p'ianstvo*) to connote the phenomenon of disease. Soviet physicians also made this distinction. Beginning in the 1860s, many Russian health care professionals built on European theories that classified alcoholism as a physical illness. They relied on concepts of alcoholism developed in French and German universities to conduct laboratory studies on the effects of alcohol on the body and mind.[44] For the most part, however, the results of this research and the various theories on the etiology of alcoholism were confined to a small group of scholars. It took the sustained efforts of the Swiss-born physician and temperance advocate E. F. Erisman, who for many years was a leading figure in Russian public health, to bring the disease con-

cept of alcoholism into a public forum and set the course for the medicalization of the drink question. In 1896 he was able to convince the Twelfth International Congress of Physicians in Moscow to establish a special division on
alcoholism as a medical problem.[45]

The idea that alcoholism was a disease requiring medical treatment
gained momentum, especially after the Twelfth Congress accepted it as a
medical concern and introduced the disease concept of alcoholism to a wide
range of physicians, psychiatrists, and laypeople. Nearly ten years earlier, in
1887, at the Congress of Russian Psychiatrists in Moscow, Dr. L. S. Minor had
proposed opening special institutions for treating alcoholics, applying Western methods as a model.[46] (Minor went on to become a noted Soviet neu-
ropathologist involved in the treatment of alcoholics.) Not until after the 1896
congress, however, did the Kazan Temperance Society establish the first Russian hospital for alcoholics in Kazan.[47] The following year, A. M. Korovin, a
physician and temperance advocate who would remain actively involved in
anti-alcohol measures under the Bolsheviks, founded a private hospital for
alcoholics in Moscow, and in 1898 the Guardianships of Popular Temperance
opened an outpatient clinic in Moscow.[48]

Beginning in 1896, alcoholism became a frequent topic in the pages of the
growing number of professional journals. Publications that regularly discussed
alcoholism included *Vrachebnaia gazeta* (Doctor's Daily), *Russkii vrach* (Russian Physician), *Zemskii vrach* (Zemstvo Physician), and *Obozrenie psikhiatr*
(Psychiatrist's Review). Temperance advocates from within the medical and
psychiatric professions also began publishing the first temperance journals
with professional medical affiliation and emphasis, including *Vestnik trezvosti*
(Temperance Herald) and *Trezvost' i berezhlivost'* (Sobriety and Thrift).

Yet the professionals who aspired to enlighten and counsel reformers on
the means of curing or preventing alcoholism could not reach a consensus on
its causes or cures. In the pages of these journals and in the discussions at various meetings and conferences devoted to alcoholism, experts agreed on the
danger of this disease, but what exactly it was; what caused it; why it seemed
to be prevalent among certain groups, especially urban workers; and how to
cure it were topics of heated debate.[49] These subjects could not be seriously
discussed, however, without critical analysis of the social and economic policies of the government. As a result, professional and philosophical divisions
within the health care community generated divergent responses to the state's
role in public health and to the optimal direction of Russia's social develop-

ment. The fragmentation within professional discourse on alcoholism high-lighted a basic fracture within society and even the autocratic state after 1905: the abstract civic values, most notably progressive social reform, of liberalism and modernization as borrowed from the West competed with both the pow-erful and persistent model of custodial statehood and a pervasive ethos of socialist collectivism that affected even the upper classes.

Temperance and the Church

Like professionals, the church had its own reasons for taking on the prob-lem of drunkenness. Concerned by a clear loss in popularity among the mass-es and threatened by an explosion of religious diversity after Nicholas II allowed for freedom of conscience following the Revolution of 1905, the church also turned its attention to temperance in a bid to restore its waning authority, to reestablish links to the community, and to retake the high ground of moral reform.[50] Among the clergy, however, there was no agree-ment about the degree to which drink was an evil; nor was there a clerical consensus as to how to combat intemperance. This lack of clerical consensus might be explained by the fact that priests drank, too, and many were notori-ous drunkards. Further, because the church was tied to the state, and the state relied heavily on liquor revenues, concerned priests had to tread cautiously around the issue of temperance.

It was not until 1889 that the Holy Synod, the supreme ecclesiastical organ in Russia, invited priests to preach on temperance.[51] Prior to 1889, various independent religious temperance societies arose in the urban parishes. Village priests also organized temperance societies, but these never gained much sup-port and in some cases met with open resistance from the rural population.

The most well known and successful parish temperance society was the Alexander Nevskii Temperance Society founded in 1898 in St. Petersburg by a young priest, Father Alexander Vasilievich Rozhdestvenskii. Rozhdestvenskii headed the Orthodox Society for Religious-Moral Enlightenment, whose mission was to counter the challenges perceived from other faiths and the growing social activism of educated society.[52] Viewing drunkenness as a vice that separated the individual from God, Rozhdestvenskii saw in the creation of the temperance society a way to strengthen the church's social role and to reinvigorate pastoral practice. His solution to drunkenness was to make the drinker take a public pledge of abstinence for a specific amount of time, typ-

ically from one to three months. Support for the newly sober came from regular church meetings and activities. In this way the society, consciously or
not, advocated consumption patterns similar to those of rural inhabitants,
who would have long periods of sobriety punctuated by bouts of extreme
drunkenness on holidays and special occasions.

Meetings and church activities appealed to workers, especially those fresh
from the village, probably because these functions gave workers a sense of
communal belonging and mirrored elements of village culture. Echoing the
earlier tippling theory, this approach also appealed to church hierarchs and
the state since it still allowed for drinking while asserting a modicum of social
control. By sobering up the *narod,* the clergy attempted to restore the moral
authority of the church. The organization of the church-sponsored temperance movement, however, was weak. Local societies usually depended on a
single energetic priest. If that priest died or left the parish, the local society
languished. Nonetheless, as Patricia Herlihy demonstrates, the existence of
several hundred church-based societies allowed the church to claim that it
alone could bring about the moral betterment of the Russian people.[53]

The struggle for sobriety was also a bid by the church to demonstrate that
it still had relevance in the modern era. As the metropolitan of St. Petersburg
declared in a summons to the clergy to struggle against alcoholism published
in the journal *Golos tserkvi* (Voice of the Church) in 1913: "The church must
here loudly raise its voice to speak this word of truth, so that the whole people hear it. We the pastors must show that we can accomplish something in
these times when those who do not wish us well are ready to throw us over-
board as garbage, as useless weeds."[54]

The Alexander Nevskii Temperance Society was wildly successful, claiming 75,889 members in 1905–1906. It became the model for other temperance
societies and movements. One of the more zealous members of the
society was Father Ioann of Krondstadt, who founded his own temperance
society in 1899.[55] His movement very quickly spread throughout the entire
province, and a great number of his followers took the pledge for life.
Interestingly, the Ioannites ran afoul of the church for being too pietistic.
According to Eugene Clay, the Ioannites were censured by the Holy Synod in
1908 for being too antiestablishment in their rejection of the authority of the
church and too devoted to Father Ioann.[56] But the Ioannites were not the only
temperance advocates to earn the displeasure of the church.

Borrowing elements of popular religiosity from the Alexander Nevskii Temperance Society and Father Ioann's movement, and rivaling their successes, Ivan A. Churikov, a peasant tradesman from Samara, headed one of the most widespread popular temperance movements in late Imperial Russia. Although a layman, Churikov converted the urban poor to sobriety by preaching the gospel, healing the sick with prayers, and hearing public confessions. By 1911 Churikov's followers, known as the *trezvenniki* (teetotalers), numbered nearly 100,000 former drunken beggars, prostitutes, and the like, who had forsworn alcohol and been reborn as hard-working, churchgoing people.[57] Almost as soon as the movement arose, however, members of the church hierarchy sought to crush it. While the church might be threatened by drunkenness, it feared sectarians and the challenge they represented to Orthodox hegemony even more. The popularity of the *trezvennik* movement stood as a painful reminder of the failure of the old order.

The Commission on the Question of Alcoholism

Clearly, from the educated elite to liberal professionals, parish priests, and the working classes, drunkenness came to symbolize the ills of the old regime. Temperance became contested ground for groups trying to establish cultural, political, and moral authority. The ideological fragmentation in the debates around alcoholism becomes apparent in examining the workings of the Commission on the Question of Alcoholism and the Means for Combating It (Komissiia po Voprosu ob Alkogolizme i Merakh Bor'by s Nim), founded in 1898. Earlier, growing interest in public health had led to the founding of the Russian Society for the Protection of Public Health (Russkoe Obshchestvo Okhraneniia Narodnogo Zdraviia) in 1877.[58] Joining together various groups with an interest in public health, including government representatives, medical practitioners, and temperance advocates, the society from the outset reflected diverse and even contradictory tendencies. The rising tide of concern over drunkenness led the society to create the commission to examine questions of alcoholism as a medical and public health problem. It is significant that the society organized the commission under the aegis of its biological section, which typically addressed questions of diseases and epidemics, thereby implying that alcoholism was a biological, and hence medical, problem rather than a moral or social problem. The medicalization of alcoholism complements other intellectual trends occurring throughout Russia and Europe as a whole, as members of educated society increasingly viewed rationalism and science as the keys to modernization.[59]

Enjoying a quasi-official status, the commission was conceived of and headed by the well-known psychiatrist and member of the board of the St. Petersburg Duma, M. N. Nizhegorodtsev. Its ninety-five charter members included many distinguished physicians and psychiatrists, prominent temperance advocates, academics, civil servants, a few clergymen, and two senior officials of the Ministry of Finance, who took a cautious interest in the proceedings of the commission. In addition, four organized groups joined the commission: the St. Petersburg Society of Psychiatrists, the St. Petersburg University Juridical Society, and the Societies of Neuropathology and Psychiatry at Moscow University and Kazan University.[60]

The commission's self-defined mandate was multifaceted. Its main objective was to determine the physiological, cultural, and economic effects and treatment of alcoholism. It also approached alcoholism as a problem with various social, legal, and political ramifications.[61] In the first four years of its existence the commission convened forty-five meetings and formed ten subcommittees to examine various social, economic, and medical aspects of the disease.[62] Given the composition of the group, it is not surprising that agreement could not be reached over the causes of and solutions to alcoholism.

Nonetheless, members of the commission shared many similar opinions. Nearly all members, for example, blamed industrial capitalism and urbanization as the chief causes of excessive drinking. Most were primarily concerned with the relationship between the spread of alcoholism and the conditions of the urban working class.[63] By focusing on alcoholism as a social phenomenon, members of the medical profession attempted to create a role for themselves as experts on public health, not only educating the masses but also advising the state on necessary social reforms in a way that provided the educated and professional elite with status and influence. At the same time, competing occupational, institutional, and political interests often divided these educated professionals. Most significant, their specialized expertise was compatible with various irreconcilable ideological perspectives that could either support or challenge the autocratic regime. The conflict resulting from the ideological diversity among members of the commission turned the issue of alcoholism into a battleground between liberal and radical reformers.

By 1900 the lines had been drawn for the contest between liberal and revolutionary members of the commission and between both these groups and the government. The liberal professionals called for state assistance and juridical reforms to increase the civil rights and living conditions of workers. These professionals included the physician N. B. Vvedenskii; D. A. Dril', an important barrister and editor of *Trezvost' i berezhlivost'* (Sobriety and Thrift); physician D. N. Borodin; and well-known physician and founder of *Vestnik trezvosti* (Bulletin of Sobriety), N. I. Grigor'ev. In the socialist camp, those linking alcoholism with capitalism and calling for a total restructuring of the social and political order included the editor of *Vrachebnaia gazeta* (Physicians' Gazette) and the commission's secretary, physician G. I. Dembo, as well as the prominent psychiatrist L. S. Minor, physician A. M. Korovin, and the founder of the first Russian clinic for alcoholics, V. M. Bekhterev, all of whom stayed involved in public health issues following the revolutions of 1917.

After two years of work, the "official findings" of the commission, which in fact were an uneasy compromise between these competing ideologies, revealed that alcoholism was "a complex social phenomenon that causes incalculable damage to the health and morality of the people and leads to the degeneration of entire classes of society." Reflecting the orientations of its members, the commission could only acknowledge the various opinions about the causes of alcoholism, which "some see only in economic terms; others in ignorance, in the lack of intellectual development, in a legal system that is unsatisfactory, in the discontent and moral revolt of individuals and of certain sections of the population. . . . [S]till others argue that misery is not the cause, but on the contrary, the result of alcoholism."[64]

Liberal-oriented professionals dominated the two most active permanent subcommittees the commission established—the Subcommittee on Education and the Subcommittee on Juridical Psychiatric Matters.[65] Dril', who in addition to being a barrister and editor was a professor of Russian law and an adviser to the Ministry of Justice, headed the Subcommittee on Education but had considerable influence in both subcommittees. Having little patience for the moralistic advocates of temperance, Dril' argued that deplorable living and working conditions led to "narcotism" among workers, primarily in the form of alcoholism. Drawing from research done on handicraft artisans (*remeslennye rabochie*) in St. Petersburg, Dril' asserted that workers had been put in unfavorable economic circumstances that they did not understand and could not control. The high rents and food prices caused overcrowding and poor diets. Workers had no means of coping with their incomprehensible situation other than to escape it through alcohol abuse. According to Dril', poor diet and crowded living arrangements made them especially susceptible to addiction to narcotic substances, including alcohol.[66]

Dril' also attacked the prevailing system of industrial apprenticeship. Claiming that the long hours and deplorable circumstances debilitated the human organism, he argued that workers were thus driven to poison themselves with alcohol or other narcotic substances. The only solution to the problem lay in government and society working together to gradually improve workers' living and working conditions. Foremost among the solutions he advocated were development of progressive industrial legislation and strict controls over enforcement of such legislation. Other measures of primary importance included the creation of trade schools and the construction of inexpensive and comfortable housing for workers.[67]

Grigor'ev's findings confirmed Dril's opinions. In a study of alcoholism among workers in small artisanal shops in St. Petersburg, Grigor'ev found that they worked fourteen to twenty hours a day and that their diet, consisting largely of liquids and starchy foods, provided inadequate nourishment. Workers and apprentices usually slept on the floor, either in the workshop itself or in an adjacent kitchen. Their low wages prohibited them from obtaining better food and lodging. Of the 470 alcoholics Grigor'ev interviewed, 132 started drinking when they were apprentices.[68] Grigor'ev also postulated that a defect of the central nervous system, which intoxication intensified, caused chronic alcoholism. He defined alcoholism as a hereditary predisposition, exacerbated by environment, psychological trauma, and excessive fatigue.[69] Recommending the establishment of government regulations to control relations between owners and workers and to improve conditions in the shops, he advocated the creation of a special inspectorate to prevent all workers from succumbing to the lure of the tavern.[70]

Many liberal members of the commission attached great importance to education, particularly early anti-alcohol training for school-aged children along with establishment of legal norms for teaching it. These commission members strove to encourage other institutions, such as temperance societies, municipal governments, and zemstvos, to support temperance education and to enlist the help of teachers, physicians, and especially priests toward that end.[71] They advocated a program for primary and secondary school curricula called "anti-alcohol sciences," an odd mix of elementary hygiene, spiritual guidance, and temperance propaganda.[72] The program sought to implant a dogmatic social morality in the minds of Russian schoolchildren. Claiming authority based on scientific truth, proponents of this program insisted they were uniquely qualified to define and teach desirable social behavior.[73] However, having little influence with a government suspicious of any educational program not based on the Bible and the Fundamental Laws, the commission's proposed school program never amounted to much. Indeed, it could not even secure permission from the Ministry of Public Instruction to give public lectures on hygiene and medicine as they related to alcoholism.

Liberals and professionals, both individually and collectively, adopted progressive values in formulating causes of and cures for alcoholism. These formulations contained an organic interpretation of alcoholism combined with a preoccupation with modernization and the negative effects of industrialization. For many, alcoholism and other negative aspects of industrialization were painful reminders of the dysfunctional qualities of urban industrial civilization and the ambiguity of progress. Professionals sought to bring existing values and institutions into conformity with Western models, on the one hand, and with the changing character of Russian society, on the other. Their attempts focused attention not only on alcoholism but also on prostitution, tuberculosis, and other manifestations of the changing social environment.[74] In addressing these social ills, Russian medical professionals emphasized the interaction between biology and society, rather than the absolute priority of biology. If alcoholics were sick rather than oppressed, then medical intervention rather than social reform was the key to reducing the incidence of drunkenness. The medical professionals' willingness to enlist state intervention in the form of legislation on the dispensation of bodies, minds, and private behaviors was a bid for authority and power, without radically altering the social structures. By contrast, the socialists on the commission were determined to turn the issue of alcoholism into a means of attacking the existing order itself.

Finding a link between the capitalist order and alcoholism in Friedrich Engels's analysis of social problems as a result of oppression, a number of temperance advocates allied themselves with revolutionary socialism. The environmentalist approach fit their sociopolitical views and provided them with a convenient tool to use against the existing order. Prior to 1905, these socialist professionals did not get much support or ammunition from professional socialists. Social Democrats were strangely silent on the issue of alcoholism, and even V. I. Lenin addressed the topic in a rather ambiguous fashion. In his most noted work, *The Development of Capitalism in Russia,* Lenin lashed out against agrarian socialists who criticized the alcoholic behavior of urban workers, implying that excessive alcohol consumption might even be progressive in relation to the life and values of the villages workers had recently left.[75]

Despite, or maybe because of, the lack of attention to alcoholism from the revolutionary intelligentsia prior to 1905, socialist physicians and psychiatrists, like their liberal counterparts, exerted their professional expertise to gain intellectual authority and political power. Defining the root cause of alcoholism among the working class as economic, a result of capitalist exploitation, Dembo, a socialist physician and the commission's secretary, succinctly outlined the socialists' position. He insisted that economic causes of alcoholism were more to blame than the Russian people's customs and traditions.[76] The commission's socialist temperance advocates attacked the views of Dril' and Grigor'ev as utopian and pious. In contradistinction to liberal arguments for the importance of education about alcoholism, the socialist physician I. I. Ianzhul, for example, argued that the real need was for the "education of the workers to their economic hardships." He asserted that the more the masses were aware of their exploitation, the easier it would be for them to improve their lives through revolutionary struggle.[77]

Enlarging on Dembo's arguments that economic and social factors encouraged excessive drinking, Korovin dismissed the idea of a hereditary predisposition for alcoholism, describing the phenomenon of loss of control that causes many alcoholics to drink without restraint after the first glass.[78] In numerous articles and public lectures, he outlined the damage done by alcoholism to the human organism, aiming his arguments at an audience of uneducated workers. Putting great emphasis on the development of workers' social and political consciousness as the solution to alcoholism, he pointed to the growing number of workers' temperance groups in St. Petersburg, Moscow, Odessa, and Tula as evidence of growing worker activism and hence consciousness.[79] However, there is little evidence to support Korovin's assertion that activist workers organized for the cause of temperance. Moreover, he failed to note that, for the most part, local priests set up and led these societies and that often the local population responded to the societies with hostility, going so far in some cases as to burn down the "temperance clubhouses."[80]

Most socialist temperance advocates alluded to the political implications of their views. Without freedom of speech, these educated professionals argued, they could not make their contributions to the general welfare, and ignorance and disease would remain the fate of the lower classes. The question of political and civil rights was, therefore, of central importance to them. Starting from the general premise that the Russian people's "lack of political rights must be recognized as one of the leading principles in the struggle with alcoholism,"[81] they attacked the forced detention of alcoholics by the police and condemned the liquor monopoly and the regime's interference in the temperance work carried out by physicians and medical associations. The socialist faction openly waged a verbal war against official temperance committees such as the Guardianships of Popular Temperance, claiming they were merely decorative, socially irrelevant, and financially wasteful.[82] Ultimately, these criticisms struck at the ethical foundations of the government and its authority, positing instead the sovereignty of the citizenry.

As with other professional groups, the socialist members of the commission were consciously restrained in their attacks of the government prior to the revolutionary events of 1905.[83] Lacking support from the Social Democratic Party or other movements of the splintered socialist Left, and often closely allied with government bureaucracies and institutes, these professionals knew all too well that overt criticism of the government would carry a high price. Toward the end of the century, however, as students openly began to defy public authorities and highly placed people engaged in acts of deliberate insubordination, socialist psychiatrists and physicians began analyzing alcoholism as one of the dangerous effects of a repressive political regime. In addition, the increasingly open expression of antigovernment views in the press fueled tensions already building within the commission, and many members, especially the socialists, began agitating for a wider national forum that would mobilize anti-alcohol groups in Russia.[84]

In 1909 this goal was realized in the form of the state-sanctioned First All-Russian Congress against Drunkenness (Vserossisskii s"ezd po bor'be s p'ianstvom). Initiated by Prime Minister P. A. Stolypin, the congress represented one of a series of public meetings, including a congress of public universities, a women's congress, and a congress of factory doctors.[85] The fact that the government sanctioned these congresses is especially significant in light of the Stolypin "coup d'état" of June 3, 1907, when the government ordered suspension of the Duma. Marking a reassertion of government control and imposed compliance with the conservative regime that lasted until 1917, Stolypin's so-called System of the Third of June changed election laws to favor conservatives, thereby disenfranchising many people. This was hardly an environment for broad-based discussion of society's ills and the government's role in creating those problems. Nonetheless, some socialists used the congress as a forum to attack the government.

In preparation for the congress, many groups previously uninterested in the question of alcoholism got involved, most notably the Social Democratic Party. It is not surprising that in the wake of the Revolution of 1905, and especially after 1907 when so many people had been silenced, the congress attracted widespread attention from members of educated society of all political persuasions, workers, the church, and the ruling elite. Many of the social ills, including alcoholism, afflicting the urban poor that predated the revolution continued unabated after 1905 and appeared as a greater threat and in sharper relief after the street violence endemic in the revolution. According to numerous sources, it was "not a rare phenomenon to see drunkards totally passed out on the street."[86] Commentators of all political orientations cited alcohol abuse more than any other factor as a sign of moral degeneracy and social decay.[87] In the wake of 1905, alcoholism appeared to be more widespread, but the social causes and loss of control associated with drunken behavior had more threatening implications. The perceived rise in rampant drunkenness and unmotivated crime among the lower classes suggested that traditional values could no longer contain the behavior of the common folk.

For professionals, and especially socialist professionals, the 1905 revolution politicized the professional context and thoroughly intertwined political and professional agendas. The period in which the alcohol question emerged as a subject of concentrated public debate coincided with the years of widespread political mobilization. After 1905, themes that had earlier preoccupied professionals in the context of their own disciplinary concerns began to attract attention in settings open to a more general audience. Perhaps nowhere was this more evident than in preparation for the national anti-alcohol congress. Even though many components of the alcohol question drew on existing discursive models, in the months prior to and during the congress the intensity of interest and the subject's heightened political charge came to a head.

In early 1909 the Special Commission on the Question of Alcoholism, founded in 1898, invited different institutions, organizations, societies, and individuals to attend the congress and present reports.[88] A committee contacted numerous workers' educational and self-improvement organizations, many of which were either directly associated with various factions of Russian socialism or had strong socialist representation in their memberships. Since the state sanctioned the upcoming congress, it was a perfect opportunity for those oppositional groups denied public political expression in 1907 to air their views. Given the intimate connection between the tsarist government and the vodka monopoly, and the fairly recent acceptance of the idea that excessive alcohol consumption caused alcoholism, the congress had great potential as a forum for legitimate criticisms of the government.

Social Democrats recognized this potential and took up the issue of alcoholism. An article in the party newspaper, *Sotsial-demokrat* (Social Democrat), demanded the "active participation" of all Social Democratic organizations in "preparing the workers for using the congress to tie the private question of alcoholism with the general aims and tasks of the workers' movement."[89] Having previously neglected the question of alcoholism, the Social Democrats frantically made plans for the congress. In a rush of furious activity, they tried to come up with an agenda to present to the congress and selected delegates for the so-called Workers' Delegation to represent socialist-affiliated workers' groups.[90] At the congress itself, the Workers' Delegation attacked the position of the clergy and liberal social reformers, arguing that alcoholism resulted from the capitalist system of exploitation and not from a personal moral failing. The Workers' Delegation asserted that society had failed the individual, and not the other way around. It also refuted as "bourgeois" the idea that poverty resulted from alcoholism: drunkenness, the delegation insisted, was in fact caused by poverty. Using surveys conducted prior to the congress, the Social Democrats demonstrated that workers who earned less drank more, worked longer, were malnourished, and lived in horrid conditions.[91]

Predictably, members of the delegation readily condemned the state liquor monopoly, accusing the government of trying to raise as much revenue as possible by "spreading drunkenness."[92] Censure of government policy, however, came from more moderate participants as well, and at least on this issue the socialists and liberals joined forces against state representatives. The most dramatic evidence of their solidarity occurred at one of the congress's final sessions. Outraged that the presidium of the congress had softened its condemnation of the state liquor monopoly, the Workers' Delegation stormed out of the congress, all the socialist physicians leaving with them.[93]

This alliance between workers and professionals merits attention because, even though most medical temperance advocates espoused reform for the benefit of the lower classes, they were reluctant to have those classes in their midst. The liberal physician Borodin went so far as to declare that "the workers' movement doesn't have any bearing on alcoholism!"[94] Most likely, frustration at the confrontational and disruptive behavior of the Workers' Delegation motivated Borodin's outburst; on several occasions throughout the congress, workers disrupted proceedings with sneers and taunts against representatives of the clergy, state, and liberal temperance societies.[95] But it is also worth considering that the activity of the Workers' Delegation, its high level of revolutionary rhetoric, and the further politicization of the alcohol question may have threatened Borodin and other liberal professionals. Having spent many years developing scientific and medical justifications for their unique right to define and solve the problem of alcoholism, these liberals feared that the socialists would steal the anti-alcohol movement out from under them.[96]

The goal of unifying all anti-alcohol groups at the congress certainly never materialized. If anything, the congress intensified controversy and conflict between groups concerned with temperance and demonstrated the impossibility of resolving struggles between various sectors of Russian society for political influence. The clergy tearfully left the congress when a proposition for religiously based temperance education failed. During heated discussion of the liquor monopoly, representatives of the Ministry of Finance angrily stormed out of the proceedings. Outraged workers led a mass exodus out of the hall when the presidium of the congress softened resolutions passed earlier. Numerous sessions were hastily adjourned when angry exchanges between liberals and socialists over the causes of and cures for alcoholism threatened to come to blows. And on at least one occasion the presidium threatened to close the congress altogether if the delegates would not control their outbursts.[97]

Because the struggle to define the causes of and cures for alcoholism was in fact a contest for power and authority, and because all groups involved in the congress bitterly opposed each other, the battle for hegemony in defining and treating lower-class drinking continued well after the end of the congress. Indeed, the battle went on, albeit in a modified form, well after the revolutions of 1917. Both liberal and socialist professionals engaged in polemics on the subject of alcoholism with increasing intensity and coverage in the public sphere until the outbreak of World War I.[98] In these discussions, the social analysis clearly served partisan ends, and all commentators manipulated the same rhetoric of alcoholic degeneracy among the lower classes to convey the menace of a dangerously unstable social environment. The urban milieu was ultimately to blame in all these accounts, with urban slums and flophouses seen as the breeding grounds of epidemics, crime, sexual deviance, moral degradation, and, of course, alcoholism.

Alcoholism and Class Conflict

From the beginning of the construction of Russia's "drink problem," members of the upper class focused their attention on the behavior, habits, and customs of the lower classes, especially the working poor. Alcoholism became a symbol of the nation's ills, most specifically of the breakdown of mechanisms of social control and the decline of the old order. The images of the lower classes that emerge in discussions of alcoholism after the 1890s endowed the working poor with a primitivism, a lack of culture, and an unwillingness or inability to assimilate respectable and civilized values. The shift from images of the poor peasant or worker as an object of curiosity and even celebration prior to the 1890s to the harsh naturalistic representations of the "moral decline" of the urban poor was closely related to the cultural conflict that resulted from the wave of migrations into the cities in the 1890s and again after 1910.[99] The sheer number of migrants altered the urban landscape, intensified social problems, and, more important, created an atmosphere of chaos and disarray. Exacerbated by the street violence during the Revolution of 1905, the behavior of the lower classes raised fears among educated society that revolutionary and criminal violence had commingled in the popular mentality and seriously threatened the immediate future.

In the last decades of tsarist rule, the construction of alcoholism as a social and medical problem provided "respectable" educated society with a means of defining the norms of respectability, both for its own self-identification and for "disciplining" the lower classes. For liberal social reformers, respectability meant the adoption of upper-class morals and amusements. For medical professionals, it meant disciplining and controlling private behaviors for the welfare of the community. For socialists, it meant a raising of worker consciousness. For the church, it meant reasserting moral authority and renewing links to the community. In all cases, the subjective, emotional, and value-laden definitions of alcoholism reflect the class conflicts and cultural disorders of the revolutionary era and the struggle to establish power, authority, and legitimacy. This struggle would be taken up again after 1917 by the Bolsheviks.

In the disorders of war, revolution, and civil war, drunkenness reached epidemic proportions, despite the government's formal institution of prohibition. As the country slid into chaos during the civil war, peasants brewed illicit alcohol in unprecedented quantities, and in cities and villages alike nearly all social interactions included the ubiquitous bottle of home brew. The discourse on alcoholism, however, and the power struggle it enacted were suspended in the preoccupation with larger problems.

In the mid-1920s, as the economy recovered and cities revived, a new process of self-identification began under the socialist state, with its own hierarchies and cultural programs. Once again, alcoholism held a central place in these discussions, this time used by political authorities to define the "respectable" proletarian worker and to stigmatize disruptive and nonproductive behaviors.

Sobering Up the Revolution

THE FIRST FIFTEEN YEARS AFTER THE OCTOBER REVOLUTION of 1917 was as an era of experimentalism as Bolshevik party leaders attempted to shift from revolutionary iconoclasm to state building and creating a new society. In the process of recasting social institutions, the Bolsheviks sought to alter traditional values, cultures, and hierarchies. In short, the Bolsheviks aimed to effect a cultural revolution while consolidating power. The party, therefore, extended reformism to nearly all aspects of daily life in a broad effort to create a new *byt*, or way of life.[1] In this attempt to craft a new society and a new type of citizen—the new Soviet man or woman—the nascent party-state introduced nationwide campaigns to revamp education, eliminate bourgeois culture and gender relations, and end illiteracy, prostitution, religion, and drunkenness.[2] The Bolsheviks' ultimate goal was to establish social control in order to achieve socialism rapidly.

All industrializing societies must solve the problem of social control in the broadest sense. The development of a wide-ranging popular consensus is one way in which social control can be achieved and cultural values imparted. The Bolsheviks understood this—the party's methods of building a new socialist culture were clearly intended to promote internalization of new values and inculcate passive controls on social behavior. This problem was critical for the

Soviet state in the 1920s as the Bolsheviks came face to face with their number one quandary: workers did not act right. The proletariat was the new ruling class, but still it was stamped with the attributes of an oppressed class.
Further, the behavior of the new working class, especially those fresh from the
village, did not meet Bolshevik expectations: they came late to work, if at all;
they broke their machines; they ignored the authority of bosses; and above all,
they drank themselves into oblivion. In light of the tension between the social
legacies of revolution and civil war and Bolshevik efforts in the 1920s to create a new socialist order, the problem of drinking and drunkenness emerges
as a reflection of the larger struggle of the party against a predominantly peasant society over issues of lifestyle and control.

Despite radical political and economic transformations, alcohol continued to lubricate many shop floor customs and dominate life after work as
well. Consequently, intemperance became the scapegoat for many social ills
that were in part a result of state policies: the breakdown of production and
exchange throughout the country, poor industrial planning, and old and
decrepit machines. Reliable statistics on the relationship between drunkenness and industrial problems are scarce, yet the party was quick to make those
associations. The party blamed drinking for a host of menacing problems,
such as crime, absenteeism, industrial waste and breakage, hooliganism, and
shirking of responsibility. The administrative organs of the People's Commissariat of Labor (Narodnyi komissariat truda, Narkomtrud) that oversaw labor
discipline reported that the primary reason for lapses in worker discipline was
widespread drunkenness. Citing unexcused absences, sickness, fights, and
assaults on managers, Narkomtrud lamented that industry might not survive
the excesses of a drunken labor force.[3]

Leon Trotsky took this one step farther. He tied a sober working class not
only to the resolution of industrial problems but also to national wealth and
cultural advancement when he declared that "to develop, strengthen, organize, and complete the anti-alcohol regime in the country of reborn labor is
our task. Our cultural and economic successes will increase as alcohol consumption falls. There can be no concessions."[4] Such rhetoric emphasized
moral reform as a prelude to economic and cultural success. Addressed to the
worker, Bolshevik rhetoric intended to tie the values of the sober, industrious
Soviet citizen to the solution of national social and labor problems.

Even as the newspaper *Pravda* (Truth) published Trotsky's remark, the
state began reviving the liquor industry and gearing up to expand production

of 40 percent vodka. By 1925 the liquor monopoly was fully reinstated. Three years later, however, in 1928, the party and state administrations launched a nationwide anti-alcohol campaign. This apparent contradiction between the repeal of prohibition and Bolshevik efforts to control private drinking behaviors suggests that the subsequent anti-alcohol campaign had relatively little to do with alcohol.

While it may have claimed to be the vanguard of the working class, in this formative period the party was controlled by events and conditions as much as it tried to shape them. The shifting, and sometimes conflicting, policies toward alcohol production and drunkenness to some extent reflect political maneuvering within the bureaucracy and state administrations. They also suggest a broader uncertainty in the purpose and goals of the party in the 1920s. The following discussion examines the institutional and organizational methods used by the Bolsheviks to resolve what many party commentators saw as one of the most pressing problems facing the new state. In doing so, this chapter reveals some of the institutional and ideological cleavages characteristic of the early Soviet state and highlights important dimensions in the complex social and cultural transformations intended by revolutionary leaders.

Prohibition, 1914–1925

Since the Soviet government inherited prohibition and the problems it generated, a brief overview of Russia's experiment in "going dry" and its impact on popular drinking practices and state revenue will highlight the tenacity of drinking behaviors and underscore some of the problems the Bolsheviks encountered in trying to create a sober socialist society. As we have seen, prior to 1914 the state had a fairly lucrative and efficient monopoly on the alcohol trade, generating significant revenues and allowing some control over the production and consumption of vodka. With the outbreak of World War I, the tsarist state introduced prohibition, thereby forfeiting millions of rubles in liquor revenue and, more important, losing control of the alcohol trade as the population sought illegal ways of obtaining alcohol.

Prohibition began as part of Russia's mobilization for war in July 1914 when the tsarist government curtailed liquor sales throughout most of the empire.[5] In the first half of 1914 a temperance lobby consisting of members of both sections of the legislative branch of the Imperial government, the Duma and State Council (Gosudarstvennyi Sovet), initiated an extensive debate on

the issue of alcohol and alcoholism. As a result, in August 1915 a number of Duma members introduced a bill making prohibition permanent, and on June 16, 1916, the Duma gave its full support to make the bill a law. Owing to the disintegration and eventual collapse of the tsarist government, this bill never made it before the State Council. Yet on March 27, 1917, as one of its first acts, the new Provisional Government implemented the law, and prohibition officially became permanent.[6]

When the Bolsheviks came to power in October 1917, they introduced measures of their own to continue prohibition. In late 1918 the new government's Council of People's Commissars (Sovet narodnykh komissarov, Sovnarkom) nationalized the liquor industry, declaring the existing stock of alcoholic beverages state property.[7] Passing a law entitled "On the banning of the manufacture and sale of spirits, alcoholic drinks, and other products containing ethanol within the territory of the RSFSR [Russian Soviet Federated Socialist Republic]," the new government in 1919 formalized near total prohibition on Soviet territory.[8] The Soviet government's "temperance" legislation fit into the larger struggle for grain procurement characteristic of the period of so-called War Communism, 1918–1921. In response to a critical food supply crisis, local soviets began requisitioning grain, sometimes brutally, from peasants who refused to sell it for depreciating currency, turning it instead into *samogon* (home brew).[9] Consistent with the militancy exhibited in this period, the law identified *samogonshchiki* (bootleggers) as enemies of the revolution, charging them with sabotaging the state's food supply policies. The ban on the manufacture and sale of alcohol was aimed primarily at conserving grain stocks and supplies of industrial alcohol rather than promoting temperance.[10] Whatever the state's goals in legislating prohibition, the effect made hard liquor legally unavailable.

There is no evidence to suggest that prohibition, tsarist or early Soviet, received popular support from working-class Russians, for whom alcohol remained central to their social, cultural, and economic lives. Despite the fact that some educated and upper-class Russians, as well as many radical vanguard workers, welcomed the new laws, the strength of custom and tradition ensured that the *narod* would find ways to evade prohibition. As one observer commented, "The population could not stand compulsory abstinence and soon began to seek ways of satisfying their traditional custom of drinking liquor."[11] Urban workers resorted to drinking anything containing alcohol,

including denatured spirits, cologne, lacquer, and varnish. For example, in 1915 production of lacquer rose by 600 percent and varnish by 1,575 percent in Moscow. That same year in Petrograd, sales of lacquer rose by 2,260 percent and varnish by 1,800 percent.[12] One can assume that in the absence of a concurrent surge in wood sales, the Russian populace had not turned to furniture refinishing for solace: A significant amount of these alcohol-based substances was being consumed.

In the countryside, where such surrogates were not available, rural populations developed and expanded a thriving illegal brewing industry. Except in some of the more remote parts of Siberia, Russia had no significant tradition of illegal brewing prior to 1914.[13] However, once introduced into a region, *samogon* spread like wildfire. A useful illustration comes from A. M. Bol'shakov's account of daily life in his home village in Tver. In this particular village, home brew was virtually unknown until 1921, when villagers first heard rumors that neighboring villages had learned how to distill grain alcohol.[14] One observer tasted it and reported back to his fellow villagers, "It stinks, but you can drink it."[15] Having tried it, some villagers attempted to brew their own through trial and error. Preparing cauldrons and tubes, these peasants opened makeshift distilleries in bathhouses and barns.[16] By the middle of 1922 almost every household in the *volost* (small rural district) made *samogon*. This seems to be the case throughout Russia. Peasants in Saratov brewed *samogon* with impunity from 1914 on. In Tomsk, home brewing was so prevalent authorities gave up trying to prosecute offenders.[17] In Kharkov, one source estimated that 70 percent of the peasants engaged in home brewing.[18] With the help of a simple still, from one pood of flour (16.4 kilograms) one could produce four to five liters of 25 to 30 percent alcohol. Another stage of distillation yielded 70 percent alcohol.[19]

Initially, the lower classes distilled solely for their own consumption, but eventually home brewing took on more commercial purposes. Bol'shakov claims that many people engaged in moonshining to replace incomes lost due to the war. In Tver, the sale of *samogon* provided an alternative income to that which villagers earned in the towns and sent back to the village.[20] More significant, when cloth exports were suspended during the war, thereby ruining the local flax trade, the women who had dominated this trade turned to illegal brewing. A Red Army soldier's widow explained to the court after she had been arrested for selling moonshine that she resorted to home brewing because she needed money to pay her taxes.[21] Distilling as a means to replace lost income was also prevalent in the cities. Unemployed urban workers comprised one-third of those arrested in Moscow for illegal distilling in 1922.[22]

While illegal distillation and the sale of grain alcohol may have boosted the incomes of many lower-class Russians, prohibition's economic impact on the government was tremendous. Not only did prohibition fail to keep Russians from drinking, as evidenced by the spread of *samogon*, but it cost the government millions in lost revenue. In 1913 the population consumed 104.6 million *vedros* (or 339.95 million gallons) of state-produced vodka, yielding just over 953 million rubles, or 26 percent of total state revenue.[23] Despite the fact that the government introduced new forms of taxation to replace the rubles it lost to prohibition, in 1914 state revenue decreased by over 500 million rubles.[24]

Government indebtedness exacerbated wartime inflation, which aggravated the social and economic crises that eventually toppled the tsarist government. The new state inherited prohibition as well as the problems it caused—decreasing state revenues, illegal brewing that reached epidemic proportions, and loss of control over commercial and private trade in liquor. Because prohibition and the war seriously shrank state coffers, many Soviet authorities saw an end to prohibition as a means for the fledgling state to attain financial solvency while simultaneously controlling the spread of illegal brewing. Further, several studies conducted in the early 1920s demonstrated that bootleggers consumed large quantities of grain in producing *samogon*.[25] If the state revived the liquor monopoly, the argument went, it would gain a measure of control over the use of grain in alcohol production. However, the idea of the new socialist state producing and selling alcohol for any reason was contrary to the utopian idealism characteristic of the early revolutionary period and sparked heated debates among party leaders.

In the end, financial considerations prevailed. In August 1921 the new government reversed its policy and legalized the sale of wine. Six months later it legalized the sale of beer, thereby beginning the slow retreat from prohibition that coincided with the party's retreat from the harsh practices of War Communism to the more benign social and economic policies of the New Economic Policy (NEP), 1921–1927.[26] Lenin called the NEP a step backward into capitalism in order to prepare the way for a surge forward toward socialism. In the same way, the party justified reintroducing the state's liquor monopoly.

Once the revenues needed for economic recovery were acquired, the state would stop producing alcohol. Therefore in January 1923 the state legalized the production and sale of 20 percent liquor, and by October 1925 it began making and selling 40 percent vodka, marking the end of prohibition and the reintroduction of the state liquor monopoly.

The Bolsheviks and Booze

Even prior to the reintroduction of the liquor monopoly, party visionaries focused their attention on the problem of working-class drinking. Given the seemingly more crucial problems facing the new regime, this attention to drinking seems misplaced unless viewed within the context of state building, the very character of which was necessarily affected by the degree of compatibility or resistance between the fundamental objectives set by the party and those of society at large. The Bolsheviks assumed that the industrial working class would provide the necessary social support for the new revolutionary regime, the "dictatorship of the proletariat," just as it had for the most part supported the October Revolution. Yet in the postrevolutionary social disintegration, the Bolsheviks found themselves the vanguard of a fragmented and undisciplined working class that shared little of the values and behavior of revolutionary activists.

At the beginning of 1917, Russia's industrial working class (including workers in the non-Russian regions) comprised about three and a half million members, with an additional million railroad workers.[27] By the end of the civil war, the total number of industrial workers had dropped to just over one million.[28] Moreover, with the beginning of industrial recovery in 1923, waves of new workers from the villages and peasant *otkhodniki* (peasants who left the village for the towns and factories in search of work during the agricultural off-season) joined the industrial labor force, radically altering the social composition of the working class.[29]

Soviet authorities viewed these peasants' attitudes and work habits as obstacles to the creation of a socialist work culture. They feared that the sheer numbers of peasant migrants seriously complicated the formation of proletarian sensibilities in broad strata of the labor force.[30] Their fears were not unfounded: In 1923–1924 there were an estimated 1.5 million *otkhodniki,* and in 1925–1926 the number swelled to 3.25 million, or nearly 40 percent of the total number of blue- and white-collar workers combined. More than 2 million peasant migrants settled permanently in the cities during the 1926–1927 fiscal year.[31]

Owing to these dramatic demographic changes, the fundamental elements of a new Soviet social order and culture had to be created.[32] Insisting on a complete break with the past, revolutionary rhetoric called into question all customs, traditions, and ways of life. Building socialism required nothing less than new men and women with new habits; human behavior had to be transformed via social engineering. Many party visionaries viewed the decade following the revolution as a period of gestation, one that would eventually lead to the birth of an ideal society—utopia in the making.[33] Two top party theorists, Bolshevik leader Nikolai Bukharin and economist Evgeny Preobrazhenskii, painted the most elaborate picture of what the new socialist state would become in *The ABC of Communism*. It predicted that full communism would flourish fairly soon, bringing with it all the solutions embedded in the classical canon of Karl Marx. In Russia, "within a few decades there will be quite a new world, with new people and new customs."[34]

Despite these utopian visions and the Bolsheviks' political defeat of the old regime and numerous other political enemies, the revolution had not eradicated the old mentalities. In fact, social and cultural contexts limited the possibilities for change and made the creation of a "new world with new people" nearly impossible. The 1920s introduced a period of dreadful poverty and social misery, an urban world of crime, unemployment, drunkenness, hooliganism, roving homeless waifs (*besprizorniki*), and open prostitution. The optimism inherent in Marxism and the revolutionary euphoria contrasted with the realities of daily life to create an unacceptably flawed present. Considered inimical to the party's basic goals for Russia's development and future, the resilient social and cultural traditions of the tsarist past had to be transformed into a new socialist culture and morality.

Alcoholism was foremost among workers' behavior deemed to be old, uncultured, and "bourgeois." Prerevolutionary socialist physicians and psychiatrists, such as G. I. Dembo, I. I. Ianzhul, and others, had defined alcoholism as a result of capitalist oppression. Their arguments informed the way Bolshevik reformers viewed the problem. Finding a link between capitalism and drunkenness in *The Condition of the Working Class in England* by Friedrich Engels, many Bolshevik leaders viewed excessive drinking as a petit bourgeois problem—a holdover from the tsarist past.[35]

Newspapers and the trade union press throughout the 1920s abound with descriptions of drunkenness as "bourgeois degeneration" and as evidence of *meshchanskyi* (middle-class) or *nepovskyi* (NEP-ish) decay. Lenin framed the problem in class terms when he complained to the chief of the political police, F. E. Dzerzhinskii, that "the bourgeoisie commits the most heinous crimes, bribing the scum of society and the déclassé elements, getting them drunk for pogroms."[36] Trotsky defined the official party attitude toward alcohol when he linked alcohol consumption to the fate of the revolution: "The very nearest future will be a period of a heroic struggle with alcohol. If we don't stamp out alcoholism, beginning with the cities, then we will drink up socialism and drink up the October Revolution."[37]

This Bolshevik emphasis on sobriety as an essential cultural value had not always been a top priority. Prior to 1917 the Bolsheviks advocated abstinence from alcohol as a necessary characteristic for "conscious" workers and criticized the tsarist state's exploitation of the vodka trade. However, most prerevolutionary party commentators were too absorbed by the larger struggle for social revolution to concentrate on temperance or to try to solve the problem of widespread working-class drunkenness.[38] Within months of the revolution, however, the Bolsheviks witnessed dramatic demonstrations of alcohol's violent potential. In November and December 1917 soldiers and civilians alike rocked Petrograd with a series of riots sparked by struggles over control of liquor supplies. In numerous towns, including Saratov and Tomsk, garrisoned soldiers along with local citizens raided shops and warehouses for alcohol in drunken orgies that lasted days. Exacerbating the situation, opponents of Bolshevism instigated liquor riots in an attempt to spread fear of anarchy and disorder.

The new authorities moved quickly to subdue this threat, but to little effect. The Petrograd Soviet's Military Revolutionary Committee ordered all stores of liquor at the tsar's Winter Palace and elsewhere to be destroyed. The Petrograd Soviet appointed G. Blagonravov "special commissar to combat drunkenness." It also established an antiriot committee chaired by V. Bonch-Bruevich, who was a socialist temperance activist before the revolution and later became a physician involved in treating alcoholics.[39] Nonetheless, the liquor riots continued in Petrograd and throughout the country, at times escalating into battles involving the use of armored cars and machine guns, maiming and killing many and destroying much property before loyal Red Guard (a workers' militia) units could restore order.

Apart from the social disorder promoted by the consumption of alcohol and the immense quantities of grain that illegal brewing devoured, authorities perceived illegal trade in liquor as evidence of bourgeois resistance.[40] Fear of profiteering by merchants and kulaks (wealthy peasants) dominated almost all Soviet discussions of the alcohol problem. *Pravda* described the rural *samogonchiki* as "kulaks, middle peasants, *otkhodniki* in the cities, and, of course, petty vendors."[41] From the party's perspective, *samogon* represented precisely the "foreign elements" and their attendant capitalist attitudes that were antithetical to building socialism.

In order to get a sense of daily life in rural areas and to assess how widespread *samogon* production might be, in 1923 a commission of the Central Committee of the Communist Party (TsK VKP[b]) traveled through the Nikol'skaia district of Kursk. In interviewing 600 peasants on the typical features of rural life, the commissioners discovered that moonshine, like vodka in the nineteenth century, held a prominent place in village life as a valuable exchange commodity: "A peasant needs *samogon* or vodka, it does not matter which. For example, if one needs to build a house, one can never find workers; but if there is vodka or *samogon,* you treat the neighbors to it, and the house is soon ready."[42] The commissioners were also shocked to learn that the overwhelming majority of those interviewed felt no obligation to cooperate with the government. One interviewee put it succinctly when he exclaimed, "Do not rely on the peasants in your battle with *samogon,* do it yourselves."[43] The commission concluded that *samogon* production "proved" the existence of capitalist relations in the countryside and exemplified the ignorance, backwardness, and counterrevolutionary nature of the peasantry.[44]

Women and *Samogon*

In reality, the bulk of the "nefarious, capitalistic" *samogonshchiki* were actually impoverished women desperate to feed their families. The legacies of European and civil wars were especially hard on women. At the close of the civil war, the population consisted of 9 million more women than men out of a total population of 131 million—the highest female-to-male ratio in all of Europe.[45] Other estimates indicated that nearly 3.5 million people had died from disease between 1917 and 1926, approximately 834,000 from typhus alone in 1920.[46] The country was in a state of near collapse due to food and fuel crises and the breakdown of industry. All these crises placed a tremendous burden on millions of working women, especially soldiers' wives and widows, particularly if they were the family's main breadwinner.

One might assume that with so many dead and missing from the war, employment opportunities for women would increase. However, just the opposite occurred. The end of the civil war saw a drop in demand for female labor: In 1921 women made up 35 percent of factory workers, but by 1924 this number had dropped to 25 percent.[47] In Moscow alone, women workers declined from 39 percent of all workers in 1920 to 25 percent in 1923.[48]

In some respects this drop in female labor can be attributed to the end of the wartime emergency that had artificially inflated the numbers of female workers. Moreover, between 1921 and 1924 the Red Army demobilized nearly five million men, a significant number of whom were urban residents and workers. In the early 1920s the government passed a series of decrees that gave demobilized Red Army soldiers preferential treatment in hiring. While technically a soldier could not simply return to his peacetime job and replace the current occupant, in practice this often happened. Typically, unions would decide to lay off certain social groups, such as women, in order to hire demobilized male workers.[49]

The problem of demobilization was exacerbated by the return of men who had migrated to the countryside during the years that food shortages plagued the cities. Between 1918 and 1920 men made up nearly 90 percent of the urban population that fled the cities. For example, while the number of female workers remained relatively constant in Moscow during the civil war, the number of male workers declined by nearly half—from 215,000 to 124,000 between 1918 and 1920.[50] Once the economy began to recover, many of those who had left returned to the cities seeking work, thereby increasing competition for jobs.

The high unemployment figures for women also reflect persistent high unemployment that accompanied the NEP as the state demanded that larger enterprises turn a profit. By insisting that factories adopt a precise system of accounting (*khozraschet*), the state ultimately placed more power in the hands of employers and forced staff cutbacks or the closure of inefficient enterprises. Massive layoffs resulted, and female workers were the first to go. Indeed, numerous articles appeared in *Pravda* and *Kommunistka* (Communist Woman) lamenting that the "NEP and its consequences have hit female labor with particular severity."[51] In 1922 nearly 60 percent of unemployed workers were women. In July 1924 women made up 45.3 percent of the unemployed.

While the absolute percentage of those out of work declined, that of women actually increased.[52]

Those women who were employed usually held unskilled positions or worked in lower-paying occupations with wages on average well below those of men. In March 1924, for example, women's wages averaged 64.4 percent of men's wages.[53] In industries typically dominated by men, the differences were even greater: in the metal industry, women earned 49.6 percent of the average male wage and in mining, 42.1 percent. In female-dominated industries the gap was smaller, yet women still earned less. For example, in the food industry women earned about 73 percent of men's average wages.[54] Reflecting a labor market divided along gender lines, these figures underscore the desperate circumstances working-class women endured throughout the 1920s.

Owing to the loss of men in the wars between 1914 and 1920, millions of women became single heads of households. Given the high level of female unemployment and the low level of female wages, many working-class women had to develop survival strategies that often placed them outside the utopian vision of a socialist society. Women from the upper classes could resort to private trading, selling their personal property, and occasionally themselves, on street corners and in markets.[55] The lower classes, however, had no such material resources to fall back on. For many of them, prostitution became the only means to survival. The 1920s witnessed an increase in the numbers of "occasional" prostitutes who were trying to supplement low pay, particularly if they had children to feed. Another more typical survival strategy practiced largely by peasant women, widows, and underemployed female workers was trade in illegal spirits. Like prostitution, bootlegging was overwhelmingly a female trade.

Throughout the 1920s *samogonshchiki* flooded the cities. Vendors sold *samogon* in factories, in private homes, and openly in small restaurants, cafés, and shish kebab stands. It was even often displayed on restaurant shelves as "lemonade in an unsealed bottle." In Moscow, one could buy it at any booth in the markets by "requesting 'lemonade' and winking at the salesman meaningfully."[56] So widespread were the production and sale of *samogon* that the press reported that home brew operations "sprang up like mushrooms after a rain."[57] With an estimated 60 percent of all peasant households making *samogon* and 70 percent of the urban population drinking it, alarmed state and local officials launched several campaigns against illegal spirits in 1922.[58]

The 1922 RSFSR criminal code labeled offenses involving *samogon* as eco-

nomic crimes punishable by forced labor for up to one year and partial confiscation of the offender's property.[59] Within six months, the central government approved a major revision of the law dealing with illegal brewing. The
law raised sanctions against home brewing for profit to no less than one and
up to three years imprisonment and confiscation of all the offender's property. Home brewing for private consumption was punishable by fines up to 500
gold rubles and six months' hard labor. In this initial call to action against
samogonshchiki, Soviet authorities did not differentiate among home brewers.
As N. A. Semashko, the commissar of public health from 1918 to 1930, argued
in the newspaper *Izvestiia* (News), "[T]he struggle must be firm and merciless. . . . We must punish every home brewer whether he wants to poison himself or others."[60]

This "firm and merciless" struggle resulted in tens of thousands of arrests.
Between 1921 and 1923 arrests for *samogon* offenses in the RSFSR increased 535
percent.[61] In the first half of March 1923 the police arrested 13,748 *samogonshchiki* (mostly women) and confiscated 25,114 gallons of liquor nationwide.[62]
Throughout the RSFSR, local militia detachments conducted thousands of
raids. In Kharkov *guberniia* (region), for example, local militia launched a
crackdown on bootleggers and between January and June 1923 arrested 5,373
people, confiscating 2,310 stills and 4,401 *vedros* of home brew.[63] In July alone,
authorities in Kharkov arrested 3,165 bootleggers, seizing 695 *vedros* of
samogon.[64] Sentences ranged from 140 days to one full year in jail plus confiscation of all of the offender's property.[65] By mid-1923 Gosplan (the State Planning Committee) reported that over 300,000 arrests had been made in the
RSFSR.[66]

A substantial majority of those arrested were women. An article in *Pravda* in February 1923 noted that "in the cities, the producers of moonshine are
mostly widows and impoverished women trying to feed their families, followed by the disabled."[67] According to the Moscow city courts, 32 percent of
the bootleggers convicted between January 1922 and May 1923 were unemployed women; 28.4 percent were female workers; 16 percent were house-
wives; 8 percent were women with no definite occupation; and 7.7 percent
were petty vendors (both male and female). Further, a 1923 investigation of
Moscow jails found that a majority of the *samogonshchiki* were women, an
"enormous proportion" of them impoverished and almost half of them widows. A similar study of Moscow in 1925 confirmed the predominance of
women and added that over 40 percent of the guilty were unemployed.[68]

In Tomsk *okrug* (district) throughout 1923 and 1924, hundreds of women were arrested for either making or selling *samogon*. Individuals representative of the types of women arrested include: Aleksandra Demidova, age nineteen, unskilled worker, member of the Komsomol (Young Communist League), unemployed; her grandmother, Marfa Ivanova Demidova, age sixty, party member since 1918, literate, unemployed widow; Ekatrina Kravets, age forty-five, semiliterate, unskilled worker, employed; Elizabet Maksimovna, age twenty-four, nonparty member, unskilled worker, widow.[69] As seen in these examples, women engaged in home brewing ranged in age from their late teens into their sixties and covered all levels of education, party membership, and work skill. All were single or widowed and could not survive on their wages alone.

Clearly thousands of women could not languish in jails for three years, nor could they afford a fine of 500 rubles. Authorities responded in late 1923 by reducing fines for those who were driven to trade in *samogon* out of unemployment or extreme family need. Nonetheless, a high number of these lower fines went uncollected as a result of the inability of the indigent violator to pay.[70] Much the same was true of arrests—many of those incarcerated in urban jails for *samogon* offenses were starkly poor women, their destitution serving as a prime motive for amnesty. However, in some areas, such as Moscow, authorities did prosecute these women to the full extent of the law, so that in 1926 nearly 60 percent of imprisoned *samogonshchiki* were women.[71]

In short, repression of the *samogon* trade fell precisely on those social groups the Bolsheviks sought to liberate from the darkness and transform into a socialist society. The production and sale of *samogon* remained a persistent problem through the 1920s and 1930s. The regime's failure to effect changes in illegal alcohol production became a glaring reminder that the Bolsheviks lacked the moral authority to establish social controls or effect a cultural transformation.

The Battle for Hegemony in Alcoholism Treatment

While central and local authorities battled *samogon* and as the party was revving up the state alcohol monopoly, health care professionals and state and party administrators were reviving the old prerevolutionary contest over hegemony in defining and treating alcoholism. Like the earlier contest, at the heart of the struggle was a bid for power and legitimacy. In the early Soviet years, many of the prerevolutionary health care professionals, such as Bekhterev, Dmitriev, Pervushin, Dril', and others, remained engaged in defining the causes of and cures for alcoholism.

Mainstream psychiatrists defined alcoholism as a form of mental illness both before and after 1917. Prerevolutionary psychiatrists, however, pinned the blame for widespread alcoholism and alcohol-related mental illness on the tsarist government, which relied on revenues from the liquor monopoly and refused to alter the socioeconomic conditions the psychiatrists believed caused heavy drinking. According to their definitions, certain individuals lacked the mental ability or emotional stability to deal with poor social and economic conditions effectively; therefore they turned to drink. Even though the reasons for heavy drinking were generally social and economic, psychiatrists saw it as an individual response rooted in some kind of mental or emotional illness. Many members of the psychiatric profession gravitated to groups agitating for radical social change and were intimately linked with the Bolshevik cause. It is not surprising that the new regime sanctioned psychiatry as the primary discipline involved with the drink question in the first decade after the revolution.

Well before 1917 the psychiatric profession experimented with the ambulatory treatment of various mental illnesses, including alcoholism, yet psychiatrists did not agree on exactly how to treat that particular mental illness.[72] Some Soviet psychiatrists continued to favor ambulatory treatment of alcoholism using existing outpatient neuropsychiatric dispensaries. Other psychiatrists insisted that alcoholics could only be cured by receiving inpatient treatment. Fewer than 25 percent of alcoholics receiving treatment were confined to inpatient facilities before the revolution, but the Soviet period witnessed considerable expansion of these facilities.[73] This debate among Soviet psychiatrists over inpatient versus outpatient facilities was not strictly about treatment facilities. It represented a fundamental aspect of the disagreement over the basic definition and profile of alcoholism and who was best qualified to treat it. Ultimately this debate fit into the larger struggle for a new revolutionary culture that swept through many professions during the cultural revolution.[74]

The initial impact of the cultural revolution on all fields of mental health and especially psychiatry intensified the drive for both remedial and preventative measures. Medical and psychiatric journals called for an end to "penitentiary psychiatry" with its "factories producing chronic inmates."[75] They hoped that a truly Marxist form of psychiatry could be discovered that would be distinct from its predecessor and a vital tool in constructing socialist society—cultivating the personality through careful organization of work and daily life. For many psychiatrists and medical practitioners, this meant focused attention on alcoholism.[76]

As early as 1923, the People's Commissariat of Health (Narodnyi komissariat zdravookhranenii, Narkomzdrav) gave its permission to expand outpatient treatment and to open many more neuropsychiatric dispensaries.[77] The outpatient dispensary aimed treatment at what psychiatry had identified as *bytovoi* (habitual) alcoholics. According to the psychiatric profile, these were people who turned to drink because they did not feel able to deal with life's small traumas. They were most likely to be unskilled first-generation urban workers or peasant migrants whose traditional culture dictated drinking to excess.[78] The alcoholics treated at outpatient dispensaries did not suffer from acute psychiatric illness, nor did they constitute a danger to society. Psychiatrists, therefore, recommended treatment consisting of work programs, psychotherapy, and restricted access to alcohol.[79] This diagnosis and therapy for the *bytovoi* alcoholic placed responsibility for alcoholism on the individual drinker and not on social conditions. In other words, it was the alcoholic who was ill, not society—an important distinction.

After 1926 social hygiene began encroaching on the hegemony over alcoholism research and treatment that psychiatry had enjoyed. Semashko, social hygiene's leading patron, described the field as "the science of the influence of economic and social conditions of life on the health of the population and on the means to improve health."[80] Emphasizing social over biological factors, social hygienists defined disease as a bio-social phenomenon and their discipline as a hybrid at the interstices of biology and sociology.[81] Soviet social hygienists borrowed heavily from German social medicine, translating German works into Russian, publishing their own research in German public health journals, and attending international conferences to collaborate with their German colleagues. The field also drew from prerevolutionary Russian community medicine, or "general hygiene," which originated among zemstvo physicians in the 1880s and studied the impact of the environment (air, water, food, and so forth) on health.[82]

In 1923 the State Institute of Social Hygiene (Gosudarstvennyi institut sotsial'noi gigieny, GISG) was founded to conduct and coordinate research on social problems.[83] Social hygienists worked from the premise that illness could only be fully understood in its social context and that cures lay in improving social conditions. Even before they became involved in research with alcohol abuse, social hygienists determined that alcoholism should be treated as a social disease whose forms were affected by social factors such as illiteracy, financial instability, and inadequate living conditions—all attributed to the capitalist past. Drawing on prerevolutionary socialist definitions of alcoholism, GISG argued that the root cause of abnormal drinking was the country's political past as well as contemporary bourgeois practices encouraged during the NEP, especially the relatively free trade in *samogon*.[84]

With reports of rising alcoholism appearing in the press, in 1926 the Sovnarkom charged Narkomzdrav with finding causes of and solutions to alcoholism and conducting a prophylactic fight against it.[85] In fact, there is no hard data to prove that alcohol consumption was actually increasing. However, because it had the attention of the press, the administration, and the party, there was a general perception that alcohol consumption was on the rise. Consequently, Narkomzdrav, headed by Semashko, passed authority for the systematic study of alcoholism as a social disease to GISG.[86] Biomedical research on alcoholism would be conducted by institutes specializing in psychiatric medicine, but GISG was to coordinate all such efforts, making it the leading center of alcoholism research. In less than six months A. V. Mol'kov, the director of GISG, opened a department for the sole purpose of studying alcoholism.[87] The department was headed by E. I. Deichman, a physician who had done considerable work on drinking among schoolchildren.

Mol'kov's stated aim in conducting research was to isolate the factors that led to alcoholism and to assess how the weight of those factors varied for different social classes. Drawing a distinction between "endogenous" (psychological) and "exogenous" (lifestyle) reasons behind the consumption of alcohol, Mol'kov presented a series of hypotheses about the importance of these factors on different social classes.[88] Endogenous factors included striving for a feeling of euphoria or the need to lose self-control, whereas exogenous factors included the desire to compensate for insufficient or unsatisfying food, exhausting or boring working conditions, poor living conditions, and a lack of cultural diversions or intellectual pursuits.

According to Mol'kov's paradigm, endogenous factors most influenced occasional or leisure drinking of the bourgeoisie and workers. Since exogenous factors were linked to living and working conditions, they affected workers most and were the root causes of abusive drinking. By contrast, Mol'kov argued that peasants drank mostly out of traditional belief and prejudice; therefore endogenous factors played a primary role in the habitual nature of their drinking practices.

Almost as soon as Mol'kov's theses linking alcoholism to social class appeared in print, Soviet health administrators adopted them as the official formula. Despite the fact that Mol'kov intended to present only preliminary hypotheses, his distinction between endogenous and exogenous factors was the core entry under "alcoholism" in the 1928 volume of the *Bol'shaia Meditsinskaia Entsiklopediia* (The Great Medical Encyclopedia).[89] At a time when nearly all professions struggled to establish conceptual and institutional identity in Marxist terms, widespread acceptance of Mol'kov's class-oriented theses is understandable.

Mol'kov developed a questionnaire to test his hypotheses, which GISG field-workers employed in conducting surveys at the local level. Using methods borrowed from sociology, GISG researchers hoped to carve out a place for themselves in public health by studying alcoholism among high-risk groups.[90] Their reliance on surveys, social statistics, and questionnaires made social hygiene distinctive in that it spawned empirical sociological analysis at a time when such analysis was officially taboo in the Soviet Union.[91]

Mol'kov's questionnaire became the standard for systematic research on the social aspects of alcoholism. It was used in at least fifteen different survey projects covering a total of more than 40,000 respondents between 1927 and 1930.[92] Several aspects of the survey are noteworthy, especially since its results determined how GISG would define alcoholism and because its assumptions and structure made the results predictable. First, the survey aimed at the habitual alcoholic and assumed consumption of alcohol as a function of lifestyle, culture, and educational level. Second, it assumed that the individual respondent's social category was worker or peasant. Finally, the questionnaire did not provide space for the drinker to explain his or her own reasons for drinking.[93] Predictably, results confirmed the importance of lifestyle, habit, and culture in alcohol abuse.

GISG's basic philosophy was that the struggle with alcoholism was not a fight against drunkenness per se but a struggle to change the cultural conditions that made habitual drinking endemic. I. D. Strashun, a leading spokesman for GISG, published an article in 1929 in which he asserted that treating alcoholics only had significance for those individuals treated. The real battle needed to be conducted among the public at large in curtailing the availability of alcohol, eradicating the conditions that led to alcoholism, and raising public consciousness.[94] As proponents of prevention, social hygienists were drawn to public temperance societies as a means to reshape public opinion. These efforts, for a time, were heartily endorsed by many high-ranking party members.

GISG researchers tried to blunt the political implications inherent in their research on alcoholism.[95] The portrait of the *bytovoi* alcoholic drawn by social hygienists depicted alcoholism as a culturally induced attachment to alcohol, reinforced by social factors. They saw alcoholics as victims of the circumstances within which they lived and worked. An individual's response to several factors in his or her milieu caused alcoholism, therefore, and not the milieu itself. In short, the alcoholic was a redeemable deviant in the grip of an undesirable habit. The regime found this portrait and the assumed redeemability of the alcoholic especially convenient. Since cultural traditions and social environments caused alcoholism, as opposed to access to alcohol, there was no implication that the state should discontinue liquor production. Moreover, in the early years of the Soviet regime, party leaders had confidence that they could alter Russia's social landscape and transform the cultural traditions of the population.

Having established the nature of the disease, GISG turned its attention to treatment. Using the portrait of the alcoholic drawn by Mol'kov's questionnaire, social hygienists devised a two-front fight against *bytovoi* alcoholism: resocialization for alcoholics requiring treatment and temperance propaganda aimed at reeducating society as a whole and softening the drinkers' attachment to vodka. The sources do not suggest a direct link between prerevolutionary temperance advocates and GISG, but their tactics were quite similar, and it is logical to assume that practitioners at GISG were influenced by prerevolutionary temperance advocates. Prerevolutionary liberal social reformers sought to cure alcoholism through propaganda and by replacing the drinker's attachment to vodka with "rational amusements." Social hygienists at GISG argued that alcoholics needed other interests, such as reading, sports, or hobbies, to replace their addiction to vodka. Both groups—prerevolutionary liberal reformers and Soviet social reformers—saw a solution in education, propaganda, and resocialization.

Narco-dispensaries were the main institutions within which social hygienists conducted resocialization, using diverse types of treatment. In most cases, they treated the mental disorders caused by alcoholism with a combination of psychotherapy, moral education, and, in extreme cases, electric shock and hypnosis.[96] Once the alcoholic was detoxified, narco-dispensaries used a program of "cultural hygiene" aimed at replacing the drinker's reliance on alcohol with new interests and hobbies, such as reading, movies, social clubs, sports, and a wide variety of other activities.[97]

The narco-dispensaries operated from the fundamental principle that *bytovoi* alcoholics did not suffer primarily from mental illness but rather that their consumption of alcohol was the result of social conditions (despair, poverty, and so forth). The emphasis on the importance of living and working conditions in the etiology of alcoholism produced an approach to treatment distinct from that of psychiatry. Whereas psychiatry sought to cure alcoholism, social hygiene focused on preventing it. Indeed, prevention became more important that its cure. Therefore narco-dispensaries, run by social hygienists, treated not just the alcoholic but the individual's family as well. They also conducted educational programs for the general public, such as alcohol awareness programs that focused on the damage done to the body by drinking.[98] This approach shifted responsibility for alcoholism from the individual drinker to society and social policy—a position that became not only self-defeating but dangerous within a few years.

Having proven themselves as the authorities in alcoholism research, social hygienists struggled against established psychiatric treatment methods to ensure their hegemony over the field. Indeed, most of what GISG viewed as significant in treating alcoholism was often formulated as a reaction against psychiatry.[99] While acknowledging some usefulness of psychiatric methods, social hygienists repeatedly attacked the field in general. For example, in a thinly veiled criticism of psychiatry, Mol'kov argued that damage was done to real anti-alcohol work by "medical meddling" and unscientific approaches to treatment. He further argued that psychiatrists' best efforts had failed at eliminating alcoholism because they ignored the root causes—poor human social conditions that caused the habitual use of alcohol.[100] In a similar vein, A. S. Sholomovich, a psychiatrist who affiliated himself more with social hygiene than psychiatry, lauded the prophylactic approach of the social hygienists and published many articles in various professional journals attacking traditional psychiatry for being focused on curing rather than preventing the occurrence of alcoholism. In one such article, he explained why social hygiene was superior to psychiatry in treating alcoholism:

> We [social hygienists] have not raised the question from the vantage point of psychopathology, of inheritance, of constitutional or acquired inclinations. We have not framed the question in terms of addiction, as did prerevolutionary psychiatry. We posed it from the vantage point of lifestyle. . . . We went from real life and showed people how to deal with their alcoholism.[101]

The conflict between psychiatrists and social hygienists continued throughout 1928–1929 as both sides attacked each other in professional journals.[102] Initially, social hygiene gained ground in the struggle to establish conceptual and institutional authority when Narkomzdrav mandated that GISG head all research projects concerning alcoholism. Yet when psychiatry launched its offensive, the prestige and respectability of social hygiene waned, and eventually the field came to an abrupt demise.[103] In late 1930 Narkomzdrav disbanded GISG, converting it into the Institute of Organization of Health Care and Hygiene, with primarily administrative duties.[104] All research on alcoholism by social hygienists ceased, and psychiatrists once again became the sole authorities on alcoholism.

There are numerous reasons for the decline of GISG. Beginning from the premise that alcoholism was a social disease, social hygienists placed the causes of excessive drinking within society. Pursued to its logical conclusion, their analysis would have revealed the root causes of alcoholism to be structural, leading unavoidably to the conclusion that to overcome alcoholism society would have to be restructured. Moreover, in advocating restricted use of alcohol, social hygiene was criticizing the state's liquor policy. In particular, Deichman, head of GISG's alcohol research department, argued in 1928 that the regime's willingness to sell vodka amounted to an abdication of responsibility, a willingness guided by the past rather than by the future.[105] Such criticism of state policy by a state-sponsored institution was not tolerated by the end of the 1920s.

By contrast, psychiatry consistently portrayed alcoholism as a mental illness. Generalizing from their studies of alcoholics treated in a variety of psychiatric facilities, psychiatrists described the alcoholic as a person who lacked the mental or emotional ability to cope with living problems. In short, it was the drinker who was ill and not society, a much more acceptable premise by 1930.

Moreover, social hygiene had not shown the kind of success it had boasted. Indeed, increasingly patients were showing up in psychiatric hospitals for alcoholism who had already been (unsuccessfully) treated at the narco-dispensaries.[106] Psychiatrists could, and did, point to empirical studies conducted on alcoholic patients in psychiatric hospitals to demonstrate that they treated alcoholism more effectively than social hygienists.[107] The social hygienists had put their faith in prevention through "cultural work" (propaganda and resocialization) aimed at breaking the drinker's attachment to vodka. This was a long-term strategy that by the late 1920s did not fit with the impatience and urgency that accompanied rapid industrialization and cultural revolution. As a result, state administrators passed authority for treating alcoholism back to the psychiatrists.

The Society for the Struggle against Alcoholism

In the *Communist Manifesto*, Karl Marx contemptuously dismissed "economists, philanthropists, humanitarians, improvers of the condition of the working class, organizers of charity, members of societies for the prevention of cruelty to animals, and temperance fanatics" as elements of the bourgeoisie "desirous of redressing social grievances in order to secure the continued existence of bourgeois society."[108] In light of this, it is ironic that top party and government officials launched a nationwide temperance campaign through the agency of the voluntary OBSA that smacked of prerevolutionary bourgeois reformism.

Voluntary organizations served as one of the primary vehicles the Bolsheviks used to mobilize and transform society. Throughout the 1920s and early 1930s these societies were ubiquitous and included organizations such as the Down with Illiteracy Society, the International Organization to Assist Revolutionaries, the All-Russian Society for Cultural Relations, and the League of the Militant Godless, to name just a few.[109] These volunteer societies brought individuals into the Bolshevik sphere, if not into the party; they built social support for the regime; and they provided individuals with a forum for social activism. Perhaps more important, these societies manifested and justified the social transformation the Bolsheviks presumed to have been achieved.[110]

OBSA was the quintessential voluntary organization. Its founders were leading party intellectuals who were drawn to the question of alcoholism because they hoped to create a new society and were imbued with what they considered a scientific view of society's ills. Like their liberal bourgeois predecessors, these social reformers sought to define and legitimize new authority. In this case, they lent their energies toward aiding socialist construction by creating a voluntary temperance society that would lead a national anti-alcohol movement.

On February 16, 1928, a group of social hygienists, doctors, and representatives from factory, state, and party organizations met in Moscow to organize the first Soviet temperance society.[111] Iuri Larin, Nikolai Bukharin's father-in-law, cofounder of Gosplan, and the country's leading economist, assembled the group and called the meeting to order, thereby officially becoming the founding father of OBSA.[112] The society's board of directors included top government and party officials: Bukharin; People's Commissariat of Internal Affairs (Narodnyi komissariat vnutrennykh del, NKVD) chief G. G. Tolmachaev; civil war hero S. M. Budennyi; party poet laureate D. Bednyi; V. I. Lenin's former personal physician, V. A. Obukh; military commander N. I. Podvoiskii; and others. At this first meeting, Larin was appointed chairman of the society, and he in turn appointed as secretary Deichman, head of the Alcohol Research Department of GISG. In looking at the founding apparat, it is clear that the high caliber of its members signaled government and party support.

Although the board did not decide on specific methods or the tempo of OBSA's future activities at the first meeting, Larin outlined the general goals of the society. Borrowing heavily from social hygiene, Larin, by way of justifying state sale of vodka, explained that alcoholism was caused by social conditions and not by the availability of vodka. He therefore urged careful examination of society as a whole in order to find ways to improve the country's material and cultural growth. With this goal in mind, the society would organize leisure activities for workers; encourage interest in sports, radio, and film; and expand alcohol treatment dispensaries.[113]

OBSA's founding coincided with the first year of the First Five-Year Plan (1928–1932), which marked the beginning of rapid industrialization. In an economy struggling to industrialize, OBSA's goals hardly seem realistic. Yet the aims of OBSA, immediate and long-term, fit perfectly with the ideological precepts of socialist construction at that time and demonstrate the atmosphere of urgency and impatience that permeated the period. The cultural transformation that accompanied rapid industrialization was fueled by the same kind of exigency that prompted calls for fulfilling and overfulfilling the Five-Year Plan and influenced OBSA's future plans. Further, the regime perceived the apparent degeneration of the working class as a real and immediate threat to the regime's survival. Bukharin made this point at OBSA's second meeting in Moscow on April 19, 1928, just a few months before his defeat and the defeat of the Right Opposition.[114] Underlining the importance of the struggle with alcoholism in the epoch of cultural revolution, Bukharin argued that if nothing was done to improve the cultural level of workers, degeneration should be feared. For this reason, OBSA's primary task would be raising the social and cultural conditions of urban workers.[115]

It is significant that Bukharin, who is generally accepted as the party's leading theorist after Lenin's death, chose the anti-alcohol movement through which to attack the problems of Soviet society. In fact, as noted above, a roster of the early members of OBSA reads like a who's who of Soviet intellectual life—these were many of the leading party theorists, academics, writers, and scholars of the time. Most of them were passionate activists whose vehement insistence on practicality can hardly be suspected of insincerity.

To understand these Communist intellectuals' use of a voluntary temperance society as a vehicle for social reform and social action, we must look at the changing role of the intelligentsia after the revolution. Prior to 1917 the revolutionary intelligentsia were by definition outside, and critics of, the structures of Russian political and economic administration. The revolution simultaneously legitimated them in their role as oppositionists to autocracy and made them obsolete as critics of state policy. As the old political structures were radically transformed by the events of October 1917, so, too, were the transformers.

As state oppositionists, the intelligentsia took on the role of an intellectual class. Communist intellectuals were suddenly the vanguard of the revolutionary transformation of society and creators of a new rational order based on the principles of scientific socialism.[116] At the same time, the new political structures did not always incorporate those intellectuals who had created them. In these new conditions, intellectuals continued to define the problems they would attack, no longer in reaction against established authority but rather in establishing and legitimizing new authority. Therefore, the Leninist emphasis on superrationality in organization and the fight against any kind of anarchism and spontaneity—including drunkenness—appealed to those intellectuals who claimed to be possessors of the teleological knowledge that would build socialism and socialist society.

In the absence of autonomous institutions, displaced *intelligents* became involved in societies and organizations as a means to utilize their unique knowledge of how society should be organized. This was particularly true for individuals such as Bukharin, Larin, and many of the other founders of OBSA. Having achieved the revolution that defined them, many of these old Bolsheviks were rejected by the system they helped to create. As early as 1929 both Larin and Bukharin came under fire for their moderate economic and political policies. As I. V. Stalin consolidated power and pushed for rapid industrialization and forced collectivization of agriculture, they turned their attention to correcting the problems of socialist construction through the organizational activities of the society. In this way they could define and solve the problems they felt themselves uniquely qualified to recognize.

OBSA's apparat applied the same zeal and fervor to eliminating alcoholism as it had in guiding a revolution. In May Bukharin issued a public appeal on behalf of the society, stating that its purpose was to "assist Soviet power in the rapid elimination of alcoholism by: developing the culture of daily life and of healthy recreation; allowing state incomes to be found from less harmful sources; and inculcating a consciousness of the personal and social harmfulness of alcoholism and weaning working people off alcohol."[117]

Over the next few weeks Larin sent letters to thousands of factory party cells; trade unions; Komsomol organizations; social, athletic, and cultural clubs; and state agencies such as Narkomzdrav, the People's Commissariat of Enlightenment (Narodnyi komissariat prosveshchenii, Narkompros), and the Supreme Council of the National Economy (Vysshii sovet narodnogo khoziaistva, VSNKh), announcing the founding of OBSA and urging them to establish and finance branches within their enterprises.[118]

The first official task on OBSA's agenda was to enlist the help of various state agencies to launch a legislative offensive limiting the production and sale of alcohol, controlling its consumption, and enforcing new legislation.[119] OBSA presented its resolution limiting alcohol production and sales on June 22, 1928, to a preparatory commission of Sovnarkom. Accepting fundamental aspects of the resolution, Sovnarkom made specific recommendations for the Five-Year Plan, which included limiting and eventually ending the production of alcoholic beverages, organizing and controlling alcohol sales and distribution, and conducting a nationwide anti-alcohol propaganda campaign.[120] Vodka sales in industrial regions were to be reduced by 25 percent of the 1927 sales. Further, Sovnarkom advised local soviets to close any bars or liquor stores located within half a kilometer of workers' clubs, schools, or factories and placed responsibility for ensuring compliance of these measures with industrial and plant managers.[121]

In keeping with OBSA's recommendations, Sovnarkom instructed Gosplan not to invest any capital in building or renovating state distilleries, taverns, or liquor stores and to prepare for full prohibition by 1938. Beginning in 1928/1929 VSNKh was to decrease production of alcoholic beverages and increase production of nonalcoholic drinks. Sovnarkom also recommended prohibiting the sale of dark molasses, an essential ingredient in *samogon*.[122] Additionally, local soviets were granted the right to close any bars or liquor stores if they decided such action would be beneficial to the "cultural and social level" of workers in the area. Sovnarkom also forbade the use of alcohol in all official soviet, trade union, cooperative, and public meetings.[123]

Sanctioning OBSA as the leader of the anti-alcohol movement, Sovnarkom gave OBSA and its departments the authority to indict and bring to trial any person or organization that violated the restrictions on alcohol sales and consumption. It also mandated that the militia should aid the society in this endeavor. Moreover, it obligated soviets, trade unions, cooperatives, and military organizations to conduct temperance instruction in their organizations according to OBSA's guidelines.

Despite these recommendations, only in Moscow and Kharkov, where OBSA had a strong presence, is there any evidence to suggest that OBSA used the power granted by Sovnarkom. For example, in Kharkov, OBSA cells at both the Petrov and Tomsk factories brought a combined total of over 200 workers up on charges of "wrecking our economic, cultural, and political life" because of excessive drunkenness at work.[124] In Moscow, OBSA sought to close numerous bars near schools and factories, but none of the sources suggest their attempts were successful.[125] By contrast, as new industrial enterprises were built in Tomsk, so, too, were new taverns and beer halls—some directly next to factories for workers' convenience.[126] In Saratov, OBSA cells existed, but there is nothing in the sources to indicate that they took any kind of legal action against individuals or enterprises. Because Moscow and Kharkov were republic capitals, it is logical to assume that central directives carried more weight and were more closely observed than in provincial areas. Local administrations in both Tomsk and Saratov, being removed from the center, had more autonomy in following or rejecting state recommendations.

Sovnarkom's acceptance of the OBSA resolution encouraged the founders of the temperance society to press for further legal and bureaucratic restrictions on the production and sale of alcohol. In 1929 Gosplan held a conference concerning amendments to the Five-Year Plan, and representatives from OBSA managed to wrangle an invitation to participate. Conceding to pressure from OBSA members at the conference, Gosplan decided to allocate 200 million rubles a year (out of the projected annual 900 million rubles in liquor revenues) for the anti-alcohol campaign. Further, Gosplan agreed to consider a plan that would allow the state to continue producing vodka during the First Five-Year Plan but beginning October 1, 1932, would reduce vodka production by 40 percent and replace it with beer and wine.[127]

By accepting OBSA's proposals, Sovnarkom and Gosplan placed the state finance and alcohol administrations in an awkward position. On the one hand, these administrations were charged with coming up with a certain amount of liquor revenues; on the other, they were supposed to reduce alcohol production. A note concerning "the operation of Tsentrospirt in the Five-Year Plan" from the People's Commissariat of Finance (Narodnyi komissariat finansov, Narkomfin) to the Central Bureau of Alcohol Production (Tsentral'noe pravlenie i ob"edinenie spirotovoi promyshlennosti, Tsentrospirt) succinctly laid out the problem:

> We need to satisfy two opposing goals—the demands of budgetary solvency and the fight against alcoholism. A year or so ago, the plan called for raising the quota of alcohol produced to 58 million *vedros* by the end of the five-year plan and to lower the cost-per-pail of hard liquor by 1 ruble 60 kopecks and table wine by 2 rubles. In 1927/28 excise taxes on alcohol netted 675 million rubles. In 1928/29 we should net 913.7 million rubles and 1,070 million by 1929/30. Yet the demands of common sobriety require minimum budgetary revenues from vodka. Herein lies our present trouble and future problems.[128]

Tsentrospirt solved this problem by flooding the countryside with vodka and reducing the amount of alcohol to be distributed to the cities. The amended plan called for a reduction in the cities from 18.5 million *vedros* in 1927/1928 to 10 million *vedros* in 1932/1933. In the villages, this trend was reversed to an increase from 24 million *vedros* in 1927/1928 to 36 million *vedros* in 1932/1933.[129] Tsentrospirt justified this move by lowering the price of vodka sent to rural areas and arguing that increased availability of cheap vodka would make significant strides in eradicating *samogon* in the countryside.[130]

In Moscow, Tomsk, and Saratov, Tsentrospirt followed this scheme—these urban areas received a total of about 8 percent less alcohol until 1930/1931.[131] However, in September 1930 Stalin instructed Molotov to "increase . . . the production of vodka" and "to aim openly and directly for the maximum increase in output" in order to raise money for the military.[132] Consequently, Tsentrospirt was reorganized and renamed Soiuzspirt SSSR. Soiuzspirt revved up nationwide production of alcohol in 1930/1931 from 58.3 million *vedros* (or 700 million liters) to 64.6 million *vedros,* an increase of about 9 percent. Further, Soiuzspirt planned a dramatic increase in the amount of alcohol to be distributed to Kharkov—upward of 25 percent. In one planning session, an unidentified person noted that supplying Ukraine with large amounts of cheaper state alcohol would not only help with the *samogon* problem there but might also pacify a population growing restive over collectivization and decreasing food supplies.[133] In less than two years Ukraine would be devastated by famine.[134]

In 1932 the central alcohol administration was again reorganized into the Central Administration of Alcohol Production (Glavnoe upravlenie spirtovoi promyshlennosti, Glavspirt) under the administration of the People's Commissariat of Supply (Narodnyi komissariat snabzhenii, Narkomsnab).[135] Along with this administrative reorganization came a further increase in alcohol production and the construction of new beer breweries and vodka distilleries in numerous oblasts in Russia. New distilleries were planned for Moscow and Tomsk in 1931. A significant number of new construction projects tackled by shock workers in 1933 were distilleries in Saratov oblast.[136]

Just as OBSA's demands for decreased alcohol production came to naught, it is doubtful that the society's legislative offensive had much practical effect either. Temperance literature at the time claimed that a few localities opted to prohibit alcohol sales, but other evidence is thin.[137] On the contrary, regional surveys demonstrate a steady increase in consumption of state-produced alcohol among urban industrial workers between 1927 and 1932.[138] In essence, OBSA's campaign to enlist the help of other state agencies was less important for its impact on drinking and sobriety than for the propaganda value in drawing public attention to the problem.

The anti-alcohol campaign, like most campaigns for a new *byt,* called upon young men and women who had come of age in "new conditions" to smash remnants of working-class behavior that were left over from the tsarist past. Children were encouraged to inculcate proper social values in their elders. This theme emerges over and over again in temperance literature aimed at youth. Temperance advocates exhorted young people to expose parents who drank, thereby subjecting the private conduct of adults to the scrutiny of youngsters. Temperance fiction often included stories about children who, having suffered some kind of lack or abuse due to their father's drinking, heroically called public attention to the parent's misdeeds. In the end, the father inevitably would recognize his poor judgment and rectify his actions.[139] While there is no evidence that children actually turned their parents in for abusive drinking, the clear message in such stories was that in the struggle for socialist culture, even children could be the agents of change. More important, it demonstrated the blurred distinctions between private and public behaviors and reflected the polemics of cultural revolution.

On a few well-advertised occasions, OBSA activists within the ranks of the Young Pioneers (a communist youth group for preteens) and Komsomols organized large groups of children to agitate against their parents' drinking. Placing themselves immediately outside the factory gates on payday, these young demonstrators would carry signs that read, "Buy us textbooks rather than vodka!" and "We demand sober parents!"[140] In 1928–1929 over 200 children's demonstrations took place in various centers such as Moscow, Leningrad, Kharkov, and even Irkutsk. However, broad general support cannot be inferred from a few well-publicized demonstrations, especially since other areas such as Tomsk and Saratov had no such demonstrations.

In fact, the expected struggle for sobriety by Soviet youth never materialized.[141] For example, throughout 1928–1930 not a word about drinking or anti-alcohol work appeared in the pages of *Molodoi leninets* (Young Leninists), the official newspaper of the Saratov Komsomol, even after OBSA had claimed numerous cells there. In both Kharkov and Tomsk, not only were the youth uninvolved in the temperance movement, but widespread drunkenness among Komsomols was a topic of great concern.[142] Numerous Komsomol reports noted that young people often skipped meetings to drink and play cards.[143] In 1928 a study conducted at the eighty-fifth school in the Moscow-Narva district revealed that 70 percent of young boys drank.[144]

Working-class women also turned out to be disappointing allies for the anti-alcohol movement. Women's participation in the temperance movement was weak—only 7 percent of OBSA's members were women.[145] Activists devoted considerable attention to how to remedy inadequate female participation.[146] Yet the fact that working-class women did not readily participate in the temperance campaign is consistent with the experience of other European temperance movements. Working-class women were not particularly active in either the German or the French temperance movements.[147] In both Europe and America, the women most actively involved in temperance were from the middle and leisure classes. No such classes existed in Soviet Russia. The sources do suggest, however, that working-class women engaged in individual actions consistent with temperance objectives, but their opposition to drunkenness was rooted in intermittent circumstances motivated by economic concerns rather than a categorical antipathy toward alcohol abuse. The most common manifestation of this was when women waited at factory gates on payday in an attempt to escort their husbands home with pay packet intact or to collect money for household needs.[148] Clearly neither cultural revolution nor domestic difficulties produced the kind of unified public struggle against alcohol use envisioned by activists.

Failing to attract Soviet youth and working-class women, OBSA membership consisted primarily of male workers. In early 1929 OBSA boasted over 250,000 members in more than 200 factory cells, thereby declaring itself a genuinely proletarian movement.[149] The first OBSA cell was organized in the Moscow factory Serp i Molot (Sickle and Hammer) and immediately began a campaign under the slogan "The Unified Front in the Struggle against Alcohol and Tobacco." Other cells quickly sprang up in the AMO factory, in the railroad repair shop at the Kursk station, and in other factories and repair shops around Moscow. From Moscow, OBSA cells spread first to Odessa, which claimed 3,000 members, and Kharkov, which reported 15,000 members.[150] By the beginning of 1929 OBSA estimated that in Saratov, nearly 6,000 new members joined factory cells. An issue of *Trezvost' i kul'tura* (Sobriety and Culture), OBSA's monthly journal, in mid-1929 reported that it had received pledges from 20,000 workers nationwide to abandon drink.[151] Yet there is no evidence that OBSA ever existed in Tomsk; in Saratov, OBSA existed mostly on paper and was certainly not active.

As the anti-alcohol campaign widened in scope, new cells seemed to lose focus and direction. Therefore in early 1929 OBSA published instructions to factory cells urging members to disseminate "correct socialist ideas" about alcohol and drug use and to influence other workers and factory organizations to join OBSA. Members were required to practice total abstinence, but a worker who still drank could be a "candidate" member until he or she gave up drink altogether.[152] In May that same year OBSA's founding apparat organized the All-Union Council of Anti-alcohol Societies (Vsesoiuznyi sovet protivalkogol'nykh obshchestv SSSR, VSPO) to coordinate the various branches' activities. The first session, held in Moscow, was attended by more than one hundred delegates from factories as far away as Ukraine, Belorussia, Azerbaijan, and Turkmenistan and included representatives from the Komsomol, Narkomzdrav, Narkomtrud, and VSNKh.[153] Within the year VSPO organized anti-alcohol demonstrations in over one hundred different towns and fifty local workers' conferences on how to struggle against alcoholism.[154]

General membership statistics do not exist owing to the destruction of OBSA's archives; therefore it is impossible to verify OBSA's claims. Yet there is little reason to doubt its working-class composition. Since most of its activities took place in industrial regions and its branches were initially organized through existing factory party cells, it is logical to assume that the bulk of OBSA's members would be workers. Since party affiliation was not an essential characteristic among members—only 22 percent were party members in 1929—the majority were rank-and-file workers.[155]

OBSA's claims of widespread working-class support and active participation, however, are much less plausible. Clearly workers joined OBSA in droves, but not all of them were actively involved in the temperance movement. In Saratov, for example, where OBSA claimed over 6,000 members, fewer than 500 had filled out membership applications.[156] In Tomsk, OBSA was either nonexistent or totally inactive.[157] In Moscow, one individual signed up the entire Moscow City Council of Trade Unions (Moskovskii Gorodskii sovet professional'nykh soiuzov).[158] Shortly thereafter, foremen in Moscow factories and repair shops enrolled their entire crews, often without the members' knowledge. Moreover, one of the complaints that appeared constantly in the pages of *Trezvost' i kul'tura* and *Kul'tura i byt* (Culture and Lifestyle) was the continued drinking and drunkenness of OBSA members.

The reasons why workers joined OBSA without necessarily being devoted to the temperance idea are closely associated with the industrialization drive and the accompanying cultural revolution. With the onset of rapid industrialization, the party sought to effect a process of political socialization among the working masses. One component of the socialization process was the use of incentives: material rewards were held out to politically acquiescent workers. In 1929 bread rationing had been introduced in Soviet towns, and during the next few years most basic food commodities and manufactured goods became rationed. Workers who belonged to voluntary societies received bonuses and increased rations, and this was also true for membership in OBSA.[159] Moreover, "politically conscious" workers, even those from the countryside, could rise in the industrial hierarchy, thereby being eligible for increased goods and services.[160] It would therefore behoove a new worker to demonstrate his or her commitment to socialist ideals by joining a voluntary society. One can only speculate that for many workers, a compelling reason to join the temperance movement would be to demonstrate political consciousness in order to increase the possibility of material advancement or, at the very least, to receive a bit more bread and meat. In short, political socialization did not make workers believe in the party's goals and values but rather secured their outward compliance and created the appearance of a politically supportive proletariat.

The Limits of Political Socialization

Throughout the 1920s state and party administrators fought a losing battle with alcohol. The politicization of the "drink question," beginning well before the revolution, made it critical for Bolsheviks to find new definitions of and cures for drunkenness. In many respects, however, the Bolsheviks resembled their bourgeois predecessors. All attempts at sobering up the revolution had essentially failed, leading to a situation in which the Bolsheviks found themselves drowning in a sea of drunkenness.

The party's decision in 1928 to force the tempo of industrial development, which resulted in the policies of rapid industrialization and collectivization, was not confined to the economy. It had its counterpart in a cultural revolution and a variety of social policies intended to facilitate the creation of new Soviet men and women. These policies were actually a part of Russia's modernizing process, which began before 1917. One of the most important areas of social reform, begun before the revolution but reincarnated in the attempt to create a new socialist *byt*, was the struggle against alcoholism. In attempting to solve the problem of alcoholism (which state agencies and theorists helped to create through definition), institutions and disciplines were created or refined to "treat" or "cure" behaviors deemed to be antisocialist. Whether it be the crackdown on illegal brewing, the rapid expansion of social hygiene's narco-dispensaries, or OBSA's extreme and immediate goals, it is clear that in the atmosphere of cultural revolution, the gradualist approach to change was rejected in favor of rapid and forced transformation in all areas of public life.

As part of the regime's efforts at political socialization, the anti-alcohol campaign defined appropriate working-class behavior, seeking to enlist the help of society at large and the proletariat in particular. OBSA's message was clear: workers should be sober, collectivist, and dedicated to advancing the goals of socialism. Yet the party's power to define appropriate values and even punish undesirable ones did not include the power to control workers' behavior or to dictate their thoughts. It more often than not simply forced workers to give the appearance of compliance while they continued to pursue their individual interests, including obtaining and drinking vodka.

The new industrial labor force that emerged through the processes of industrialization and collectivization defied the party's definitions of "working class." Rejecting the identity of new Soviet men or women, workers collectively and as individuals resisted the behavioral norms officials sought to impose on them, relying instead on older, more fundamental cultural traditions. Unable to impose social controls through legislative action or voluntary societies, reformers hoped propaganda would inculcate passive controls through the vilification of drink.

Demon Vodka: Anti-alcohol Propaganda and Cultural Revolution

WITH THE ONSET OF RAPID INDUSTRIALIZATION IN 1929, the ranks of the proletariat greatly expanded into a new workforce, created virtually from the peasantry. Anxious to create a truly Soviet working class, the leadership was concerned not only about workers' political attitudes but about their social and private behaviors as well. This ultimately meant that the regime had to initiate a process of socialization that it expected workers to accept. It also meant the politicization of private life: private behaviors, such as drinking, carried political connotations. Since party leaders had defined most forms of working-class drinking as antithetical to the goals of socialism, workers had to be either persuaded or coerced into giving up their attachment to "excessive" drinking. Yet throughout the 1920s and 1930s workers collectively and as individuals rejected official values and clung to their traditional cultures and modes of socialization, especially their drinking behaviors, just as the state clung to its reliance on liquor revenues. The state's need for liquor revenues and society's continued drunkenness presented a challenge to the Soviet leadership: how to sell the idea of sobriety to workers while still selling them alcohol.

To solve this problem, Bolshevik reformers employed ideological and rhetorical devices to construct drinking in political terms that reflected larg-

er cultural and political conflicts between state and society during the early Soviet period. Having found themselves helpless to curb the flow of illegal alcohol, unable to generate acceptable forms of revenue to replace alcohol revenues, and utterly incapable of changing traditional drinking habits, the Bolsheviks attempted to school workers on correct drinking practices in two ways: through the nationwide temperance society, OBSA, and through the dissemination of propaganda.

Nearly twenty years ago Peter Kenez dubbed the Soviet Union the first modern "propaganda state."[1] In the course of 1918 the Bolsheviks put into motion an impressive and extensive propaganda apparatus to a degree previously unknown. Institutions of mass mobilization became an integral part of the Soviet state. The intention here is not to argue whether the Bolsheviks used propaganda to school workers on proper drinking behavior; of course they did. Curiously, relatively little scholarly attention has been paid to the content of that propaganda. Most studies that include an analysis of Bolshevik rhetoric focus on the revolution or the civil war and not on the polemics of cultural revolution.[2] Yet throughout the late 1920s and 1930s the Bolsheviks remained profoundly committed to reconstituting society and the individual in accordance with their ideological precepts. To do so they exploited a monolithic apparatus that exposed millions upon millions of Soviet citizens to propaganda on the street, in the workplace, and throughout the public sphere.

As with most modernizing European countries, the Soviet temperance campaign was one important aspect of this mass indoctrination. Temperance propaganda found expression in written, oral, and visual media. Since newspapers and pamphlets were the least expensive way to reach large numbers of workers, activists relied most heavily on written means to cajole, coerce, or convince workers to give up their attachment to vodka. Drawing on a number of rhetorical devices, they manipulated language to frame drinking in political terms and to demonize alcohol and alcoholics. Anti-alcohol poems and stories were quite prominent in the popular press. The party also used visual images to define political issues for workers and to stigmatize "un-Bolshevik" behavior. These included plays, mock trials, and agitational films. Obsessed with the creation of a Soviet worker culture, party members employed visual images to indoctrinate the bulk of the illiterate or semiliterate working class. In order to engage the audience and entice workers to attend these events, party activists used fantasy, melodrama, and humor to vilify or ridicule alcoholics. By focusing on the content of anti-alcohol

propaganda, this chapter reveals how the regime defined itself and its perceived enemies and offers insights into the making of Bolshevik-defined socialist society.

Alcoholism and Socialism Are Incompatible

OBSA took the lead in launching a massive propaganda campaign to sway public opinion against drinking. Under the slogan "Alcoholism and Socialism Are Incompatible," OBSA began its public antidrinking campaign using agitation, propaganda, demonstrations, exhibitions, and enlistment drives. From the very start it was clear that the thrust of the campaign was aimed at industrial workers and that it was not a general struggle against alcohol abuse but a fight for complete abstinence.

The highly visible campaign generated a lot of attention, even though it never really attracted wide public support. For example, within the first five months of the campaign, OBSA organized 2,000 mass meetings, lectures, and exhibitions attended by nearly 150,000 people.[3] In 1928 Narkomzdrav and Sovkino (the state film agency) teamed up to produce and release a number of anti-alcohol films.[4] In April 1929 a special anti-alcohol "cinema exhibition" toured the country showing temperance films, giving lectures, and organizing OBSA cells in industrial enterprises and mining operations.[5] This exhibit made its way from Moscow to Kharkov, Saratov, and Siberia, although it missed Tomsk. Muscovite temperance activists from OBSA traveled with the exhibition, signing up individual members and whole enterprises. Since the exhibition did not reach Tomsk, it is no coincidence that OBSA never got a foothold in Tomsk.

In addition to organizing exhibitions, OBSA members flooded journals, magazines, and newspapers with articles carrying titles such as "For a Sober Life," "Down with Vodka," "Join the Struggle with Alcoholism," and even "Shoot Drunks!" In 1929 nearly 5,000 articles appeared in newspapers on workers' resolutions to swear off alcohol and join the anti-alcohol campaign.[6] That same year each issue of the regional newspapers and trade union journals in Moscow, Kharkov, Saratov, and Tomsk carried at least one article on alcoholism or anti-alcohol work, a trend that appears to have been nationwide. Even though OBSA had no presence in Tomsk, the local press carried as many temperance-related articles as in Saratov or Kharkov. It is logical to

assume that this was true for other parts of the country as well and that OBSA's propaganda was more far-reaching than its ability to organize factory cells.

Temperance advocates used two sets of linked metaphors to stigmatize drinking behaviors not conducive to Communist-defined socialist values. The first depended on a military metaphor to characterize the battle with alcoholism. This can be seen as an extension of what Mark von Hagen has termed the "militarization of political culture" already apparent during the civil war and characteristic of the 1920s.[7] Throughout the years of the anti-alcohol movement (1928–1933), reformers conceived of the arena of anti-alcohol activity as a "front" and sober workers as an "army." The first OBSA cell organized in the Moscow factory Serp i Molot immediately began a campaign under the slogan "The Unified Front in the Struggle against Alcohol and Tobacco." Further, every issue of *Trezvost' i kul'tura* opened with the following declaration:

> We can defeat alcoholism through broad agitation and propaganda, personal example, the unmasking . . . of wreckers of socialist construction who are active on the alcoholic front. We will be able to claim victory over alcohol through merciless struggle with home brewers and tavern keepers, and through the replacement of bars and other places for the sale of spirits by Soviet teahouses and other cultural institutions.[8]

A 1929 issue of *Trezvost' i kul'tura* declared that over 20,000 workers nationwide had already abandoned drink and that the Soviet Union possessed the "most sober army in the world."[9]

In addition to militaristic rhetoric, one of the most obvious features of OBSA's propaganda was the extremism in definitions of alcoholism and calls for sobriety. It identified alcoholism with the total destruction of the cultural revolution, the First Five-Year Plan, socialist construction, and worker discipline. According to OBSA literature, drinking necessarily led to alcoholism, and alcoholism necessarily led to criminality, insanity, death, murder, mayhem, disease, and, worst of all, "bourgeois degeneration."

The society's propaganda emphasized the damage to health caused by drinking. Displaying pictures of livers that resembled Jerusalem artichokes and images of swollen, blackened hearts, many of OBSA's journals and books detailed the physical horrors that awaited one in taking a few drinks.[10] OBSA routinely published columns of statistics on suicide and criminality; graphs of rising accident, sickness, and death rates; and photographs of drunkards and deformed babies of alcoholics, thereby keeping the verbal and visual evidence of the most heinous effects of alcoholism in the public eye.

This emphasis on the extreme degradation caused by drinking was tactically and psychologically maladroit. While it might have scared a few people into abstaining and may have encouraged some to join the temperance movement, it more likely offended both common sense and human nature. The ordinary Soviet worker must have had a hard time believing that the traditional glass of vodka would lead directly to prison, to the asylum, or into the welcoming arms of capitalist enemies.

A second metaphoric system, which overlay the first, split society in a Manichaean fashion into heroes and villains, darkness and light, sinners and saviors.[11] Rooted in a profound conviction that Marxist principles would lead them to a socialist utopia and confident in the success of the revolution, the Bolsheviks initially adopted quasi-religious moralistic tones toward drunken workers and peasants. Bolsheviks were the saviors; drunkards were the wayward "sinners." This attitude toward the continued existence of drunkenness reveals much about how the Bolsheviks viewed themselves in relation to society. When the object of moral reform—the person who has violated the norms of the reformers—can be perceived as a deviant rather than an enemy, the social status of the reformer is enhanced.[12] The reformer's norms are the ideal and the dominant operative standards for society. When the norms violator is defined as an enemy, the social status of the reformer is threatened. A social group that perceives its culture as defining the ideal and publicly valid norms of society will approach the deviant as someone to be helped in attaining the habits that can ensure improvement in the deviant's social condition. The response to social problems is assimilative: "Be like us." This in turn reinforces the reformer's belief in his or her social supremacy.

The assumption that the norms violator recognizes the legitimacy or domination of the normative order is contradicted when the violator becomes the enemy. His or her behavior raises the question "Who dominates?" Such an individual cannot be dealt with as someone to be assimilated and converted but as someone who is hostile and must be coerced or forced to accept the dominance of the reformer. When the drinker is seen as an enemy, he or she presents a challenge to the domination and legitimacy of the reformers and threatens their power and prestige, their superior position vis-à-vis the drinker.

In the early 1920s both assimilative and coercive attitudes toward drunken workers and peasants were present in anti-alcohol propaganda, indicating not only contrasting and conflicting impulses within Bolshevik policy but also perceived changes in the party's dominance and authority. Initially, the Bolsheviks held a predominantly assimilative attitude toward drunken workers and peasants. Assuming they possessed the moral and cultural authority to create a new society, party leaders portrayed the drinker in the kindly images of a sufferer or sinner, a victim of capitalist oppression, to be uplifted and saved by the Bolsheviks. For example, soon after the October Revolution, Semashko declared, "For centuries the tsar made the people drink and held them in ignorance and lack of knowledge. The worker or the peasant often did not have the opportunity to spend his leisure other than to get drunk and forget the nightmares of his dependent, slave-like existence."[13]

Semashko's statement reveals much about the assumptions and agenda of Bolshevik leaders. From the party's perspective, the masses were *nekul'turnye* (uncultured). They could seize factories and farms, but they did not know how to run them as would an industrialized modern labor force. The culture they lacked was much more than technical knowledge; it included all elements of *samodiatelnost'*—the intelligent self-activation of a modern people. Culture meant striving for emancipation from the realm of darkness (*temnoe tsarstvo*), from the self-assertive pigheadedness of the master and the self-effacing irresponsibility of the slave.[14]

The illiterate peasant and the alcoholic worker became symbols of those for whom the Bolsheviks would light the way out of the darkness, freeing them from past oppression by propagating political consciousness and leading a cultural revolution. This perspective was based on a fundamental assumption that the masses wanted to be saved, bolstered by the Bolsheviks' conviction of the legitimacy of Bolshevik-defined socialist culture as the dominant set of cultural values. Such an assumption presupposed a common class culture—proletarian—and a social consensus on the "rightness" of Communist morality. The assumed redeemability of the alcoholic through rational persuasion in the state's resocialization programs reflects the regime's belief in its own dominance and validity as moral reformer.

Anti-alcohol Literature

The assimilative mood of the Bolsheviks can clearly be seen in the anti-alcohol literature of the early 1920s. Soviet writers took up the call for moral reform as a spate of temperance-oriented literature appeared in the pages of journals, magazines, and books throughout the 1920s and into the 1930s. Newspapers such as *Pravda, Izvestiia,* and *Rabochaia gazeta* (Workers' Gazette); popular journals such as *Begemot* (Hippopotamus), *Lef* (Left), and *Literaturnaia gazeta* (Literary Gazette); and many trade union and factory newspapers carried articles, poems, stories, and cartoons about drinking in almost every issue. Some of the leading Soviet writers who published temperance fiction, poems, and plays about drinking included A. A. Blok, A. N. Tolstoi, V. V. Maiakovskii, I. Ilf and E. Petrov, and D. Bednyi.

The most popular form of temperance literature was poetry. Many of the early poems invoked images reminiscent of religious motifs, such as the devil tempting the righteous or a Christ-figure redeeming the sinner. A poem entitled "Devilish Glass and a Drunk from Lipetsk" by Bolshevik poet laureate Dem'ian Bednyi is representative of this type of imagery. It is about a peasant who never drank, never entered a tavern, and lived an entirely honest life. The devil constantly tempted him, but he was able to stand firm until economic hardship struck in his fortieth year. The devil promised him a sack of money if he would commit "just one little sin"—adultery or murder. When the peasant refused, the devil persuaded him to at least get a little drunk. Eventually the peasant could no longer resist and got "devilishly drunk." To the devil's delight, while under the influence, the righteous peasant raped his neighbor's wife and killed his neighbor. The poem ends in a moralistic tone:

> A cunning Devil, say from the Kadet's camp,
> Can trick the Soviet peasant.
> "You will have all sorts of wealth
> Just kick the Soviet power under its ninth rib."
> Now take a look at the drunk from Lipetsk,
> How he clutches the devilish glass.
> It is impossible to pull him out of the Beast's jaws.
> Alcohol is the worst enemy of Soviet power.
> A drunk is able to drink Soviet power away.

We ought to baptize drunks with Soviet holy water,
And sprinkle them so well,
That next time the drunk sees the Devil with his brew
He would avoid the Devil like the plague.[15]

In this poem, the righteous peasant is not to blame—alcohol, the devil, even the Kadets are the enemy.[16] Even bolstered by Soviet power, the peasant is able to stand firm against the devil only so long. Ultimately the devil wins, but the purifying and empowering influence of holy "Soviet water" sprinkled on drunks as if upon sinners by a priest can once again restore peasants to their righteousness.

These types of poems appeared in the most popular journals that circulated among tens of thousands of people throughout the Soviet Union between 1923 and 1929. The most important vehicle for temperance literature was OBSA's monthly journal, *Trezvost' i kul'tura*, which was founded in 1928 and claimed a print run of between 45,000 and 60,000 circulating throughout Russia and Ukraine. Funded largely from alcohol revenues, copies of the journal made their way to all four of the cities under study, and one may assume it reached all corners of the empire.

Many publications represented drinking as a major cause of the misfortunes of urban workers and their families. A typical example is the following poem by an anonymous author, taken from the pages of a popular journal. It has a tone of sadness, despair, and suffering, all common motifs in poems and stories about drinking in the early 1920s:

At the dirty, sticky table,
Head bent down,
Stands the wife with Antip,
Shaking him.
—Why are you here?
Mumbles the drunken husband.
—Let's go, you're already drunk.
And the sounds of the violins cry
And the singer is completely hoarse.
Silently Antip hands her
A saucer of peas,

His beret trembling in his hand.
In the morning there will be
Not even a little to eat,
The entire paycheck was disposed of
On the father's debauch.
—Get up, why put on airs?
You are a sinner even in front of the children!
I wanted to laugh,
But nothing was funny.[17]

This poem conveys the sympathy of the righteous toward those too weak to help themselves. The subject is downtrodden and suffering. He is a sinner who can repent, one who probably wishes to be saved but cannot help himself. Often these poems carried the implicit suggestion that once the transition to socialism was made, such suffering would wither away—that socialism would save those who could not save themselves.

Explicit in the rhetoric of Communist intellectuals during the 1920s was the assertion that socialism would cure these ills: "That which in capitalist society is squandered by the capitalists in gluttony, drunkenness, and riotous living will, in Communist society, be devoted to the needs of production . . . all members of society will be occupied in productive labor."[18] The capitalist past would soon be transformed into the socialist future, bringing with it the flowering of an ideal society, the end of oppression, and the liberation of the masses.

From Victims to Enemies

Coercive reform is a reaction to a sense of declining dominance.[19] Coercive reformers do not perceive the subjects of their reforms with sympathy and warmth. They are not victims who can be assimilated into the reformer's communities or converted to his or her culture. The violators of norms are enemies who have repudiated the validity of the reformer's culture. This orientation, not evident in the prerevolutionary socialists' temperance agenda, surfaced in the early 1920s but began to take precedence in policy after 1927 as a mood of militancy and alarm swept through the party.

Toward the end of the 1920s, one can see a subtle shift in the tone of much of the temperance propaganda from assimilative to coercive. Whereas earlier pieces used dichotomies of sinner/savior, later pieces employ dichotomous images of enemy/victim or villain/hero. By 1928, with the imperatives of rapid industrialization, the perceived threat of foreign "capitalist encirclement," and the saturation of the industrial labor force with peasant migrants, the party shifted from vanguardist, leading a revolution, to militant, coercing the masses to comply. This was in part a reaction to social realities that created intensifying tension between a predominantly peasant society and an increasingly etatist party representing itself as the instrument of socialist construction. In the countryside, the peasants fiercely resisted abandoning traditional ways of life and institutions for an uncertain and undefined "socialist transformation." In the factories, worsening conditions undermined skilled workers' support for party policies. Added to this, campaigns to control new workers intensified their disorientation and hostility to the regime, resulting in various forms of passive resistance.

The party was continually being confronted with situations that could only be interpreted as a failure to establish cultural dominance—the party was leading, but the masses were not following. The following complaint was cited in a Moscow party plenum as indicative of the mood of the workers: "*Communists* are the enemies of the working class. Why should we follow them? . . . For ten years the party has been leading us, but it is still not clear to where!"[20]

This shift to coercive reform was signaled in a speech at the Seventeenth Moscow City Party Conference by Iuri Larin, the founder of OBSA. Addressing the problem of alcoholism, he warned that the greatest danger to Bolshevik hegemony was from "repulsive bourgeois and petit-bourgeois elements" in the party and especially "those hundreds of thousands of workers who in recent years have entered our factories from the countryside and from the middle-class."[21] Much was blamed on these new workers, including drunkenness, hooliganism, and poor labor discipline. From 1927, the Bolsheviks increasingly described the drinker as the enemy of socialist construction and drinking as a threat to both the party and state.

In 1927 E. I. Deichman articulated the party's more militant attitude toward drunkenness. He admonished state administrations to mercilessly expose "drunken parasites," warning that the harm caused by alcoholics could undermine "the authority and trust in Soviet power and the party."[22] Aspects of coercive reform found their way into official policy in the last months of 1927 when Narkomzdrav and the NKVD published "Instructions on the Forced Treatment of Alcoholics."[23] These instructions gave health care organs permission to use force against anyone who, due to alcoholism, "violated the standards of socialist conduct" or was deemed to be a "wrecker" or "squanderer." Moreover, it advised that existing alcoholic dispensaries introduce such measures and prepare facilities for such treatment.

By the end of the 1920s the anti-alcohol campaign offered very few positive incentives for buying the idea of sobriety. Given the Bolsheviks' failure to establish cultural dominance, they experienced a loss of control over the society they were creating. It is not surprising, therefore, that their responses to drinking became more hostile and coercive. Further, during the cultural revolution a mass campaign called socialist competition swept through the Soviet Union. Beginning with the Komsomol in the Ukrainian metallurgical industry, workers organized themselves into model, or shock, brigades, and acted as a vanguard in the factories promoting not only production competitions but other social and political mobilizations as well.[24] Ridiculing and harassing new workers from the countryside, shock brigades intensified bitter conflicts among workers. Contemporary accounts speak of struggles between shock workers and kulaks. Peasant migrants labeled shock brigades as "detachments of the Antichrist."[25]

Tagging alcoholics as enemies of the people, OBSA members organized shock brigades to police the shop floor, thereby constructing and reflecting the polemics of cultural revolution. Arguing that the struggle against alcoholism was a battle for full achievement of the Five-Year Plan in four years, temperance advocates declared that every drunken worker was an enemy of socialist construction.[26] Becoming more strident and more frequent toward the middle of 1931, this theme appeared repeatedly in temperance rhetoric throughout the early 1930s and provided the political justification for members of OBSA to attack workers they deemed to be drunkards. In singling out workers and accusing them of excessive drinking, OBSA shock brigades branded offenders with the label "fraudulent shirkers of responsibility."

OBSA shock brigades operated in various factories in Moscow, Kharkov, and elsewhere. In general, members of OBSA cells would organize themselves into sixty-member brigades to investigate absences from work.[27] The brigades would go to the absent worker's home, and if the worker was drunk or hung over, he or she would be reported to administrative and trade union officials. The largest shock brigade, the Red Putilov Workers (Krasnyi Putilovtsy), was located in Leningrad at the Putilov factory. In Moscow, OBSA shock brigades were quite active in the larger factories, such as Dinamo and Serp i Molot. The same was true in Kharkov. In Saratov, however, OBSA cells did not form shock brigades, probably because of the weakness of local leadership. One may assume that individual chapters of OBSA had a fair amount of autonomy in deciding what types of anti-alcohol activities to pursue. There appears to have been no consequences for poor performance by or within a local chapter.

In those areas that did have shock brigades, anyone coming under fire from OBSA for drinking or shirking responsibility would be subject to ridicule, suspension, and, in some cases, arrest. Legally, an enterprise would be within its rights to fire errant workers, remove their ration card, and kick them out of company housing.[28] This would mean that the offender would not only be unemployed but homeless and hungry as well.

In Ukraine, where peasant resistance to collectivization was greatest, OBSA brigades also went into the countryside, theoretically to help collectivization and to spread anti-alcohol propaganda to the peasantry.[29] In the spirit of cultural revolution, many of these brigades were imbued with a militant zeal for change and contempt for peasant backwardness, which most likely translated into rudeness and violence against the peasantry. However, in Kharkov, numerous members apparently mistook their mandate and were later purged from OBSA for "drinking with kulaks."[30]

OBSA was not the only organization that purged members for drinking. Drunkenness among party members was a matter of great concern and debate for the leadership. As early as 1921 the party began disciplining its own ranks for drinking, in part responding to greatly increased numbers of members resulting from a series of recruitment drives.[31] Just as the working class had gone through a transformation between 1924 and 1930 owing to industrial recovery and expansion, so did the party. The old prerevolutionary organization of political intellectuals and politically active workers had all but disappeared as civil war and NEP recruits altered the social composition of the party. A mass enrollment campaign in December 1923 admitted 100,000 workers into the party. In 1924 and 1925 two recruitment drives, known as the Lenin Levy, increased party membership by 638,070 people.[32]

In Moscow after the Lenin Levy, an overwhelming majority of party members were male workers under the age of thirty-four, 48 percent of whom were employed in manual labor.[33] Party membership went through similar transformations in Kharkov, Saratov, and Tomsk as semieducated first- or second-generation industrial workers joined the party. With their cultural traditions, it is little wonder that they engaged in drinking, at times to excess.

Beginning in 1923, habitual drinking became a common reason to expel members from local party cells. These early purges do indeed seem to be about drinking, as the party set out to be the example for Soviet society to emulate. Moreover, they dovetailed with the leadership's commitment to "reproletarianize" the party by establishing purge commissions in 1924 to root out social aliens from party and educational institutions. Since the party defined drunkenness as a petit bourgeois activity, it sought to purge its ranks of "drunks, hooligans, and other class enemies."[34] A resolution issued by the Party Central Committee and sent to local party organizations called for diligent struggle to clean the party of drunken bourgeois elements.[35] By 1928 drinking became the number one reason people lost their party membership. According to a NKVD report dated May 5, 1928, over 22 percent of those who lost their party membership did so for being "habitual alcoholics."[36] Purging party members for drunkenness was a nationwide trend repeated by local party organizations in all four areas under study.

Drinking also became a convenient excuse to get rid of members if no other charges would stick—even nondrinkers were purged for drunkenness. In one such case a certain Dmitriev was charged with being a Trotskyist. No proof of Dmitriev's Trotskyist activities could be found, and after a long hearing in which several people testified on behalf of his political soundness, the commission expelled him for drunkenness, even though no one had previously commented on his drinking.[37] In another case in Saratov, I. Bormotov was purged from the party and fired from his job in 1929 for "lack of discipline and habitual alcoholism," even though he had not been reprimanded since 1921. Born in 1897, Bormotov joined the party in 1917 and started working in Saratov factories in 1920. In 1926 he moved to Moscow, where he worked without incident until he was accused of drinking and purged.[38] At his hearing, five other workers with similar biographies and circumstances were purged. The real reason for such purges remains a mystery, but it is easy to imagine that scapegoating and personal rivalries at times were behind the guise of cleaning the party of drunks.

As in official policy, cultural representations of drinking began to reflect an attitude of coercion, the central themes most often being conflict between enemies or heroes versus villains. Take, for example, another poem published in 1930 by Bednyi:

> Those who drink,
> Drink not only liquor,
> But other people and things as well!
> We are not the bourgeois states,
> Where everything is blamed on poor people.
> We are the USSR!
> We fight for a different future,
> And should carry on a fight with drunks
> Without hypocritical measures,
> But harsh ones!
> (A prison will suppress the drunken energy
> Of drinkers motivated either by need or stupidity),
> And with words, which are terrible to forget:
> In the battle with drunkenness we battle for our culture
> And for this: to save our own skins from our enemies![39]

This appeal for sobriety is not based on an effort to convert the sufferers but rather on moral indignation—to punish those who violate socialist norms. Drinking is portrayed not as an isolated activity but as a destructive force that will annihilate all the gains made by the revolution. The hostile and angry tone of the poem is a reaction to the threat to Soviet domination that the existence of drinking on a wide scale implied. In this context, such admonitions against drinking are symbolic representations of the party's struggle to extend its cultural authority to define appropriate morality and lifestyle.

The coercive strain of the Bolsheviks' reform framed drinking in political terms in order to sanction certain behaviors that would defend the Bolsheviks' social and political superiority. Believing it had the moral authority to wipe out old cultural traditions, the party called upon "conscious" workers to discipline and punish backward ones. Maiakovskii illustrates this theme in a poem entitled "Hey, Workers":

> And now, drunken workers miss work
> Not only at night like (prerevolutionary) traders did

But even during the day.
Now these workers waste not the capitalists' money,
But their own—the money of the Workers' State.
And production is ruined
And the Workers' State is spoiled.
We can no longer beat these drunks,
Like a father would a drunken son.
So comrades, spit on them, swear at them,
And punish these drunkards yourselves!
Remember that every alcoholic worker brings us grief
And brings joy to our enemies.[40]

Similarly, another poem by Maiakovskii is representative of hundreds of poems that appeared in the pages of the popular press in the early 1930s:

Crime throughout the system,
The shouts and screams of hooligans,
The tarnishing of daily life.
All are simply a measure
Of how much beer and vodka has been drunk today.

Clearly there were reasons other than alcohol for crime, hooliganism, and daily problems, but temperance advocates developed several rhetorical associations to vilify and stigmatize drinking. Drinking became associated with many social ills—crime, prostitution, and venereal disease, of course, but also tuberculosis, smoking, hooliganism, street fights, poor labor discipline, and illiteracy. As the 1920s wore on and the party leadership confronted the problem of declining legitimacy and control, policies toward working-class drinking became more hostile and coercive. The more benign attitudes of the NEP in the early 1920s gave way to a harsher militancy by the decade's end.

"Acting" Drunk: Plays and Mock Trials

The anti-alcohol campaign also used visual images, employing a new type of propaganda known as agitation trials (*agitatsionnye sudy,* or *agitsudy*). Performed in a number of venues, including workers' clubs and factories, these trials were plays scripted in the form of courtroom scenes. According to Elizabeth Wood, such dramatized trials became an important part of the political fabric in the 1920s, helping to illuminate "correct" political, social, and cultural values of the new regime.[41] Like written media, these agitation trials registered a shift in propaganda from vandguardist to coercive.

The earliest mock trials, between 1920 and 1923, were designed to show the correctness of the policies of Lenin and the Bolshevik Party. Generally in these plays, leaders submitted themselves to the will of the people and were acquitted, thereby being vindicated and elevated to the status of heroes for all to emulate.[42] *Pravda* reported a number of such agitation trials that proceeded against the heroes of the revolution, including trials of the Russian Communist Party, the Red Army, Soviet authorities, and Lenin and Trotsky. Wood argues that most of these trials contained charges that reflected genuine complaints and concerns appearing in public discourse, rumors, and the émigré press.[43] The *agitsudy* also were designed to teach audiences Bolshevik ideals regarding a number of critical problems, such as the antireligious campaign, the battle against illiteracy, the struggle for sanitary health, and, of course, the battle against drunkenness.[44]

By the middle of the decade, however, negative role models became dominant in these trials, and the staged polemics were designed to vilify "incorrect" behavior and elicit strong emotions to convince audiences of the "right" path. These *agitsudy* depicted conflict between good and evil, with trial testimony imbued with a clear moral purpose. A classic example can be seen in *Sud nad p'ianitsei* (The Trial of a Drunk) by physician Boris Sigal, which was widely performed throughout 1929–1931.[45] In this trial, Ivan Stepanov, a thirty-five-year-old worker in Leningrad, is charged with drunkenness, hooliganism, unexcused absences from work, assaulting his boss, and beating his wife and children. Several witnesses are called, including his wife, a former comrade, and a doctor. As each witness takes the stand, the tale of Stepanov's degeneration unfolds. Once a good man, industrious and true, he began to visit the beer hall after work with a rather dubious co-worker (who was not a party member). In a short time he starts drinking vodka and *samogon,* ultimately becoming addicted. He begins drinking at work, "for his health." His boss recounts how Stepanov's behavior at work sometimes would turn murderously violent. The doctor cites Stepanov's failing health and quotes several statistics on how many people die each year from alcohol and what happens to the physical organism of a drunk, and he tries to dispel myths that vodka and wine can be used to treat certain ills.

The most dramatic moment in the trial comes when Stepanov's wife, sobbing nearly uncontrollably, testifies that she and the children have been repeatedly beaten within an inch of their lives—a fact that Stepanov cannot remember owing to drunken "blackouts." Further, his wife relates how Stepanov used all the money for booze, leaving the family nothing to eat. Initially defiant and denying the charges, Stepanov ultimately confesses and repents before the court. Weeping shamelessly, he begs forgiveness and implores the court to punish him severely. He is sentenced to six months' hard labor and forced treatment for alcoholism. By the end of the play, there is no doubt that while Stepanov is bad, alcohol is the real enemy.

Formal instructions for performing the *agitsudy* indicate that they were to be as realistic as possible in order to draw in and enliven the audiences. The script for *Sud nad p'ianitsei* even contained directions not to present it as a "play about a trial" but to advertise it as a "show trial" (*pokazatel'nyi sud*) of a drunk.[46] The ritual of contemporary courtrooms was observed in minute detail: The entire auditorium rose when the judge entered; court officials brought witnesses to the stand and took them away; a deputy verified the name and charges of the accused. The point was to make the trial sufficiently lifelike so that both the audience and performers could easily believe they were not in a club but rather participating in a real trial.

Organizers hoped that the dramatic visual presentation of ideas under the illusion of reality would be more effective at schooling an illiterate or semiliterate audience of workers than political speeches. As Julie Cassidy argues, the melodramatic unmasking of the enemy and his or her tearful contrition were intended to move the audience to tears and encourage the spectators to go through a similar process of self-criticism (*samokritka*), so that they, like the enemy, could be rehabilitated into proper Soviet citizens.[47] The propagandistic value of the *agitsudy* lies in the blurring of the distinction between the real and the fictional so that audiences could see themselves as potential victims/villains and give up alcohol before they suffered Stepanov's fate.

The theme of an enemy who repents and is redeemed appeared in other stage productions as well. Between 1926 and 1930, the Theater of Sanitary Culture (Teatr tsentlal'nogo instituta sanitarnogo prosvesheniia), under the direction of the Institute for Sanitary Culture, performed hundreds of plays in workers' clubs across the Soviet Union, including Moscow, Kharkov, Saratov, and Tomsk. These plays dealt with a range of "moral and sanitary" issues, such as drinking, prostitution, venereal disease, and cleanliness. When the plays were performed in workers' clubs, attendance was voluntary and admission was usually a few kopecks—OBSA members were given discounts. Some were also performed in factories during work hours, and attendance at these was compulsory. They were also performed in cafeterias, workers' barracks, and apartment courtyards free of charge.[48] Often, *anketi* (questionnaires) were circulated after the play to register the audience's response to the show. In general, these *anketi* reveal that audiences enjoyed watching the plays and agreed that drinking was harmful, but audiences expressed no desire or need to temper their own drinking.[49]

A number of the temperance plays portrayed the alcoholic as having drunk away the family's chance for happiness and on the verge of losing all when, through heroic struggle and vigilance, the alcoholic is able to overcome the "green snake" and once again become a useful member of society. Such temperance drama depended on reconciliation and return in order to lay the foundation for what the Bolsheviks expected to become the status quo. Reflecting Bolshevik tendencies to privilege public over private concerns, these plays were usually set in factories, thereby inviting audiences to judge the drunk's behavior on its impact on the collective.

One such play, *On a New Path: Victory Over Alcohol,* depicts the man of the house as a drunken, wife-beating louse who alienates his children and becomes unable and (worse) unwilling to work. He finally responds to his wife's pleas to abandon the bottle, gains the respect of his children, and makes amends at work by becoming a model worker.[50] This particular example underscores the role of women in anti-alcohol rhetoric. According to temperance propaganda, a woman's "most important obligation" was to prohibit the use of alcohol in the home.[51] Even though women were not necessarily supposed to have total control over the behavior of their husbands, they were often blamed for it. As one article in 1929 noted, when a husband drank up the pay packet, the wife was the "culprit" because she was "the cause of all the evils of family life."[52]

Placed side by side, these two examples from temperance propaganda provide contradictory cultural representations of women. On the one hand, women are portrayed as the bearers of the light who can redeem their husbands from alcoholism and save the family from moral and financial ruin. On the other, women are the bearers of evil and misfortune simply by the fact of their existence. This contradiction reflects various debates and factions within the party as to the social role of women in new socialist circumstances. To a large degree, women were viewed much the same as peasants—as backward, uneducable children.[53] At the same time, a patriarchal romanticism of the purity and innocence of women persisted within the culture and within the party.

A much more representative play, and one that was performed in workers' clubs from Moscow to Kharkov and from Saratov to Tomsk, was *Pautina* (Spider Web) by Mikhail Verestinskii. Employing all the melodramatic contrasts of good/evil, victim/villain, hero/enemy, the play's cast of characters include a kulak, a prerevolutionary factory owner, an American engineer, several hooligans, several Komsomol members, and the alcoholic who was an old bourgeois specialist. As in most temperance drama, this play highlights the struggle between virtuous community and anticommunity. On one side are models of socialist consciousness, embodied by the Komsomoltsy, who, by their example, will lead others toward a socialist rebirth. On the other side are those, like the kulak and the hooligans, who represent the old slavish ways of prerevolutionary Russia.[54]

The action takes place in 1928 in a factory on the Volga. The central plot of the play is the battle for the soul of Prokhor Vasil'evich Sutyagin, the old specialist in the machine shop. There are several subplots, such as the physical and moral destruction caused by alcoholism and hooliganism, the struggle for healthy working conditions, socialist competition between factory shops, the evil influences of capitalism, and spies and traitors who have infiltrated the factory's workforce.

The protagonist, Sutyagin, is a master at his craft and a good proletarian who trains and disciplines unskilled workers. Yet he is still vulnerable to deviation and degeneration. As the play opens, one of the Komsomol members is warning a drunk Sutyagin that bad things will come from his drinking. Sutyagin argues for his "right" to have a drink now and then. Sutyagin represents what Lars Lih calls waverers—those who have doubts about the Bolshevik program and cling to their individual pursuits of happiness. He is one still steeped in the old ways of valuing the private over the public and the individual over the collective. Such waverers can join the virtuous community only if they reject the influences of anticommunity and accept the collective as their true self-identity.[55] To illustrate this, one of the Komsomoltsy recites a poem by Maiakovsikii:

The question regarding one's private happiness is not simple
When the republic is attacked by thugs.
Private happiness will come
With the growth of the wealth and power of our republic.[56]

Throughout the play, hidden villains commit several acts of hooliganism, sabotage, and wrecking. Further, there is constant tension between the "heroes" of socialist construction, the Komsomols, and the backward, drunken degenerates. At one point, as drunken voices sing to a harmonica in the background, the secretary of the factory's Komsomol cell complains, "We have reached the accomplishments of technology with a speed that the Americans would envy and at a scale no other country can match. Along with that we have a rotten, stagnant way of life—American technology and Russian *byt*."[57] In the end, a drunken Sutyagin gets his hand caught in a machine. His hand is mutilated, and a finger has to be amputated.

The final scene takes place two years later. We find that the evildoers have been unmasked and banished from the factory. The virtuous have received just rewards—education, promotions, marriages, babies. The workers have new, clean apartments, and the American is accepted into the Communist Party. Having seen the error of his ways and rejected the lure of individual pleasure, Sutyagin quit drinking and has been sober for two years. In his final speech, he addresses the audience, holding up his mangled hand: "All of you, look at this! I have been drinking for thirty years. I drank myself under the table and I drank myself to this. This is the end. There is no more vodka for Sutyagin. I took it with the garbage to the dump. I quit drinking—forever!" Sutyagin ultimately joins the Bolshevik cause, thereby reinforcing and reflecting the party's myth of moral authority and cultural dominance.

Other temperance plays include *Arapy* (Swindlers), *Abort* (Abortion), and *Bez Gal'ma* (No Stopping), all dealing with the social and psychological effects of alcohol abuse. It is impossible to tell how many workers saw these plays, but judging from the *anketi* and other archival evidence, it must have been hundreds of thousands across the Soviet Union. In Saratov, *Arapy* was performed in numerous factories and workers' clubs, as was *Pautina*. Few *anketi* were distributed here, but the documents refer to from 50 to 400 spectators in each venue.[58] In Kharkov, *Bez Gal'ma* alone was attended by a few thousand workers in numerous clubs and factories. Several hundred *anketi* were collected.[59] Generally, the audiences enjoyed the drama and tragedy but complained about the play's moralistic tone. In Tomsk, several of these plays, including *Pautina* and *Arapy,* were quite popular and well attended, probably because there were few other amusements for workers.[60]

These plays were not simply dramatizations of political doctrine; they were, as Lars Lih argues, accurate expressions of the narrative myths that energized political doctrine.[61] In many ways they were much more pertinent and important for disseminating those myths than the doctrines put forth by party theorists.

The Use of Ironic Overstatement

Another device used by temperance activists was humor and ironic over-statement. The sarcastic tone of much anti-alcohol rhetoric expressed Bolshevik reformers' frustration with their own lack of moral authority to transform a predominantly peasant society into a conscious proletariat. Besieged by the tide of peasant migrants into factories in the late 1920s, threatened by the increased mechanization, their labor devalued by assembly line production and increased demand for semiskilled labor, vanguard workers and party members responded with anger and frustration. A telling example comes from the Komintern factory in Kharkov, where the head of the machine shop and chairman of the factory party cell was brought to task for getting involved in fisticuffs with new workers. When confronted at a committee meeting in 1928, he bellowed, "The real working class is quantitatively small and it is impossible to turn these drunken peasant hicks into proletarians. To think so is utopian!"[62]

The anti-alcohol propaganda that engaged in ironic overstatement both reflected and intensified this mood of powerlessness and frustration. One such example comes from a play entitled *Smychka* (Alliance). The title itself evokes the Leninist policy of establishing an alliance between the peasantry and the proletariat. The play, performed at workers' clubs in numerous cities throughout the Soviet Union by the Theater for Sanitary Culture, consisted of only four characters: Samogon (moonshine), Syphilis, a "new" worker (clearly fresh from the countryside), and a prostitute.[63] Waylaid on his way to a lecture at the workers' club by both Samogon and Syphilis, the hapless worker is enticed into drinking moonshine, which then leaves him drunk and vulnerable to the lascivious suggestions of Syphilis. The ploy works, and the worker and the syphilitic prostitute share a bottle of hooch as they walk past the club on their way to engage in more debauchery. As the play closes, Samogon and Syphilis agree that the *smychka* is mutually beneficial and laugh heartily at the prospect of the worker trying to locate a dispensary to cure his imminent ills—alcoholism and venereal disease.

The Struggle for Cultural Dominance

As part of the regime's efforts at political socialization, the anti-alcohol campaign figured prominently in defining appropriate working-class behavior. The Bolsheviks exploited an extraordinary propaganda apparatus and spent a great deal of time, energy, and resources to impart their vision of socialist society. Seeking to enlist the help of society at large and the proletariat in particular in establishing cultural hegemony, Communists used moralistic force. Toward this aim, the regime employed various rhetorical strategies to stigmatize drinking and advance the cause of sobriety. In the early 1920s, laboring under delusions of established moral authority, the Bolsheviks initially sought to convert and transform the errant or suffering members of society. Poems, plays, and stories conveyed important Soviet political myths and portrayed the Bolsheviks as benevolent patriarchs guiding Russia's working class toward socialist salvation.

As the decade wore on, however, traditional Russian culture exerted as much influence on official culture as the other way around. Finding themselves unable to establish cultural dominance, the Bolsheviks shifted from being assimilative social reformers to using coercion to impose socialism on a population they saw as fraught with enemies and counterrevolutionaries. By the end of the 1920s the utopian efforts at genuine cultural creation apparent in the first ten years after the revolution gave way to a more militant conservatism that would dominate the 1930s. Further, the discourse on alcoholism revived an old trope from the civil war by framing cultural conflicts in a form that maximized struggle as the operative theme: the struggle of Soviet power over its enemies; the struggle for a new lifestyle; the struggle of the proletariat against traditional (that is, peasant) culture. The struggle of the party to establish cultural dominance underlay it all.

Did political and cultural indoctrination through propaganda have an effect? Did the agitators, volunteer societies, journals, meetings, and plays influence changes in the working class? The implied condemnation of workers' drinking was a clear refutation of worker values and culture, whether former peasant or old worker. This challenge to their traditional ways of life by representatives of the workers' state was met by resistance—many workers, of course, continued to drink. At the same time, many workers did give up drink. What was their motivation?

These questions are impossible to answer. One may assume that workers resented such perceived challenges to their rights as workers and as individuals to exert their own wills in structuring their leisure and social institutions. The next chapter examines working-class drinking after 1917 and looks at the social utility of alcohol in socialist factories.

Liquid Assets:
The Working Classes and Vodka

O NE OF THE INHERENT WEAKNESSES OF BOLSHEVISM WAS the belief that the Bolsheviks could succeed only by convincing the population to adopt party-defined socialist values. The less workers and others shared those values, the more the state coerced them, resulting in stronger resistance and further alienation of precisely those groups the Bolsheviks intended to convert. Indeed, the irony of the types of passive resistance employed by members of the working class was that the regime's vilification of certain passive behaviors of resistance, followed by repression, actually strengthened older cultural traditions and identities. The cultural traditions of urban hereditary workers and peasant migrants that predated 1917 continued to determine the behavior and attitudes of the toiling masses into the 1930s, at times polarizing the working class. Throughout the 1930s the party increasingly relied on coercion to change workers' attitudes and behaviors, especially those relating to alcohol consumption.

As we have seen, one of the primary cultural traditions was the shared experience of drinking as an important symbolic vehicle for affirmation of the social relations that formed the basis of Russian preindustrial society. Not to drink was tantamount to complete withdrawal from a socially meaningful existence. Toward the end of the nineteenth century, the demands of mechanized factory production and the accelerated pace of urbanization

contributed to a restructuring of social patterns of work and leisure, including the evolution of drinking behaviors. During the rapid industrialization
of the First Five-Year Plan (1928–1932), these processes were even further
accelerated, accompanied by the Bolsheviks' insistence on the hegemony of
socialist culture.

Transforming working-class cultural values was complicated by how the
Bolsheviks defined proletarian. For the Bolsheviks, the working class was
understood in ideological and symbolic terms. A "real" worker was not a
peasant or a woman. He was a hereditary worker who behaved in certain ways
and whose parents had also been workers with no ties to the village. Most
important, he was far removed from the traditions, beliefs, and worldview of
rural inhabitants. In large measure, class was defined by behavior. Despite
Bolshevik definitions, the millions of peasants who swarmed into industrial
cities during the First Five-Year Plan brought with them their own social
organization, cultural expressions, work habits, and attitudes, creating deep
divisions and hierarchies within the industrial workforce. These newly urbanized workers, at least in the 1920s and early 1930s, did not have a sense of
themselves as belonging to a specific social class, were not defined as proletarians by the Soviet leadership or vanguard workers, and did not feel themselves
the benefactors of the dictatorship of the proletariat.

This chapter examines modes of drinking and modes of sobriety as
expressions of self-identity and social identity that differed greatly among
social groups within the working classes. As exercised on the shop floor or in
working-class neighborhoods and taverns, drinking simultaneously deepened
the fracture lines within the working class, strengthened solidarities among
various social groups, and was a symbolic affirmation of domination and
power. The following discussion focuses on the association between drinking
practices within the working-class milieu, on the one hand, and divisions in
the social structure, on the other, in order to explore how these divisions
played out on the shop floor. It also refracts light on how Bolshevik-defined
social categories exacerbated conflicts between social groups and helped to
undermine the regime's efforts at cultural revolution.

The Soviet Industrial Workforce

Before discussing patterns of drinking among workers, a brief survey of
the social composition of the working class in the late 1920s is in order.

Although such a quick once-over must inevitably distort complex and changing patterns, two basic characteristics of the Soviet working class stand out: its constantly changing composition and the intensification of conflicts between "old" (that is, skilled, urban) and "new" (that is, unskilled, peasant) workers.

During the period of the NEP, industrial jobs were in short supply, and unemployment was high.[1] The party leadership, trade unions, and labor authorities wanted to keep jobs as much as possible for "real proletarians"—male urban dwellers preferably of working-class origin whose prerevolutionary industrial experience qualified them generally as "skilled." In the early 1920s the ranks of these valued workers expanded somewhat, but in 1926 Gosplan reported that "the supplies of skilled labor on the labor market have been exhausted."[2] This meant that industry had to draw on the pool of unskilled workers, women, and peasant in-migrants to fill the labor demands of expanding production. However, women were largely excluded from typically "male" industries such as mining and metallurgy. As Wendy Goldman reveals in her well-researched study of female labor in Soviet industry, between 1923 and 1928 women's share of every industry, with the exception of traditional female trades, dropped considerably.[3] Industrial managers and trade union officials viewed women and peasants as undesirable recruits to the industrial labor force. On occasion, managers even impeded women's and peasants' efforts to join unions and gain employment. At the same time, skilled urban workers displayed antagonisms against peasant workers in general and female workers in particular. In the words of one worker in 1925, "[U]rban workers view the unemployed who come from the countryside as dangerous competitors. . . . [R]ivalry between them and the urban workers speaks negatively to the solidification of the union of the working class and the peasantry."[4] Nonetheless, a steady stream of rural migrants swelled the ranks of the working class throughout the 1920s.[5] The influx of new workers, as well as conflict and antagonism on the shop floor, accelerated dramatically at the end of the 1920s as the party moved to implement a plan of rapid industrialization.

The new policies that initiated these changes ultimately resulted from the victory of Stalin and his supporters over first the Left Opposition, then the Right Opposition headed by Nikolai Bukharin and his supporters. From 1923 to 1927 Leon Trotsky headed the Left Opposition, which rallied against party discipline on a wide array of issues. In a polity where loyalty and opposition were deemed incompatible, the Left Opposition was doomed from the start. Trotsky pursued his advocacy of "permanent revolution" as Stalin promoted his theory of "socialism in one country." At the same time, L. B. Kamenev and G. E. Zinoviev broke with Stalin over the issue of socialism in one country and continuation of the NEP. Nonetheless, through skillful maneuvering, Stalin increasingly secured control over the party apparatus, eroding what little power base the oppositionists had. Consequently, in 1927 Trotsky, Kamenev, and Zinoviev were removed from the Central Committee and replaced by Stalin's handpicked successors, thereby enhancing the position of the Right.

Until early 1928 the platform of the Right coincided with the policies of the Soviet government and the Politburo. Headed by Bukharin, the Right included A. I. Rykov, M. I. Tomskii, and their then-ally Stalin. They held a majority in the Politburo until 1926. Their good fortune changed, however, following the decisive defeat of the Left Opposition at the Fifteenth Party Congress in December 1927. Having supported Bukharin and the Right's position on the cautious implementation of the NEP, Stalin, in 1928, abruptly reversed his position and adopted the rapid industrialization program of the Left. He and his new majority in the Politburo then attacked the Right Opposition over various issues, including forced grain requisitions, the antispecialist campaign, and industrial production targets for the First Five-Year Plan.

Under attack politically, Bukharin, Rykov, and Tomskii signed a statement acknowledging their "errors," which was published in *Pravda* in November 1929. Nonetheless, Bukharin was removed from the Politburo that same month. The following year Rykov and Tomskii were also expelled from the Politburo. By the end of 1930, the trio was removed from all positions of leadership, and moderates throughout the party were purged, which officially marked the defeat of the Right Opposition. Having already destroyed the Left Opposition, Stalin was now the uncontested leader of the Soviet Union.[6]

Once he consolidated power, Stalin was able to push forward his plan of rapid industrialization. The first year of the official policy of rapid industrialization, 1928, also marked the beginning of collectivization of agriculture, which fundamentally realigned the contours of agrarian life and methods of cultivation. Collectivization shattered old rural structures and caused millions of peasants to flock into the towns. These peasants filled the unprecedented demand for labor that large-scale industrial development and rapid economic expansion required. At the same time, the Bolsheviks sought to destroy any remaining vestiges of "bourgeois" power and influence. As the regime launched political attacks against specialists and stripped them of their authority, thousands of workers gained entrance into educational institutions, creating a technical intelligentsia of working-class origins. Thousands more workers were promoted from the shop floor into positions of administration and management.[7] Peasants, skilled workers, bosses, and the party all pursued their own interests, intensifying cultural conflicts and turning factories into contested space.[8]

According to the census of December 1926, Russia's most reliable since 1897, 18 percent of the population (or twenty-six million people) lived in towns. Thirteen years later, in January 1939, 33 percent of the population was classified as urban.[9] During 1931, the peak year for migration, over four million peasants settled permanently in cities. The bulk of these peasants left the countryside during collectivization. Some left voluntarily because the prospect of industrial employment meant hope for a higher standard of living; others fled possible arrest and deportation. Millions more remained rural inhabitants but were employed in industry. According to the 1926 census, nearly all rural residents claimed to be employed in agriculture, but by 1939 there were thirty million people registered as rural inhabitants employed in state enterprises outside the agricultural sector.[10]

During this period of tremendous out-migration from the villages, the composition of the Soviet working class underwent a profound transformation. From being an old, experienced working class with long traditions of struggle and organization, it became a predominantly young, peasant-based, unskilled workforce with little proletarian culture.[11] Between 1928 and 1932 the number of blue-collar industrial workers increased by 92 percent, and the number of construction workers jumped by 293 percent, the majority of whom were unskilled male peasant in-migrants.[12] By 1933 fewer than 20 percent of workers in most industries had worked previously as wage laborers.[13] A survey of workers in Ukraine graphically illustrates this trend, especially in the Donbass region, the heart of Soviet coal mining and the location of the most important steel- and iron-producing centers. Between 1930 and 1932, 80 percent of new iron- and steelworkers and 75 percent of the new coal miners came from the peasantry.[14]

Rapid industrial expansion also created an enormous need for skilled technicians, industrial managers, and low-level supervisory personnel, which resulted in a great degree of social mobility. Many older experienced workers advanced directly from the shop floor to administrative posts, while party activists recruited many of the younger ones into higher education. In addition, experienced workers who remained on the shop floor were often promoted to the fast-growing number of posts for foremen. The new workers who filled positions vacated by these promotions consisted primarily of males in their late teens or early twenties. Unskilled and poorly paid, they tended to drift from factory to factory in search of higher wages.[15] Of the new industrial recruits in 1931, over 50 percent were under twenty-three-years old and had parents who were peasants.[16] Having no long-term experience or residence at any one industrial enterprise, they could not have developed a sense of being part of an older work culture and community. They therefore most likely perceived themselves (and were themselves perceived) as outsiders, on the margins of the working class.

The cultural dimensions of these developments greatly affected both the character and identity of the working class. Peasants who moved to the city did not remain rural prototypes, nor did they assimilate established shop-floor culture. The urban environment to which older workers were accustomed and that new workers encountered was constantly changing, reflecting aspects of both city and village.

Classifications and Representations

Clearly, then, Russia's industrial proletariat was a heterogeneous and changing social class with variegated and complex social identities, complicated by the Soviet authorities' attempts to define and categorize the urban proletariat.[17] Recognizing that not all workers embraced its vision of a socialist state, the party labeled those who identified with their programs and policies as "enlightened" or "conscious" and berated those who did not as "backward" or "bourgeois."[18] More often than not, however, these relational definitions were contradictory and conflict ridden, couched as they were in terms of class war.

Simplistic, bifurcated categories dominated party discourse and propaganda. The term "conscious" as used in the factory, trade union, and political press denoted an exalted status, often interchangeable with the respectful term "cadre workers." Conscious workers were predominantly represented as factory veterans and heroes of the October Revolution. Members of this group too young to participate in the epic events of the early Soviet years were nonetheless considered "conscious" because of their urban backgrounds and work experiences. Public discourse characterized them as sober, disciplined, literate, actively participating in factory meetings, and involved in political and social organizations. The party looked to this stratum of workers to educate novice workers in selfless work efforts and technical skills. Countless examples were given in the press of "conscious" workers taking a principled stand against falling standards on the shop floor or helping errant workers improve themselves.[19] How grounded in fact these stories were is a matter of speculation. It is logical to assume that there were cases where veteran workers acted as patrons to newer ones, but there is no evidence to suggest that this was common.

The Bolsheviks attached the label "backward" to workers of peasant origin and "petit bourgeois" to their social and political outlook. Older workers judged them to be uncultured, ridiculing them in derogatory terms such as "yokels," "sandaled hicks," or "dark people."[20] During the first years of rapid industrialization, as factories filled with more and more migrants from the countryside, this group of workers received considerable attention within the party and the press. The images of factory peasants were generally negative: They were backward, were illiterate, were not interested in political matters, did not master the skills of industrial work, and had no qualifications and did nothing to acquire them.[21] Often accused of drunkenness, laziness, or cunningly avoiding work, peasant migrants were portrayed as wreckers, hooligans, slackers, and drunkards who were dangerously vulnerable to "socially alien" enemies of socialist construction.[22] In short, behavior defined class. No longer a tight sociological category, class became ascribed.

The terms "backward" and "conscious," however, obscure more than they reveal about the working class. The categories roughly corresponded to the backgrounds and characteristics of certain groups of workers, but one should not assume that such classifications related strictly to social background or that they were static. In the convoluted negotiations between state and society, workers most likely accepted parts of the party's policies and rejected what was against their perceived interests, irrespective of ideology or classification. In their daily lives, individual workers could express elements of both "consciousness" and "backwardness" simultaneously. Conduct indicative of old workers frequently coexisted with behaviors attributed to former peasants.

Indeed, it was quite common for skilled workers to use their privileged positions to drink on the job and then attend a factory committee meeting after work.

Cultural representations of workers generated by Soviet officialdom simultaneously reflected and created these workers' sense of themselves as members of a social class. Given the party's monopoly on the press and other aspects of Soviet life, however, it is difficult to determine how much of workers' cultural expressions was actually real and how much was created as an image to inculcate values, such as sobriety, desired by the state. Moreover, it is difficult to tell to what degree the press and party members fabricated negative images of new workers in order to discredit and punish behaviors and attitudes perceived to be "petit bourgeois."

The accuracy of these perceptions and representations of the working masses is not the issue here. What is important is that each of these representations and judgments expressed values and functioned to structure workers' self-identification and relationships with other workers, the party, and the state. Both positive and negative representations were discursive constructions that enhanced the real or symbolic power of the party's elite. They are a part of what James C. Scott terms the public transcript—the discourse of power and domination.[23] According to Scott, the act of domination and the accompanying discourse necessarily engender resistance and a hidden discourse (words, gestures, acts of sabotage, and so forth) of corresponding richness by the powerless. This discourse by the powerless, what Scott refers to as the hidden transcript, usually does not find public expression.

In all discursive representations in Russia, alcohol was a symbol of social status and class: Conscious workers were sober, and new workers were drunks. Drunken workers were petit bourgeois (peasant), and sober workers were socialist. In daily life, however, one of the more important cultural expressions of both peasants and workers was drinking. As we have seen, in both cultures alcohol was an important symbol of community and an idiom of social exchange. As these two cultures merged and collided on the shop floor during the First Five-Year Plan, the consumption of alcohol took on greater social, cultural, and political meanings. Indeed, various drinking rituals and practices became exclusionary and part of the public transcript of skilled workers, as drunkenness became part of the hidden transcript of subordinate workers.

With the influx of new workers, the disruption of established hierarchies in the factory, and labor policies resulting from the regime's decision to institute rapid industrialization, the workplace became an arena of conflict and struggle for influence and control. Describing the atmosphere on the shop floor, one official observed that new workers developed hostile attitudes toward skilled workers and envied their better working conditions. For their part, experienced workers adopted a haughty, scornful attitude toward new workers, often beating them and demanding from management the exclusive right to occupy the best positions in production.[24] The struggle for hegemony in the workplace extended beyond the control of the best jobs. Skilled workers claimed that only "cadre workers" had the right to run in elections for local councils or serve in positions of authority on factory committees. Fistfights between old and new workers over issues of control were common.[25]

The instruments in the struggle for control of the workplace were in part institutional, but they were also rhetorical and definitional. A skilled worker's complaint about an unskilled worker's drunkenness mirrored the language of the party propaganda and reflected a myriad of attitudes, beliefs, and values. Expressing social and cultural frames of reference, drinking was an important behavior in which workers participated both individually and in groups. The rest of the chapter focuses on the ideas, attitudes, and values of the working class as expressed through drinking behaviors.

Domination and Resistance

Older skilled workers, whom the party relied upon to be the cultural leaders of the Soviet working class, were a small but "aristocratic" group. These workers, having been the party's solid base of support, experienced what Hiroaki Kuromiya termed "the crisis of proletarian identity" in the late 1920s.[26] Besieged by the tide of peasant migrants, threatened by increased mechanization, their labor devalued by assembly line production that increased the demand for semiskilled labor, these older skilled workers attacked drinking in part as a device to assert their superiority and maintain their status and control in the factory. While individual vanguard workers may have wished to uplift and enlighten new workers, this goal did not lessen overall expressions of condemnation and hostility from skilled workers as a group toward in-migrants. Often these vanguard workers acted directly to punish other workers guilty of drunkenness or moral laxity with public shaming, fines, or expulsions from the shop.[27] They asserted that sobriety and moral discipline went hand in hand with progress in the workers' movement, while few of them adhered strictly to these principles.

In her study of workers in St. Petersburg, Laura Phillips claims that vanguard workers embodied the values of the state, especially sobriety and discipline.[28] While this may be true of a very small number of worker-*intelligents* in St. Petersburg, there is very little evidence to suggest that the majority of skilled or "conscious" workers themselves actually adopted a sober lifestyle or curtailed their own drinking. On the contrary, there is much evidence to suggest that skilled workers and foremen promoted from the ranks of vanguard workers could, and did, drink more or less with impunity on the shop floor. There are numerous testimonies in the official temperance journal of older workers who gave up drink. However, according to regional consumption figures and data from questionnaires, great numbers of workers did not put down the bottle.

In 1928–1929 the Department of Moral Statistics of the Central Statistical Bureau (Tsentral'noe statisticheskoe upravlenie, TsSU) conducted extensive investigations of workers' consumption of alcohol, broken down by region, industry, and skill level.[29] According to these surveys, skilled workers in Kharkov and Moscow drank just slightly less than skilled workers in the periphery. In all areas, unskilled workers drank more than their skilled comrades. For example, per capita consumption of vodka among skilled workers in Kharkov and Moscow averaged between seventeen and nineteen bottles a year. Skilled workers in Saratov drank slightly more—an average of twenty-one bottles per year. In Tomsk, alcohol consumption among skilled workers averaged between twenty-three and twenty-five bottles a year.[30] Because state and party organizations were stronger in the capitals, it makes sense that some of these workers might be influenced by the ideals and values espoused by the party leadership. Moreover, participation in OBSA was stronger in Moscow and Kharkov than in Saratov and Tomsk, so perhaps anti-alcohol agitation in the factories had some effect. At the same time, unskilled workers in all four locations consumed more than skilled workers—between thirty-two and thirty-seven bottles a year.[31] One can only speculate as to why unskilled workers consumed more.

The results of these surveys are misleading, however, because they do not take into account consumption of *samogon*. Further, average consumption levels were estimated for the entire population of a given region, including women, children, and the very old. Obviously, real consumption levels for individual workers were much higher. Most of the evidence suggests that highly skilled workers drank as earnestly as unskilled workers. An investigation of workers' drinking by Narkomtrud at the Krasnoe Sormovo factory in 1929 revealed similar findings: unskilled workers engaged in hard labor were the heaviest drinkers, followed by highly skilled workers and foremen.[32]

Until the mid-1930s, however, skilled workers were rarely punished or received only light reprimands for drinking on the job. For example, in 1933 the head electrician at the Mikhailovskii combine in Kharkov came to work drunk and promptly fell asleep. He therefore did not notice that one of the cooling pumps was malfunctioning, and it burned up. Despite the fact that the factory was without water and could not operate for two days, he was not reprimanded.[33] At one regional factory committee meeting in Moscow, a member of the factory committee cited five highly skilled workers who were repeatedly written up for being drunk at work, but the factory could not fire them because their skills were needed. Noting that, by contrast, unskilled workers or workers with ties to the countryside were regularly fired for coming to work drunk, he argued that production in the factories would stop altogether if skilled workers were fired for drunkenness.[34]

In 1928 at *raikom* (regional party committee) meetings in Kharkov, Saratov, and Tomsk, the focus was on the "systematic drunkenness" of older party members heading factory party cells.[35] It seems that in all factories, vanguard workers had established systems of patronage. They were not disciplined for drinking and other infractions of labor discipline, not only because their skills were valuable but also because they were allied with the administration in what the party termed "protectionist policies."[36] This complaint was echoed repeatedly in trade union meetings and noted in factory reports by the Workers' and Peasants' Inspectorate (Narodnyi komissariat rabochekrest'ianskoi inspektsii, RKI) in all cities under study.[37] In Kharkov, for example, the problem was so prevalent that the RKI presented a three-page list to the Central Committee of the Ukrainian Communist Party (TsK KPU) of factory supervisors who were regularly drunk at work. None of them were disciplined.[38]

Despite their own drinking behavior, vanguard workers employed the party's rhetoric to level the charge of drunkenness against workers of peasant backgrounds. A telling example comes from the Komintern factory in Kharkov, where the head of the machine shop, who was also the chairman of the factory party cell, was brought to task for getting involved in fisticuffs with new workers. He was notorious for punishing new workers for their lack of discipline or for their drunkenness by hitting them, and they often struck back. When confronted at a committee meeting in 1928, he went into a rage, bellowing that peasants could never be turned into conscious workers. Unfortunately, he was drunk at the time he made this pronouncement and was subsequently purged from the party.[39]

Alongside exhortations for factory newcomers to put down the bottle, older skilled workers often demanded payment in vodka from new workers before they would train them. As one new worker complained, "If you want to begin something, if you want to learn or understand . . . vodka is necessary. . . . If you don't play along, you can study for two hundred years, but nothing will ever get started."[40] Individual apprenticeship was everywhere linked to this type of payment—trainees had to "pay what they must and keep quiet."[41] For example, recruits at one textile mill in Moscow were invited to buy vodka for the foreman in order to secure a decent loom. Trainees were also advised to make a contribution to the trainers' liquor cabinet unless they wanted to be reported to the factory committee for receiving unofficial recruitment and training.[42] At a trade union meeting at the Krasnoe Sormovo factory in Moscow, it was revealed that the shop supervisor demanded a bottle of vodka from new workers before he would allow them to begin work. New workers complained that they should be allowed to work first since they could not afford to buy vodka until they earned a paycheck. Their complaints, however, were dismissed owing to the fact that the supervisor shared his "booty" with the administration.[43] When a highly skilled vanguard worker at the Lenin factory in Saratov was promoted to overseeing the training of unskilled recruits, he used his position to stay drunk at work and extract vodka from his charges, where previously he had been a model worker.[44] So widespread was the practice of extracting alcohol from trainees that in 1928 *Golos tekstilei* (Textile Workers' Voice) published cartoons showing new recruits approaching a mill loaded down with vodka and food while members of the factory committee looked on through their fingers.[45] Not surprisingly, trade union reports in 1930 criticized apprenticeships for not providing the individual instruction they were supposed to give.[46]

Vanguard workers' demands for payment in vodka for training seem to be a reversal of the traditional practice of "wetting the bargain." None of the sources suggest that these workers invited the newcomers to drink with them. Shared drinking would symbolize a mutual, equitable exchange and shared respect, if not friendship.[47] As discussed earlier, drink rituals were firmly embedded in a reciprocal lifestyle that governed social relationships in the village. Helping a neighbor with the mowing, for example, was often part of that local system of mutual obligation, and the liberal provision of vodka was a means of symbolizing one's acceptance of the mutuality, friendliness, and communality of the event.

In contrast to tradition, privileged workers' demands for vodka served as a symbolic gesture of domination that manifested and reinforced a hierarchical order. Because relations of domination are, at the same time, relations of resistance, they necessarily cause friction and can only be sustained through continuous demonstrations and enactments of power.[48] The demand for vodka by vanguard workers implied negation of equality and solidarity with newcomers and marked a clear delineation between dominant and subordinate workers, skilled and unskilled, labor aristocrats and supplicants, thereby reinforcing social distances and hierarchies between the two groups. Skilled workers who received vodka would often share it with foremen or administrators, perhaps to curry favor but at the same time signaling their solidarity with management against new workers.[49]

That skilled workers preferred association with socially mobile bosses suggests that there was more social distance between old and new workers than between old workers and the *nachalstvo* (factory administrators, managers, bosses, and so forth). Indeed, as the First Five-Year Plan progressed, vanguard workers, touting their skills and proletarian backgrounds, became the core of the *nachalstvo* as they were promoted into new managerial positions created by the drive for industrialization.[50] Some young workers with urban backgrounds also received promotion, but the number of former peasants advanced to supervisory positions in the 1930s was insignificant.[51]

Skilled workers' "right" to receive vodka from newcomers and to drink without much fear of retribution intensified new workers' resentment of their subordinate status and served to create hidden transcripts against the experience of being dominated. An incident at the rolling mill workshop at the Enakievo metallurgical plant in Ukraine is particularly illustrative. Reacting to old skilled workers' refusal to work in protest against an increase in output quotas, the party secretary of the factory, N. A. Voznesenskii (who would become chairman of Gosplan in 1937), summoned all workers to a meeting in the factory club. Emphasizing how important the increase was for building socialism, he attacked skilled workers for frequent drinking and absences. His speech evoked a cry from the audience, "That's right! How much can we put up with [from them]? Chuck them out!" Voznesenskii replied by saying,

"Today, when each and every skilled worker is so important to us, we allow him a lot. But this is temporary. . . . Tomorrow we won't pardon anybody for drinking and truancy."[52]

This exchange clearly expresses new workers' resentment toward their "betters" on the shop floor and constitutes a public expression of resistance to domination. Skilled workers' demands for vodka in exchange for training and their license to drink at work were symbolic gestures of domination, underscoring the marginality of new workers' positions. Indeed, without the designation as skilled, workers had no hope of receiving better work and improving their social and material conditions or being accepted into the community of established workers.

Skill ranking was a powerful instrument. It affirmed patterns of domination and excluded new workers from the most desirable jobs. Skill ranks in Soviet industry ranged from one (unskilled work) through eight (highly skilled work). Some specializations required years of training and experience.[53] At the same time, technical innovations permitted many tasks to be learned on the job, yet such jobs continued to be categorized as "skilled."[54] In the factory shop, unskilled positions given to new workers and women were typically the lowest-paying and most physically arduous jobs. Higher-paying, less physically demanding skilled positions were reserved for established workers, who also often occupied supervisory positions in the factory.[55] Skill ranking, therefore, not only connoted experience and proficiency at a trade, it was also used to exclude newcomers from prized positions. It reinforced social hierarchies by segregating skilled and unskilled workers on the shop floor.

Such domination by skilled workers and the *nachalstvo* must have provoked feelings of both alienation and anger in new workers. The party's labeling and condemnation of new workers as petit bourgeois, their segregation from the ranks of skilled workers, and their exclusion from drunken camaraderie on the shop floor led some workers to seek acceptance and integration. One tactic was to become more "soviet" than vanguard workers by enthusiastically participating in the regime's productivity campaigns such as shock work, socialist competition, and the Stakhonovite movement.[56] But most often domination and marginality led to collective protest, association, and passive forms of resistance.

Elements of passive resistance that James Scott terms the "weapons of the weak" include popular discourse, feigned ignorance, and false compliance.[57] Scott's interpretation broadens the scope of resistance to encompass expressions of popular culture(s) that exist alongside and interact with the dominant culture. Indeed, as Michel Foucault and others have demonstrated, where there is power, there is resistance. Yet this resistance, in Foucault's words, "is never in a position of exteriority in relation to power."[58] This was certainly the case with Soviet peasants and in Soviet factories.[59] Throughout the cultural revolution, as the regime attempted to create an industrial elite and a socialist working class, a different kind of cultural revolution emerged. New workers' sense of alienation in many respects prompted them to form solidarities in opposition to the oppressive and alienating culture of the regime and vanguard workers—a type of passive revolt against domination by their socialist "liberators."

One might expect unskilled workers to have acted more aggressively in defending their interests, but it is important to remember that migrants' attitudes were rooted in village tradition. Workers of peasant origin brought with them from the countryside an attitude of suspicion and circumspection toward authority. For centuries, Russian peasants had deferred to the authority of the village elders or landlords while passively resisting their demands. The recent experience of collectivization reinforced such caution. Given the power of the elites and officials, the struggles of peasants and new workers took the safer form of anonymous attacks on property, foot-dragging, and evasion—tactics learned in the village and reinforced by peasant popular culture.

However, since the October Revolution was carried out in the name of all workers, and in public discourse and iconography the worker was an exalted member of the Soviet state, some new workers reacted with open hostility to the duality of rights and privileges, especially when this dual standard challenged their way of life and material well-being.[60] As Scott points out, whenever subjects find themselves unjustly treated but unable, without considerable cost, to respond in kind, they can be expected to show signs of aggression as soon as the opportunity presents itself.[61] Usually workers expressed their resentment through sustained daily resistance and hidden transcripts, yet on rare occasions they aggressively challenged the authority of skilled workers and foremen, craftily using official channels and invoking the rhetoric of the party.

Since new workers were often openly accused of being drunkards and hooligans, they would employ this same charge in defiance against foremen and skilled workers to trade union committees, party cells, and other workers' organizations.[62] In one such example, a worker complained to an inspector from RKI that it was impossible to meet production norms because of the drunkenness of the *nachalstvo*. He claimed that his shop supervisor was more often drunk than sober, relating how his supervisor carried on drunken orgies in the factory with his cronies, ruining materials and slowing production. When the worker had complained to the foreman, his complaints were dismissed. He finished by saying:

> This proves that the fate of many thousands [of rubles] are in the hands of unprincipled drunks who don't care about people's property, and whose drunken interests and arrogance are more dear than the people's interests. . . . With this drunkenness at the top, I, as a Russian citizen, cannot even protest in my own factory, where the interests of the state are sacrificed to the interests of drunken, hooligan, scandalous bosses. I am begging you to take some appropriate action.[63]

The speaker in this case clearly invoked the language of socialist construction in his protest. What he emphasized was not poor working relations with his boss, or any of a number of other problems present in such a situation, but rather that his superiors were wasting *his* money in *his* factory.

In another case, unskilled workers at a trade union meeting at the Rykov factory in Moscow attacked both the administration and the trade union, arguing that both promoted "tailist attitudes, formalism, and spinelessness."[64] They gave the example of an overseer who got drunk and stole material from the factory and was not reprimanded. In their formal complaint filed with the RKI, these workers demanded that the overseer return the materials to the factory and be fired after being brought up on charges at a disciplinary court. They declared, "[I]n this case the trade union has yet to [address the problem] openly. We ourselves are powerless to struggle against such violations if the trade unions and administration do not pay attention to infractions occurring within their midst."[65] The derogatory terms "spinelessness" and especially "tailism" (*khvostizm*) were frequently used in the press and in party meetings at the time to chastise and condemn workers' behavior considered to be "antisoviet" and were usually directed against new workers and bourgeois specialists.[66]

Old workers' consciousness as members of a class was forged through prerevolutionary struggle against their capitalist oppressors. Despite the fact that the party leadership continually asserted that there was neither exploitation nor oppression in Soviet factories, new workers ironically often bonded through struggle against their socialist oppressors. Indeed, the old workers and worker-*intelligents* held the best factory positions and received preferential treatment from the administration. Advocating values alien to the bulk of former peasants, these workers must have been seen as enemies of the working class to its newest members. The revolutionary ideology of workers' control and power that garnered support for the Bolsheviks from among the working class in the 1920s came to have very different meanings to most of the rank-and-file workers of the First Five-Year Plan. For them, workers' control did not mean that workers controlled the means of production but rather that they had control over their time and bodies to structure their work as they had in the village—with regular breaks for talking, smoking, and drinking.

In resisting the domination they encountered on the shop floor, new workers forged and strengthened solidarities among themselves.[67] Since they suffered from the same humiliations and subordination, unskilled and new workers had a shared interest in jointly refuting or negating the authority of skilled workers and bosses, thereby creating a discourse of dignity.[68] In addition to lodging collective complaints against old workers' drinking, they joined together to defend the common worker's right to drink in the factory.[69] Expressing solidarity among their own ranks, new workers often rallied to protest the firing of one of their comrades for drunkenness.

In one such case, a certain Votskyi was dismissed after receiving six pink slips for truancy and coming to work drunk. His fellow workers petitioned the trade union to reinstate him, arguing that the offenses did not merit dismissal, especially since this punishment was not applied to all workers uniformly.[70] In another case, the actions of an unskilled metalworker who came to work drunk, refused to leave, and started a fistfight with the night watchman were defended by his comrades, who argued that he was not to blame since he was suffering a "nervous breakdown." Further, they claimed that the administration had violated labor codes in dismissing him.[71] When workers at the Kriukovskii factory in Kharkov were reprimanded for drinking, they blamed the executive committee of the regional soviet for their lapses in discipline, noting that the soviet had allowed a beer hall to operate next door to the factory.[72] Implying that drinking was a natural part of working-class life, workers defended their right to stop in for a shot or two before and after work and pointed out that they were actually doing their part to increase the soviet's budget.

Appropriating Public Space for Private Behaviors

In both the village and the factory, drinking rituals and practices were embedded in prerevolutionary patterns of work and sociability. Although some working people responded to the party's antidrinking propaganda and adopted a sober lifestyle in the interests of socialism, much larger numbers remained attached to their traditional drinking habits and customs. The ways in which workers drank and the places they chose to drink often segregated new workers from old, thereby strengthening social hierarchies.

Prior to the 1914 ban on alcohol, taverns and beer halls were located in working-class neighborhoods or adjacent to factories.[73] Wherever laborers worked or lived, a drinking establishment was probably nearby. It is likely workers frequented the same tavern and met the same group of drinking companions every week, usually companions with similar living standards, social backgrounds, and occupations.[74] This came to an abrupt halt with prohibition. Then, when the Soviet government revived the sale of alcohol beginning in 1921, the drink trade in its previous incarnation no longer existed. The number of taverns in the 1920s never again rivaled the number witnessed in the tsarist period, and patrons had to travel farther from home or factory to find a favorite watering hole.

Although the complex lines of fraternization that occurred within taverns is impossible to document, it is logical to assume that while workers from diverse crafts may have gathered in a particular tavern, the boundaries of and exclusions from this community existed along social and cultural lines just as they did in the factory. For example, in Leningrad, seasonal workers and migrants from the countryside headed for a tavern on Gorodskaia Street.[75] In Moscow, the Stenka Razin pub was known for its tumultuous clientele consisting predominantly of new peasant migrants.[76] And in Kharkov, city officials complained that new workers gathered at a tavern called Bam before and after work.[77]

These bars were cited in the press because of their notoriety for attracting peasant clienteles, hinting at the segregated nature of worker sociability outside work. To a significant degree, the location of a tavern determined its clientele. Peasants who migrated to cities traditionally settled in outlying districts or settlements clustered around factories, rather than in the central regions. Perpetuating traditional patterns of chain migration, peasants who moved to the cities in the 1930s joined relatives or fellow villagers already living there. These village networks could provide the newcomers with the information, work, and shelter they needed.[78] Because public transportation did not service the outlying areas to any meaningful extent, migrants who settled in these areas remained isolated from established workers, who tended to live in more central districts.[79] Even in areas where newcomers lived close to old workers, they remained largely segregated by building. For example, at the housing settlement at the Serp i Molot plant in Moscow, old workers lived in one barracks, and all newcomers lived in another.[80] New workers, therefore, oriented their leisure, and hence their drinking, around the particular culture and establishments that grew up on the outskirts of town, rather than around the urban culture in the center of town. It is highly doubtful that old workers, who refused to socialize with in-migrants or unskilled workers in the factory, would travel to the outlying areas to patronize taverns where new workers congregated.

Perhaps more important, neighborhood taverns were locations where the unspoken responses, the stifled anger and frustration created by domination and humiliation in the factory, could find expression.[81] For new workers, frequenting their own neighborhood taverns simultaneously expressed and created a solidarity with others who shared common work and subordination, beyond the gaze of foremen. For many, the tavern's importance lay less in the drinking it fostered than in the opportunity it provided for antihegemonic discourse—a place of unmonitored assembly for lower-class neighbors and workers.[82] A conversation reported in a Saratov newspaper between two former peasants living in the Asserin district reveals the attitudes of many new workers: "Here, in the tavern I am my own boss. What I want to do, I do. . . . Today, let's drink until we are dead drunk."[83] Ultimately such drunken camaraderie expressed desires common to nearly all former peasants—a wish to be a "fellow among fellows." They desired to escape for a time the filth, monotony, dank smells, and alienation of the workplace; to live according to their own rules and norms; and to be recognized as no worse than other people.

Since taverns were not always accessible, workers quite frequently appropriated public parks, dining halls, cooperatives, private homes, neighborhood streets, and even workers' clubs for drinking and socializing. There is abundant evidence that many workers drank in various public areas where official regulations prohibited the consumption of alcohol. Since the Soviet regime and factory administrations would not tolerate the casual informality that had characterized work in the prerevolutionary factory or in the village, workers found or created new temporal and physical loci to engage in forms of discourse, such as gambling, gossiping, fighting, swearing, and especially drinking. For example, workers' clubs, intended by the regime to be centers of culture and enlightenment, were constantly besieged by drunken workers or were passed up by workers on their way to the beer hall.[84] In one account, two metalworkers who had been excluded from the trade union for drunkenness arrived at a club, ate, drank vodka, and threatened to shoot anyone who disturbed them.[85] Similarly, a trade union paper noted that drunken youths frequently visited the club and started brawls when asked to leave.[86]

Workers also appropriated dining halls for rough and drunken sociability, despite the administrations' attempts to prevent it. In Kharkov, where a factory party cell had banned the sale of beer in the dining hall, workers nonetheless brought their own. A reader of the *Kharkovskyi proletarii* (Kharkov Proletariat) complained that

> many have already written about, and even more have talked about the fact that the workers' dining hall doesn't sell beer. Well, it doesn't matter. On paydays the dining hall is turned into a tavern anyway and it is impossible to eat there. It is always full of troublesome drunks. There is smoke, swearing, and fights because everyone brings vodka in with them.[87]

This same paper ran a cartoon under the caption, "The Dining Hall as It Really Is." The cartoon depicted a scene of chaos with drunken workers retching on the floor, others passed out on tables, and still others engaged in drunken fisticuffs. The waiter, holding up a bottle of vodka, asks a drunken patron with a huge red nose, "Lunch? To drink here or to take [and drink] out?"[88]

The implied condemnation of workers' drinking was a clear refutation of worker values and culture, whether former peasant or old worker. Workers clearly resented such perceived challenges to their rights as workers and as individuals to exert their own wills in structuring their leisure and social institutions. Consequently, they resisted this challenge to their traditional way of life, creating or appropriating places where they could participate in a dissident subculture without punishment or ridicule.

While perhaps not actually drinking at the same table or bench, or even at the same pub, club, or dining hall, the use of these places by both new and old workers demonstrates workers' passive as well as outright resistance to the regime's calls for workers to adopt a sober lifestyle. It also implies a form of common male worker solidarity against what they perceived to be unjust demands made on them by the state: to spend their work time in the sober creation of socialist production and their leisure time in sober, cultured entertainment. In this case, workers as a class asserted and expressed their collective culture as workers despite the split into two strata. The rejection of official values in favor of peasant or prerevolutionary worker culture amounted to an act of resistance and of self-definition for members of the industrial workforce. When they went to the beer hall instead of the club, they were rejecting the official model of proper behavior for workers. Such activity not only reflected their culture but also reaffirmed and consolidated their sense of social identity.

Social Divisions within the Working Classes

Between 1928 and 1932 many "working classes" existed side by side. The physical separation of public space for workers' leisure activities, as well as segregation on the shop floor, both influenced and reflected the tenacity of workers' traditional cultures in the new urban milieu and led to deepening social divisions within the working class. New workers challenged the authority of established workers and bosses, and their own domination, through daily resistance to the established urban hierarchies and culture. They did so by asserting their own right to drink. Attempts to coerce them into adopting socialist values led to a strengthening of resistance and a deepening of older traditional cultures. At the same time, skilled workers asserted their superiority and further marginalized former peasants by excluding them from their own forms of worker sociability and by allying themselves with the *nachalstvo*.

In this way, old notions of class and culture were turned upside down as the regime sought to effect a cultural revolution. Older workers, who had gained consciousness of themselves as a class through struggle against their oppressive employers in the prerevolutionary period, became the oppressors, more clearly aligned with bosses and supervisors than with new workers. And new workers formed common bonds and solidarities, most likely viewing themselves as members of an oppressed class, as they struggled against the alien and hostile domination of the vanguard.

An interesting question at this juncture is whether the *nachalstvo*, created from the ranks of vanguard workers, formed more of a class than the working class did in the 1930s, given the absence of common identities and cultures. One is tempted to answer in the affirmative, yet at times old and new workers exhibited a tenuous solidarity in resisting the authority of the regime to define and control their behavior. They did so in numerous routine and everyday ways, including frequent drinking and defining the uses of public space, thereby creating at least the rudiments of a community among themselves and a dissident subculture.

Giddy with Success: The End of Alcoholism in the Soviet Union

I N 1933 I. V. STALIN, REVERSING THE STATE'S PREVIOUS CALLS
for the creation of a sober working class, encouraged workers to reward
themselves for a job well done with a "little glass of champagne." Within a
few months, discussion of workers' drunkenness in the press, which had
occupied a central place in public and official discourse on creating a new
socialist society, and especially new Soviet men and women, ceased. A large
and vital temperance movement fell silent, all OBSA factory cells were dis-
solved, and their leaders were purged. Mental health and social welfare
authorities, who a few years earlier had defined alcoholism as a social disease
resulting from poor living and working conditions, were quietly removed
from their positions in clinics and hospitals. Alcoholism disappeared as a
social problem in the Soviet Union.

The closing of GISG and the dissolution of OBSA mark not only a change
in official policy and politics as directed from the center but also suggest an
uneasy compromise with society on the part of the state. The complete transformation of everyday life proved to be an impossible goal. When it became
obvious that Soviet cultural authorities lacked the resources and moral hegemony to create rational and sober leisure activities for the working class, they
softened their position against drinking. Having failed to transmit new values

and principles to Soviet society, and faced with the growing need for revenues, the party and state agencies reversed their position on alcoholism and simply defined it out of the picture.

The Demise of OBSA

By early 1930 social hygiene ceased to be a valid field of health care, and Narkomzdrav converted GISG into the Institute of Organization of Health Care and Hygiene.[1] Within two years the medical interpretation of alcoholism changed, and the broader approach of the social hygienists was replaced by a narrower focus on individual psychology. Alcoholism became an individual mental illness. Medical and health care workers stopped all social research on alcoholism and published no more statistics on alcohol production or consumption.[2] Biological research on the effects of alcohol on the body and mind continued, but not in relation to the disease of alcoholism. Medical researchers, for example, carried on numerous experiments on fetal alcohol syndrome, but they did not link it to the mother's alcoholism.

Accompanying the changes at GISG, Narkomzdrav gave OBSA instructions to shift its focus from "narrow anti-alcohol work" to an all-out struggle for "improvements in the conditions of everyday life."[3] The temperance journal *Trezvost' i kul'tura* explained to its readers that the temperance movement had been misdirected—there was no need to combat alcoholism since socialism and the "socialist way of life would destroy drunkenness."[4] In keeping with this shift, the following month the journal changed its name to *Kul'tura i byt* (Culture and Lifestyle). Denouncing OBSA's old leadership for being antigovernment demagogues, V. P. Voznesenskii, the acting secretary of the Moscow Oblast OBSA (MOOBSA), announced upcoming changes in the society's apparat. Most likely Voznesenskii was responding to attacks on the leading temperance advocate, Iuri Larin, a former Menshevik who was removed from his position in Gosplan in 1930 and fell under fire for his political and economic views. For example, in 1928 Larin had called for the "complete elimination of alcohol" from the Soviet Union's budget.[5] On Larin's suggestion, the Sixteenth Party Congress in 1929 approved a program for the "de-alcoholization" of the economy. Yet in May 1930 a Central Committee resolution took issue with his views, denouncing the "totally unfounded, fantastic and therefore extremely harmful attempts of some comrades [including Larin] to leap over all the obstacles of socialist construction in a single bound."[6]

Following suit, *Kul'tura i byt* published a searing condemnation of both Larin and Deichman:

> You may see in the removal of our former comrades from [OBSA's] leadership (Deichman, Larin, and others) our acknowledgement of their specific mistakes. They built their careers on an administrative struggle against alcoholism without considering the necessity of socialist construction. . . . Only by restructuring daily life in new socialist conditions may we successfully combat alcoholism.[7]

In September 1930 OBSA held a plenum in Moscow to officiate changes in the society. Appointing Voznesenskii as president over the more likely Semashko, who had been a member of OBSA's founding apparat, the society finalized its divorce from social hygiene. In addition, at the plenum Voznesenskii attacked Sholomovich (an active member of OBSA since 1928 and a staunch defender of social hygiene) for seditious political activity—a charge that was completely unfounded.[8]

At the Moscow plenum, OBSA decided to change the direction of the temperance movement and dropped all discussion of administrative measures to curb alcohol production or sales. The objectives of restricting access to alcohol, limiting the production of vodka, eventual prohibition, or any other measures that could be construed as criticism of state liquor policies were no longer part of the society's agenda.[9] OBSA's shift coincided with Stalin's directive to V. M. Molotov in 1930 to increase the production of vodka to the maximum output possible.[10] Since state agencies that made and carried out decisions to increase vodka production were "organs of proletarian dictatorship," any criticism of them would be a "crude political mistake."[11] The confidence and bravado OBSA had exhibited a few years earlier with Sovnarkom and Gosplan had evaporated, and the so-called restructuring of anti-alcohol work amounted to little more than continuing a much watered-down propaganda campaign.[12]

After the Moscow plenum, OBSA announced that it planned to work in conjunction with the League of the Militant Godless and the Society against Illiteracy to create the Society against Three Evils. Arguing that religion and illiteracy cause alcoholism, OBSA declared that such a move would "enhance socialist construction, reach a greater mass of workers and peasants, and increase membership."[13] OBSA's shift from defining alcoholism as the result of social and economic conditions to being caused specifically by religion and illiteracy pinned the blame on the drinker. Alcoholism was now deemed to be caused by individual behaviors—like believing in God or not learning to read. By extension, then, the state was absolved of responsibility for making alcohol available since the drinker was now conceived of as a conscious actor and not a victim. Such ideological distancing from social criticism by OBSA, however, did not go far enough.

The merger that would have produced the Society against Three Evils never materialized, and the literature does not clarify why. In March 1931 OBSA officially changed its name to the Society for Healthy Living and ceased all anti-alcohol agitation and propaganda. The society continued to publish *Kul'tura i byt* until 1932, but the journal no longer addressed problems relating to alcoholism. From November 1930 to February 1932 it published only eight articles on the temperance movement. At the same time, newspapers and journals that had reported regularly on OBSA's activities and published temperance propaganda, such as *Pravda, Izvestiia, Trud,* and *Rabochaia gazeta,* dropped all mention of the anti-alcohol movement.[14]

When it was founded by top party intellectuals in 1928, OBSA's purpose was clear: to influence government policy and public opinion away from alcohol production and consumption in order to aid socialist construction and eradicate one of society's gravest ills. In 1930 OBSA reversed its position as an innovator of social policy to one of following the lead of state and party administrations. In 1931 OBSA was again restructured to become barely recognizable as a temperance society. By the end of that year OBSA ceased to exist.

The most obvious reason for the decline of the temperance movement lies in OBSA's close ties with state and party administrations, which made it vulnerable to changes and shifts in politics and policy. OBSA's fate hinged on the leadership's policies regarding the state alcohol monopoly. As Stalin consolidated power, OBSA fell out of favor with the government. The party program of 1919 had committed the new regime to fighting social diseases such as tuberculosis, syphilis, and alcoholism.[15] In 1921 Lenin refused to consider reviving the state liquor monopoly, arguing that trade in spirits would lead Russia "back to capitalism and not forward to communism."[16] Two years later he was just as emphatic in a speech at the Eleventh Party Congress that there would be "no trade in rotgut."[17] In contradistinction to Lenin, Stalin was equally convinced that the Soviet Union needed liquor revenues to survive. Addressing a press conference in 1925, Stalin made his position clear: "What is better, the yoke of foreign capital or the sale of vodka? This is the question facing us. Naturally we will opt for vodka because we believe that if we have to get a bit dirty for the sake of the victory of the proletariat and the peasantry, we will take this extreme measure in the interest of our cause."[18] Again at the Fifteenth Party Congress in 1928, Stalin reiterated that vodka in the state budget was a regrettable circumstance that the state could not afford to do away with.[19]

By 1930 the Stalinist state had abandoned the quest for a sober society in the interests of financial expediency. Moreover, this reversal suggests that the regime considered pragmatic accommodations and even retreat preferable to further antagonizing its already uncontrollable and unreliable constituency. Consequently, Tsentrospirt came under stronger central government control and began accelerated construction of new distilleries and alcohol factories.[20] Over the next several years the state expanded the liquor industry, so that by 1940 there were more shops selling alcohol than meat, fruit, and vegetables put together.[21]

Even though OBSA had made it clear through the removal and renunciation of the old leadership that it would not challenge the state's alcohol policies, ideologically OBSA had become a liability. Party theoreticians defined alcoholism as a bourgeois excess left over from the tsarist past. Therefore, if success was being achieved in socialist construction, alcohol abuse would naturally wither away, just as it had disappeared from public discussions. In 1933 Stalin endorsed the modest use of alcohol by workers to reward themselves for a job well done. In 1936 a book published by the state publishing house on food and drink declared that concerns about Russian drunkenness were unfounded. Since socialism had been achieved in the Soviet Union, workers no longer suffered from alcoholism as in capitalist countries. The book suggested that workers drink champagne for holidays and vodka with meals.[22]

Despite the dramatic events and upheavals in Russia's political, economic, and social structures in the first decades of the twentieth century, the daily lives of ordinary workers, as evidenced by overall alcohol consumption patterns, changed little. Even though prohibition may have at first resulted in a decline in consumption of alcoholic beverages, the working masses soon found ways to brew their own. Neither dramatic change at the top, nor radical legislation, nor ideological constructions were sufficient to motivate workers to alter their traditional forms of sociability and fraternization. Perhaps more important, drinking rituals and practices retained their symbolic meanings through the years of war, revolution, civil war, and cultural revolution.

Laura Phillips has argued that, for workers in St. Petersburg after 1917, ritual drinking that had been "integrated into the life of pre-revolutionary workshops dissipated."[23] I find no evidence of this in Moscow, Saratov, Kharkov, or Tomsk. While some workers must have accepted various aspects of the party's policies, workers in general clung to traditional drinking norms and rituals. For example, despite minor regional variations, unskilled workers in all areas consumed a little more than their skilled counterparts.[24] Skilled workers tended to drink a bit less in Moscow and Kharkov than in Saratov. In Tomsk, skilled workers drank almost as much as unskilled workers. One can only speculate as to why there were regional variations in consumption patterns.

Greater numbers of skilled workers in Moscow, Saratov, and Kharkov had been a part of the revolutionary vanguard in 1917; they therefore might have tended to more readily adopt socialist morality than workers in Tomsk. Perhaps skilled workers drank less in Moscow and Kharkov because in the capitals, other forms of leisure such as clubs and theaters were more available. Since OBSA had a stronger presence in Moscow and Kharkov, one can guess that anti-alcohol agitation had a greater effect in those locations. It is impossible to tell from the sources. It is clear that while a select group of workers may have altered their alcohol consumption, most did not. Whatever the reason, it is logical to assume that, in general, the cultural traditions of workers and peasants that predated 1917 continued to determine their behavior and attitudes after the revolution.

The existence of two major cultural strands within the working class created conflicts between workers and had profound implications for the legitimacy of the Soviet state as the fledgling regime sought to redefine and shape working-class culture. In the late 1920s the rapid rise of Soviet industrial society, therefore, entailed an attempt by the Bolsheviks to impose their own moral standards on the population while at the same time prohibiting the cultural and spatial segregation of the working class that would allow working-class culture to develop a separate and unified self-identity. The result was that during the First Five-Year Plan, traditional modes and mentalities persisted among Russian workers, even as the regime tried to delegitimate them.

While the Bolsheviks insisted on social and cultural unity, Bolshevik policy was not everywhere the same. As evidenced by the anti-alcohol campaign, state-sponsored programs were not uniformly implemented and were often contradictory. For example, Sovnarkom charged Tsentrospirt with simultaneously decreasing alcohol production while increasing alcohol sales and revenues. At the same time, OBSA shock brigades from Kharkov went into the countryside to conduct anti-alcohol agitation while the state increased the distribution of vodka to rural Ukraine by nearly 25 percent.[25] More temperance plays and mock trials were performed in the capitals, and OBSA had a much stronger presence there than in Saratov or Tomsk. Although documentary evidence is scarce, it is reasonable to assume that Moscow and Kharkov, as republic capitals, received more funding for anti-alcohol work than did the other two locales.

One possible explanation for the uneven attention to alcohol policy and anti-alcohol work was funding. The state lacked the resources to fulfill its ambitious goal of transforming daily life. OBSA and state officials earnestly intended to replace drinking with more rational leisure activities, yet they had no money to do so in a compelling manner. With the top priority of Soviet leaders being industrialization, little funding was left for workers' clubs, palaces of culture, and sports arenas.[26] Even when the state increased alcohol production, the lion's share of the revenues went toward industrialization. Consequently, planners had to prioritize the regions that would receive funding for cultural work.

That the capitals received more funding and attention toward the anti-alcohol campaign is not surprising. Katerina Clark has argued that during the 1930s, the Bolsheviks transformed Russia into a colony. In describing the development of socialist realism, Clark suggests that the Bolsheviks provided new myths and a new cultural identity for Russia, much like a colonizing power would.[27] According to Clark, in the process of colonizing Russia, the Bolsheviks created a new center for the country—Moscow—that had to be repurified and recast. Certainly as evidenced by alcohol policy and the anti-alcohol movement, the Bolsheviks acted as a colonizing force. Social deviants, in this case drunks, had to be expelled from Moscow and, to a lesser degree from Kharkov, to clean up the capitals in preparation for the increasing colonization and centralization of the country that would occur during the Second Five-Year Plan (1933–1937). Less alcohol per capita was distributed to Moscow and Kharkov than to the other cities, and legislation intended to rationalize and limit the sale of alcohol was more readily enforced in the capitals.

Clearly then, the state used alcohol policy as an economic and political tool, much like a colonizing power would. Elena Osokina has demonstrated how the Soviet state used food rationing and distribution strategies to reward or punish various social groups.[28] The same was true with alcohol policy. Where and how alcohol was distributed depended upon a variety of political and economic agendas. For example, in Ukraine, state planners used alcohol distribution as a way to subdue potential problem areas. Moreover, since Ukraine produced the bulk of the ingredients for alcohol production, one must wonder what effect increased alcohol production in 1931 had on the famine of 1932–1933 and to what extent alcohol policy was intended to punish Ukrainian resistance to collectivization.

Regardless of state policy, drinking continued to function to structure the workers' milieu. Expressing self and social identity, modes of drinking and modes of sobriety differed greatly among social groups. Simultaneously deepening fracture lines in the working class and strengthening solidarities among social groups, drink functioned to structure divisions within the working masses. As exercised on the shop floor, in taverns and clubs, and in working-class neighborhoods, drinking was not just a way to spend leisure time. It was also a primary symbolic vehicle for generating and maintaining social relationships and, as such, was fraught with political implications in the Soviet period.

The politicization of the alcohol question highlights the fact that the aims of the revolution went beyond simply transferring the means of production to the proletariat. The Bolshevik understanding of "revolution" entailed not only a transfer of political and economic authority. It also provided for a transformation of social and cultural institutions, as well as values, norms, popular images, and traditions—in short, a cultural revolution. The men and women who led the October Revolution aspired to more than power in the raw hegemonic sense. Rather, the process of "building socialism" made imperative the inculcation of a new worldview. Society would have to learn to understand its collective experience in a new way, resulting in new values, myths, traditions, and behaviors.

Against the backdrop of prerevolutionary drinking and temperance, Soviet intellectuals and professionals adopted many of the same goals and tactics as their bourgeois predecessors. As we have seen, those in power, both before and after the revolution, defined working-class drinking as problematic and sought cultural modernization through addressing Russia's "drink problem."

In this sense, then, cultural revolution was a process tied to Russia's modernization that began before 1917 and continued into the 1930s. It also had much in common with general European movements to modernize and rationalize society. Soviet norms of sobriety, hygiene, literacy, and the like mirrored more general ambitions in many modern European countries to civilize the masses and establish social control. What made the Soviet experience unique was the Bolsheviks' insistence on collectivity, unity, and cultural dominance and a reliance on coercion when persuasion failed.

Preexisting Russian cultural traditions and behaviors presented formidable obstacles to the creation of a new society and a new culture. Excessive drinking among workers in particular impeded any social transformation based on the Bolsheviks' principles of discipline and sobriety. In this context, the more important conflicts of the initial decades of Soviet rule did not occur between classes or institutions but took the form of a clash of cultures. The failure of Soviet authorities to fashion a conscious, sober proletariat, despite the fact that control over the media and other resources allowed them to establish the dominant discourse, reflects the tenacity of traditional cultural practices and underscores the limitations of revolutionary vanguardism. Continued drinking expressed dynamics of control and resistance among workers that ultimately forced party leaders to seek ideological retreats and accommodations.

Perhaps the Stalinist leadership realized that it could not have its Stakhanovites and have them sober, too. In this sense cultural revolution ended with a productivism that had no place for the utopian visions of a world of sober rationality. From another viewpoint, the abandonment of serious efforts to control alcoholism in the Soviet Union marked a compromise between state and society—a compromise spurred by the more critical issue of social and economic stability. The state would make inhumane demands on its workers, but it would stop trying to control their use of the true opium of the masses—vodka.

Epilogue

At the Seventeenth Party Congress in 1934, Stalin declared that socialism had been built and that the First Five-Year Plan had eradicated the last vestiges of capitalism as well as the exploiting classes.[29] Since the Bolsheviks defined alcoholism as a result of capitalist exploitation, beginning in 1934 the alcohol problem in the Soviet Union was "solved." According to the entry under "Alcoholism" in the 1950 edition of the *Bol'shaia Sovetskaia Entsiklopediia* (The Great Soviet Encyclopedia), "In the USSR, where we have completely liquidated the exploitative classes, where we have improved the living standards of all the people, we have wiped out the social roots of alcoholism."[30]

Indeed, in September 1932 Tsentrospirt was reorganized into the central Bureau of Alcohol Production (Glavnoe upravlenie spirtovoi promyshlennosti) under the administration of Narkomsnab. The reorganization created twenty-one alcohol trusts, including one that was to oversee the building of new breweries. At the same time, state production of alcohol increased dramatically: in 1930 the state produced 618 million liters of alcohol; in 1933, 700 million liters; in 1936, 776 million liters; and in 1939, 1,095 million liters.[31] Clearly both the party's and OBSA's commitment to limit alcohol production had been abandoned.

In the main, a new stage in the state's relationship to drinking began in 1932 and lasted until the reforms of Mikhail Gorbachev in the mid-1980s. The state primarily used legal and administrative measures for combating public drunkenness. It punished individual offenders with fines, arrest, and ultimately incarceration either in prison or in mental institutions for years. In short, alcoholism became the problem of doctors and judges, not of society. Since drinking was no longer a problem for socialism or society, throughout the post-1930 Stalinist period alcohol was abundant and cheap. The average working-class salary was 331 rubles a month, and the average bottle of vodka cost 6 rubles 15 kopecks.[32]

Stalin's successors, especially Nikita Khrushchev (1953–1964) and Leonid Brezhnev (1964–1982), did not waver much from Stalin's post-1932 alcohol policies. Alcohol sales once again became one of the most important sources of revenue, especially in the difficult years following World War II, comprising approximately 29 percent of all state revenues. In the 1950s the state increased the tempo of alcohol production, restoring breweries damaged during the war and building new ones. By 1950 the state had revived alcohol production to 75 percent of its prewar level, and by 1960 alcohol production far exceeded 1940 levels: the production of vodka was 1.5 times greater, beer production doubled, and wine production quadrupled.

Consequently, per capita alcohol consumption increased by over 300 percent between 1950 and 1970. Because of the vagaries of Soviet accounting, it is difficult to discern exact annual per capita consumption figures. One source claims that annual per capita consumption of pure alcohol in 1950 was 1.85 liters; by 1970 it had jumped to 6.8 liters.[33] Gone were the exhortations for workers to give up their attachment to vodka and adopt sober lifestyles. On the contrary, it was in the state's best financial interest to have them drink. Just as Stalin had encouraged workers to reward themselves with alcohol for a job well done, a popular advertisement during the Khrushchev years extolled the virtues of vodka. It read, "Delicious, cheap, and nutritious—drink vodka. Absolutely!"

From time to time the party would give lip service to combating drunkenness and alcoholism. Indeed, every Soviet leader since Stalin attempted to deal with Russia's (nonexistent) alcohol problem. Some even launched nationwide anti-alcohol campaigns, however brief and ineffectual. And after each campaign, the level of alcohol consumption in the country nearly doubled.

The first such temperance campaign began under Khrushchev on December 15, 1958, when top party and state organs called for a determined struggle against alcoholism. The campaign mainly took the form of propaganda and education aimed at fostering intolerance toward drunks and drunkenness. The state also placed some restrictions on the sale of alcohol in shops and public eateries and closed a significant number of liquor stores and kiosks selling alcohol. Laws against brewing or selling *samogon* were strengthened. In 1960 the criminal code provided for compulsory therapy along with harsh sentences for those arrested for drunkenness more than once.

Brezhnev, himself a notorious drinker, also called for efforts to control alcohol abuse, but to little avail. In 1966 the state introduced a series of fines for public intoxication and established a network of labor rehabilitation centers (*lechebno-trudovye profilaktorii*, LTPs). Amounting to little more than squalid jails, LTPs provided compulsory treatment and labor reeducation for alcoholics. Despite repeated calls from both the Khrushchev and Brezhnev administrations for more determined efforts to curb alcohol abuse, state alcohol output increased and per capita consumption rose. Laws regarding restrictions on alcohol sales and abuse were very sporadically enforced, indicating a lack of will on the part of state administrations to give more than scant attention to the problem.

In the brief period between Brezhnev's death in 1982 and the accession of Mikhail Gorbachev (1985–1991) to the post of general secretary, both Yuri Andropov (1982–1984) and Konstantine Chernenko (1984–1985) sought to strengthen public order and morality. An attempt to reduce public drunkenness was an integral part of their campaigns. In 1983 Andropov introduced new penalties for drinking in the workplace. Chernenko, quite openly expressing concern over the failure of earlier temperance campaigns, began planning a national anti-alcohol movement. He even discussed introducing total prohibition and creating a national temperance society. Chernenko died, however, before he could implement any of these plans.

When Gorbachev became the Soviet leader, he took up the issue of alcoholism as a top priority of his administration.[34] To that end, state and party organs issued decrees restricting the amount of alcohol an individual could buy, limiting the hours stores could sell it, and prohibiting alcohol consumption in numerous public places. The state reduced production of vodka and wines by more than 50 percent: from 29.5 million liters of vodka in 1980 to 14.2 million liters in 1988 and from 32.2 million liters of wine to 17.9 million liters for the same years.[35] Further, in 1985, in an attempt to promote sobriety throughout the Soviet Union, party and state officials created the All-Union Society for the Struggle for Temperance that closely mirrored OBSA. By May 1986 the society claimed 350,000 branches with more than eleven million members. That same year the society revived the old temperance journal, *Trezvost' i kul'tura,* with over 600,000 subscribers.

The results of Gorbachev's anti-alcohol campaign were disastrous. Sugar, used in the production of *samogon,* disappeared from the shelves as bootlegging became epidemic. Vast numbers of people poisoned themselves with other intoxicants, such as brake fluid and rubbing alcohol. For example, one source estimates that in 1987 alone 11,000 people died from drinking alcohol surrogates.[36] The government lost nearly two billion rubles in alcohol revenues precisely when its financial needs shot up, in part owing to the costs of cleaning up the nuclear accident at Chernobyl. The population became angered by the abrupt unavailability of alcohol, seriously undermining Gorbachev's authority and support. A popular joke that circulated widely in the 1980s describes one poor chap in a very long line to buy vodka, who couldn't stand it any longer. "I'm going to the Kremlin to kill Gorbachev," he said. An hour later he came back, and everyone in the line was still there. "Did you kill him?" they asked. "Kill him?" he exclaimed. "The line for that is even longer than this one!"

Within three years Gorbachev retreated from his anti-alcohol policies, but the damage had already been done. It took the government more than four years to recover lost revenues. Unable to get alcohol, some people took to drugs. During these years, the number of people treated for alcoholism declined by 29 percent. At the same time, the number of those addicted to other drugs more than doubled.[37]

Perhaps more important, there is no evidence to suggest the campaign had any effect on the level of alcohol consumption. According to one estimate, current annual consumption is roughly four gallons of pure alcohol per capita, of which over half is vodka.[38] This figure is misleading, however, since it is averaged over the entire population. Obviously, the very young and the very old consume significantly less. Moreover, it does not take into account samogon. It is estimated that rural populations consume as many as four and a half bottles of samogon for every bottle of vodka.[39] Actual consumption figures, therefore, are much higher, making Russia rank ahead of France as the heaviest drinking nation in the world.

NOTES

CHAPTER 1: "DRINKING . . . WE CANNOT DO WITHOUT IT"

1. "Vodka: Russia's Holy Devil," *Pravda ru*, December 2, 2005, 1.

2. Magnus Huss, *Chronische Alkogolkrankeit oder Alkoholismus Chronicus* (Berlin, 1852).

3. Alexander II's regime instituted the Great Reforms (1855–74) that freed the serfs and created a liberalized tsarist system. See, for example, Bruce Lincoln, *The Great Reforms: Autocracy, Bureaucracy, and the Politics of Change in Imperial Russia* (DeKalb, 1990).

4. In his recent book, David Hoffmann has taken great strides to place Russia's modernization within a European context. See David L. Hoffman, *Stalinist Values: The Cultural Norms of Modernity, 1917–1941* (Ithaca, 2003).

5. Since Sheila Fitzpatrick published her pathbreaking article on the cultural revolution in 1978, there has been an explosion of histories dealing with the cultural aspects of the Bolshevik Revolution. Sheila Fitzpatrick, "Cultural Revolution as Class War," in *Cultural Revolution in Russia, 1928–1931*, ed. Sheila Fitzpatrick, 8–41 (Bloomington, 1978). A renewed debate over the definition of cultural revolution has been spurred by a recent article by Michael David-Fox, who argues that the Bolsheviks intended cultural revolution as a process involving both internal and external transformations. See Michael David-Fox, "What Is Cultural Revolution?" *Russian Review* 58 (April 1999): 181–201.

6. Some representative works include Katerina Clark, *Petersburg: Crucible of Cultural Revolution* (Cambridge, 1995); Wendy Goldman, *Women, the State, and Revolution: Soviet Family Policy and Social Life, 1917–1936* (Cambridge, 1993); Peter Kenez, *Cinema and Soviet Society, 1917–1953* (Cambridge, 1992); and Richard Stites, *Revolutionary Dreams: Utopian Vision and Experimental Life in the Russian Revolution* (New York, 1989).

7. See Christopher Read, "Values, Substitutes, and Institutions: The Cultural Dimension of the Bolshevik Dictatorship," in *The Bolsheviks in Russian Society: The Revolution and the Civil Wars*, ed. Vladimir N. Brovkin, 298–319 (New Haven, 1997).

8. For some of the best examples, see Frances Bernstein, "Prostitutes and Proletarians: The Soviet Labor Clinic as Revolutionary Laboratory," in *The Human Tradition in*

Modern Russia, ed. William Husband, 113–28 (Wilmington, 2000); Hoffmann, *Stalinist Values*; William Husband, *"Godless Communists": Atheism and Society in Soviet Russia, 1917–1932* (DeKalb, 2000); Paula A. Michaels, *Curative Powers: Medicine and Empire in Stalin's Central Asia* (Pittsburgh, 2003); Karen Petrone, *Life Has Become More Joyous, Comrades: Celebrations in the Time of Stalin* (Bloomington, 2000); and Donald J. Raleigh, *Experiencing Russia's Civil War: Politics, Society, and Revolutionary Culture in Saratov, 1917–1921* (Princeton, 2002), especially chapters 7–11.

9. For the Soviet period, see T. P. Korzhikhina, "Bor'ba s alkogolizmom v 1920-e— nachale 1930-kh godov," *Voprosy istorii* no. 9 (1985): 20–32; Boris Segal, *The Drunken Society: Alcohol Abuse and Alcoholism in the Soviet Union* (New York, 1990); S. N. Sheverdin, "Iz opyta bor'by protiv p'ianstva i alkogolizma," *Voprosy istorii KPSS* no. 9 (1985): 103–17; and Vlad Treml, *Alcohol Use in the USSR: A Statistical Study* (Durham, 1982). Stephen White, *Russia Goes Dry: Alcohol, State, and Society* (Cambridge, 1996), is the only examination of the 1985 temperance movement launched by Mikhail Gorbachev.

10. Among the few studies that address Russian prerevolutionary drinking and temperance, the best examples include David Christian, *"Living Water": Vodka and Russian Society on the Eve of Emancipation* (Oxford, 1990); Patricia Herlihy, *The Alcoholic Empire: Vodka and Politics in Late Imperial Russia* (New York, 2002); W. Arthur McKee, "Taming the Green Serpent: Alcoholism, Autocracy, and Russian Society, 1890–1917" (Ph.D. diss., University of California, Berkeley, 1997); Boris M. Segal, *Russian Drinking: Use and Abuse of Alcohol in Prerevolutionary Russia* (New Brunswick, 1987); and David Christian and R. E. F. Smith, *Bread and Salt: A Social and Economic History of Food and Drink in Russia* (Cambridge, 1984).

11. Laura Phillips, *The Bolsheviks and the Bottle: Drink and Worker Culture in St. Petersburg, 1900–1929* (DeKalb, 2000).

12. Ibid., 145.

13. See Christian, *"Living Water."*

14. See Herlihy, *Alcoholic Empire.*

15. For discussion of the process and results of this migration to Moscow, see David Hoffmann, *Peasant Metropolis: Social Identities in Moscow, 1929–1941* (Ithaca, 1994).

16. For discussion of Saratov and its workers in 1917, see Donald J. Raleigh, *Revolution on the Volga: 1917 in Saratov* (Ithaca, 1986). Chapter 1 details the historical development of the city. See also Raleigh, *Experiencing Russia's Civil War.*

17. Tsentral'nyi Gosudarstvennyi Arkhiv Moskovskoi Oblasti (Central State Archive of Moscow Oblast, TsGAMO), f. 738, op. 1, d. 33, l. 29.

18. Laura Phillips provides evidence that female workers had their own distinctive drinking behaviors. See Phillips, *Bolsheviks and the Bottle,* 96–99.

Chapter 2: Swimming in a Drunken Sea

1. *Trudy vserossiiskogo s"ezda prakticheskikh deiatelei po bor'be s alkogolizmom* (Petrograd, 1914), 3:1147–49.

2. E. Ch. Skrzhinskaya, ed., *Barbaro i Kontarini o Rossii* (Leningrad, 1971), 228–29.

3. See Giles Fletcher, *Of the Russe Commonwealth,* ed. Richard Pipes (Cambridge, 1966), 44, 112.

4. Samuel H. Baron, ed., *The Travels of Olearius in Seventeenth-Century Russia* (Stanford, 1967), 142.

5. See, for example, James H. Billington, *The Icon and the Axe: An Interpretive History of Russian Culture* (New York, 1965); I. G. Pryzhov, *Istoriia kabakov v Rossii (v sviazi s istoriei russkogo naroda)* (1868; reprint, Moscow, 1991); and I. P. Takala, *Veselie Rusi: Istoriia alkogol'noi problemy v Rossii* (St. Petersburg, 2002).

6. For detailed discussion of vodka in Russia, see Christian, *"Living Water."*

7. The government's claim to a monopoly was asserted in the Law Code (*Ulozhenie*) of 1649. This made it illegal to buy or sell vodka except through government *kabaks* (taverns), and all revenues from the sale of alcohol were by law a part of the royal purse. See Count D. Tolstoi, *Istoriia finansovykh uchrezhdenii Rossii s vremeni osnovaniia gosudarstva do konchiny imperatritsy Ekateriny II* (St. Petersburg, 1848), 134–73. For discussion of alcohol taxation, see, for example, John P. LeDonne, "Indirect Taxes in Catherine's Russia: The Liquor Monopoly," *Jahrbucher fur Geschichte Osteuropas* no. 24 (1976): 173–207; John P. LeDonne, *Ruling Russia: Politics and Administration in the Age of Absolutism, 1762–1796* (Princeton, 1984); and N. I. Pavlenko, *Istoriia metallurgii v Rossii VXIII veka* (Moscow, 1962).

8. P. A. Khromov, *Ekonomicheskoe razvitie Rossii v XIX–XX vekakh, 1800–1917* (Moscow, 1950), 440–45, 494–511. Khromov bases his figures on statistics from *Ministerstvo finansov, 1802–1902,* 2 vols. (St. Petersburg, 1904).

9. All the sources make at least a brief mention of a distinction between peasant and urban drinking cultures. Here I am building on ideas in Christian, *"Living Water,"* 69–99. See also Patricia Herlihy, "The Joy of Rus': Rites and Rituals of Russian Drinking," *Russian Review* 50, no. 2 (April 1991): 131–47; and Segal, *Russian Drinking,* 138–52.

10. Kvass generally is 1.0–2.5 percent alcohol by volume, as the fermentation of lactic acid during its production inhibits the formation of alcohol. In nineteenth-century Russia, making kvass was a basic household skill. See Brokgauz-Efron, *Entsiklopedicheskii slovar'* (St. Petersburg, 1890–1904), 1st. ed., 27:864–65.

11. V. I. Dal', *Poslovitsy russkogo naroda: Sbornik* (Moscow, 1957), 817–18.

12. E. Georg, "Vzgliad po istoriiu i sovremennoe sostoianie piteinykh sborov po velikorossiisskim guberniiam," *Vestnik promyshlennost'* no. 3 (1858): 102–3.

13. This continues to be the defining characteristic of Russian drinking.

14. S. A. Pervushin, *Opyt' teorii massovogo alkogolizma v sviazi s teoriei potrebnostei* (St. Petersburg, 1912), 52–58.

15. M. I. Fridman, *Vinnaia monopoliia* (Petrograd, 1916), 2:462.

16. See, for example, N. A. Minenko, "The Living Past: Daily Life and Holidays of the Siberian Village in the Eighteenth and First Half of the Nineteenth Centuries," in *Russian Traditional Culture: Religion, Gender and Customary Law,* ed. Marjorie Mandelstam Balzar, 195–217 (Armonk, 1992).

17. Olga Semyonova Tian-Shanskaia, *Village Life in Late Tsarist Russia,* trans. and

ed. David Ransel (Bloomington, 1993), 110–11; D. N. Voronov, *Alkogolizm v gorode i derevne v sviazi s bytom naseleniia* (Penza, 1913), 37–41.

18. A. P. Zablotskii-Desiatovskii, "O krepostnom sostoianii," in *Graf P. D. Kiselev i ego vremia: Materialy dlia istorii imperatorov Aleksandra I-go, Nikolaia I-go i Aleksandra II* (St. Petersburg, 1882), 4:312.

19. Minenko, "Living Past," 200.

20. For description of typical village celebrations, see A. Preobrazhenskii, "'Volost' Pokrovsko-Sitskaia Iaroslavskoi gubernii Molozhskago uezda," in *Etnograficheskii sbornik izd. Imperatorskim Russkim geograficheskim obshchestvom* (St. Petersburg, 1830–34), 1:99–100.

21. Christine D. Worobec, "Masculinity in Late-Imperial Russian Peasant Society," in *Russian Masculinities in History and Culture,* ed. Barbara Evans Clements, Rebecca Friedman, and Dan Healy, 76–93 (London, 2002).

22. *Moskovskie vedomosti* no. 22 (1913): 3; N. Gersevanov, *O p'ianstve v Rossii i sredstvakh istrebleniia ego* (Odessa, 1845), 68; Tian-Shanskaia, *Village Life,* 110; Voronov, *Alkogolizm,* 37–41.

23. D. N. Voronov, *Zhizn' derevni v dni trezvosti* (Petrograd, 1916), 20.

24. *Moskovskie vedomosti* no. 69 (March 21, 1859); no. 75 (March 28, 1859); no. 106 (May 6, 1859); I. S. Belliustin, *Description of the Parish Clergy in Rural Russia: The Memoir of a Nineteenth-Century Priest,* trans. Gregory Freeze (Ithaca, 1985), 145–47; Voronov, *Zhizn',* 21; Tian-Shanskaia, *Village Life,* 92.

25. D. N. Voronov, "Analiz derevenskogo alkogolizma i samogonnogo promysla," *Voprosy Narkologii* no. 3 (1926): 57.

26. Ibid., 54.

27. See, for example, D. Thorner, Basile Kerblay, and R. E. F. Smith, eds., *A. V. Chayanov on the Theory of Peasant Economy* (Homewood, 1966), 118–34; A. Chayanov and G. Studenskii, *Istoriia biudzhetnykh issledovanii* (Moscow, 1922); *Statisticheskye tablitsy Rossiiskoi Imperii za 1856 g.* (St. Petersburg, 1858), 269; and Tian-Shanskaia, *Village Life,* 155.

28. *Svedeniia o piteinykh sborakh* (St. Petersburg, 1860–61), 1:99–100; Tian-Shanskaia, *Village Life,* 111; Cathy Frierson, trans. and ed., *Aleksandr Nikolaevich Engelgardt's Letters from the Country, 1872–1887* (Oxford, 1993), 47.

29. N. M. Druzhinin, *Gosudarstvennye krest'iane i reforma P. D. Kiseleva* (Moscow, 1946), 1:347. See also Frierson, *Letters,* 48–50.

30. Tian-Shanskaia, *Village Life,* 164; Frierson, *Letters,* 188.

31. Frierson, *Letters,* 34.

32. See, for example, Worobec, "Masculinity," 78; and Stephen P. Frank, "Popular Justice, Community, and Culture among the Russian Peasantry, 1870–1900," *Russian Review* 46, no. 3 (1987): 249.

33. For discussion of work parties, see Smith and Christian, *Bread and Salt,* 319–22; and Herlihy, "Joy of Rus'."

34. Belliustin, *Description,* 128–30.

35. Voronov, "Analiz," 54.

36. Ibid.

37. Ibid.; Frierson, *Letters*, 58–59.

38. Voronov, "Analiz," 54.

39. Ibid. See also Tian-Shanskaia, *Village Life*, 110–11; Preobrazhenskii, "'Volost,'" 1:103–4; and Voronov, *Zhizn'*, 23–24.

40. Worobec, "Masculinity," 81; Herlihy, "Joy of Rus'," 139.

41. Minenko, "Living Past," 160.

42. Frierson, *Letters*, 161.

43. Voronov, *Alkogolizm*, 46–48.

44. Quoted in Minenko, "Living Past," 160.

45. Belliustin, *Description*, 139–41.

46. Laura Phillips challenges the notion of a shift in drinking behaviors related to urbanization and modernization. See Phillips, *Bolsheviks and the Bottle*. Chapter 4 contains a detailed discussion of taverns in St. Petersburg. See also Pryzhov, *Istoriia kabakov;* and Takala, *Veselie Rusi*, 37–39.

47. Christian, *"Living Water,"* 21–50; Takala, *Veselie Rusi*, 37–39. For discussion of the introduction of distilled spirits in Russia, see Gersevanov, *O p'ianstve,* 4–7.

48. Christian, *"Living Water,"* 21–50. See also Pryzhov, *Istoriia kabakov.*

49. Pryzhov, *Istoriia kabakov,* 229.

50. See, for example, Ben Eklof, John Bushnell, and Larissa Zakharova, eds., *Russia's Great Reforms, 1855–1881* (Bloomington, 1994). For discussions on village economies and peasant culture in postemancipation Russia, see Esther Kingston-Mann and Timothy Mixter, eds., *Peasant Economy, Culture, and Politics of European Russia, 1800–1921* (Princeton, 1991); Stephen P. Frank and Mark D. Steinberg, eds., *Cultures in Flux: Lower-Class Values, Practices, and Resistance in Late Imperial Russia* (Princeton, 1994); and Ben Eklof and Stephen P. Frank, eds., *The World of the Russian Peasant: Post-Emancipation Culture and Society* (Boston, 1990).

51. V. K. Dmitriev, *Kriticheskoe obsledovanie o potreblenii alkogoliia v Rossii* (Moscow, 1911), viii–ix.

52. *Svedeniia*, 1:189.

53. Ibid., 3:247.

54. For discussion of the growth of taverns in the nineteenth century, see Christian, *"Living Water,"* 99–102; Christian and Smith, *Bread and Salt*, 288–326; Pryzhov, *Istoriia kabakov,* 226–36; and *Svedeniia*, 3:48–50, 73–110.

55. G. I. Uspenskii, *Sobranie sochinenii* (Moscow, 1956), 5:103.

56. See Jeffery Burds, "The Social Control of Peasant Labor in Russia: The Response of Village Communities to Labor Migration in the Central Industrial Region, 1861–1905," in Kingston-Mann and Mixter, *Peasant Economy*, 52–100; and Heather Hogan, *Forging Revolution: Metalworkers, Managers, and the State in St. Petersburg, 1890–1940* (Bloomington, 1993), 5–24.

57. *Russkii dnevnik* no. 34 (February 12, 1859).

58. Frierson, *Letters,* 141–43.

59. Burds, "Social Control," 54–60.

60. See Victoria Bonnell, *Roots of Rebellion: Workers' Politics and Organizations in St. Petersburg and Moscow, 1900–1914* (Berkeley, 1983), 20–21; and Hogan, *Forging Revolution,* 26–28. For further discussion of peasant migration, see, for example, Barbara A. Anderson, *Internal Migration during Modernization in Late Nineteenth-Century Russia* (Princeton, 1980); and Robert Johnson, *Peasant and Proletarian: The Working Class of Moscow in the Late Nineteenth Century* (New Brunswick, 1979).

61. S. A. Smith, "Masculinity in Transition: Peasant Migrants to Late-Imperial St Petersburg," in Clements, Friedman, and Healy, *Russian Masculinities,* 95.

62. R. E. Zelnik, *Labor and Society in Tsarist Russia: The Factory Workers of St Petersburg, 1855–1870* (Stanford, 1971), 247.

63. Charters Wynn, *Workers, Strikes, and Pogroms: The Donbass-Dnepr Bend in Late Imperial Russia, 1870–1905* (Princeton, 1992), 80.

64. Ibid.

65. V. Ia. Kanel', *Alkogolizm i bor'ba s nim* (Moscow, 1914), 383, 384, 385.

66. Ibid., 358–59.

67. P. A. Ignatov, *Zhizn' prostogo cheloveka* (Moscow, 1965), 114.

68. David Christian, "Traditional and Modern Drinking Cultures on the Eve of Emancipation," *Australian Slavonic and East European Studies* 1, no. 1 (1987): 61–84. For description of working women's drinking, see Laura Phillips, "In Defense of Their Families: Working-class Women, Alcohol, and Politics in Revolutionary Russia," *Journal of Women's History* 2, no. 11 (Spring 1999): 101–3; and Phillips, *Bolsheviks and the Bottle,* 99–102.

69. See Rose Glickman, *Russian Factory Women: Workplace and Society, 1880–1914* (Berkeley, 1984), 120, 130–31.

70. *Trudy pervogo vserossiiskogo s"ezda po bor'be s p'ianstvom* (St. Petersburg, 1910) 2:184 (hereafter cited as TPVS). See also Wynn, *Workers,* 79.

71. E. A. Oliunina, *Portnovskii promysel v Moskve i v derevnakh Moskovskoi i Raizanskoi gubernii: Materialy k istorii domashnei promyshlennosti v Rossii* (Moscow, 1914), 256; A. Buzinov, *Za Nevskoi zastavoi: Zapiski rabochego* (Moscow, 1930), 23–24.

72. Wynn, *Workers,* 81.

73. Reginald Zelnik, *A Radical Worker in Tsarist Russia: The Autobiography of Semen Ivanovich Kanatchikov* (Stanford, 1986), 57. See also Phillips, *Bolsheviks and the Bottle,* 50–51.

74. Buzinov, *Za Nevskoi,* 24. A variation on this ritual, known as *prival'naia,* is discussed in Phillips, *Bolsheviks and the Bottle,* 50–51, 58–60, 71.

75. G. I. Uspenskii, *Rasskazy i ocherki* (Moscow, 1948), 118.

76. Voronov, *Alkogolizm,* 7–10.

77. Kanel', *Alkogolizm,* 130.

78. *TPVS,* 2:889. For more surveys, see V. K. Dmitriev, *Kriticheskie issledovaniia o potrebleniia alkogolia v Rossii* (Moscow, 1911); N. I. Grigor'ev, *Alkogolizm i prestupleniia*

v Peterburge (St. Petersburg, 1900); and *Trudy postoiannoi kommissii po voprosu ob alkogolizme,* vols. 1–14 (St. Petersburg, 1913).

79. *TPVS,* 3:1412. These figures for detention in *vytrezvitely* should be viewed with caution, however, as the high numbers could reflect a larger number of militia on the streets on the weekends.

80. *Svedeniia,* 3:36, 48.

81. S. A. Pervushin, *Vliianie urozhaev na potreblenie spirtnykh napitkov v Rossii* (St. Petersburg, 1909), 1.

82. *Polnoe sobranie zakonov,* 2nd ser., 37197, "Polozhenie o piteinom sbore." For details of the 1863 reform, see, for example, David Christian, "A Neglected Great Reform," in Eklof, Bushnell, and Zakharova, *Russia's Great Reforms,* 102–14.

83. The French tax farm was abolished by a law promulgated on March 27, 1791. For a classic study on tax farming in France, see G. T. Matthews, *The Royal General Farms in Eighteenth-Century France* (New York, 1958). For one of the few English-language studies on Russian tax farming, see Paul Bushkovitch, "Taxation, Tax Farming, and Merchants in Sixteenth-Century Russia," *Slavic Review* 37, no. 3 (1978): 381–98.

84. For details of liquor farming, see, for example, Christian, *"Living Water,"* 99–218.

85. See *Svedeniia,* 4:278–81, 455–61; Druzhinin, *Gosudarstvennye,* 1:370; and Pryzhov, *Istoriia kabakov,* 270.

86. Pryzhov, *Istoriia kabakov,* 287.

87. For details of the excise system, see *Ministerstvo finansov,* 1:516–20.

88. See Khromov, *Ekonomicheskoe,* 440–45, 494–511.

89. Pryzhov, *Istoriia kabakov,* 266–68.

90. D. N. Borodin, *Itogi paboty pervogo vserossiiskogo s"ezda po bor'be s p'ianstvom* (St. Petersburg, 1910), 6.

91. Khromov, *Ekonomicheskoe,* 494–511.

92. The effects of the reform on popular drinking are not documented in the sources. The impact of the liquor monopoly was debated at length by contemporaries in the following years. See, for example, Borodin, *Itogi;* and *Ministerstvo finansov,* 2:530–36.

93. *Vestnik popechitel'stv o narodnoi trezvosti* no. 22 (June 5, 1904): 527. See also Borodin, *Itogi.*

94. E. I. Deichman, *Alkogolizm i bor'ba s nim* (Moscow, 1929), 77.

95. See, for example, Borodin, *Itogi;* and *TPVS,* vol. 3.

96. Fridman, *Vinnaia monopoliia,* 491.

97. See Laura Phillips, "Everyday Life in Revolutionary Russia: Working-Class Drinking in Taverns in St. Petersburg, 1900–1929" (Ph.D. diss., University of Illinois at Urbana-Champaign, 1993), 140–44.

98. S. B. Okun', ed., *Krest'ianskoe dvizhenie v Rossii v 1857–1861 gg.: Dokumenty* (Moscow, 1963), 736.

99. V. I. Lenin, "'The Peasant Reform' and the Proletarian-Peasant Revolution," in

Collected Works (Moscow, 1960–63), 17:122. For Soviet interpretations of the "sobriety movement," see, for example, V. A. Fedorov, "Krest'ianskoe trezvennoe dvizhenie 1858–1860 gg.," in *Revoliutsionnaia situatsiia v Rossii v 1859–1861 gg.*, ed. M. V. Netchkina, 107–26 (Moscow, 1962); and Ia. I. Linkov, *Ocherki istorii krest'ianskogo dvizheniia v Rossii v 1825–1861 gg.* (Moscow, 1952).

100. See Christian, *"Living Water,"* 286–352; and David Christian, "The Black and Gold Seals: Popular Protests against the Liquor Trade on the Eve of Emancipation," in Kingston-Mann, *Peasant Economy,* 261–93.

101. *Svedeniia,* 1:202, 3:24.

102. Druzhinin, *Gosudarstvennye,* 1:374–75.

103. Okun', *Krest'ianskoe dvizhenie,* 189.

104. Peter Kolchin, *Unfree Labor: American Slavery and Russian Serfdom* (Cambridge, 1987), 303.

105. For details of the riots, see Fedorov "Krest'ianskoe trezvennoe"; and Christian, *"Living Water,"* ch. 11.

106. For descriptions of violence and disorder in 1905, see Abraham Ascher, *The Revolution of 1905: Russia in Disarray* (Stanford, 1988); and John Bushnell, *Mutiny amid Repression: Russian Soldiers in the Revolution of 1905–1907* (Bloomington, 1985).

107. For discussion of rising crime and violence as reported in the popular press, see Joan Neuberger, *Hooliganism: Crime, Culture, and Power in St. Petersburg, 1900–1914* (Berkeley, 1993), 71–110.

108. Buzinov, *Za Nevskoi,* 36; Phillips, "Everyday Life," 137–38; Glickman, *Factory Women,* 191–92.

109. Glickman, *Factory Women,* 191–92.

110. *Peterburgskii listok,* June 27, 1906, 3; *Novoe vremia,* June 27, 1906, 8–9.

111. *Peterburgskii listok,* August 8, 1906, 1; *Peterburgskaia gazeta,* August 1, 1906, 3; August 7, 1906, 1.

112. *Gazeta kopeika,* July 8, 1914, 3; July 9, 1914, 3; July 10, 1914, 2.

CHAPTER 3: TIPPLING AND TEMPERANCE

1. Patricia E. Prestwich, *Drink and the Politics of Social Reform: Antialcoholism in France since 1870* (Palo Alto, 1988), 284.

2. See Olga Crisp and Linda Edmonson, eds., *Civil Rights in Imperial Russia* (Oxford, 1989); Daniel Brower, *The Russian City between Tradition and Modernity, 1850–1900* (Berkeley, 1990); and Joseph Bradley, *Muzhik and Muscovite: Urbanization in Late Imperial Russia* (Berkeley, 1985). For discussion of the influence of Western liberalism on medical professionals in Russia, see Laura Engelstein, *The Keys to Happiness: Sex and the Search for Modernity in Fin-de-siècle Russia* (Ithaca, 1992).

3. See, for example, Simon Dixon, "The Church's Social Role in St. Petersburg, 1800–1914," in *Church, Nation, and State in Russia and Ukraine,* ed. G. Hosking, 167–92 (New York, 1991).

4. Here I am building on ideas discussed in Herlihy, *Alcoholic Empire.* See also

George Snow, "Socialism, Alcoholism, and the Russian Working Classes before 1917," in *Drinking Behavior and Belief in Modern History,* ed. Susanna Barrows and Robin Room (Berkeley, 1991).

5. The most notable of these was a brief temperance campaign led by Saint Tikhon of Voronezh in the eighteenth century. See N. I. Grigor'ev, "Obshchestva trezvosti v Rossii," in *Trudy kommissii po voprosam ob alkogolizme i merakh bor'by s nim* (St. Petersburg, 1900), 4:230.

6. Christian, "Black and Gold Seals," 261–93.

7. Christian, *"Living Water,"* 255–85. See also L. V. Tengoborskii, *O proizvoditel'nykh silakh Rossii,* vol. 2, pt. 2 (Moscow, 1857–58).

8. N. V. Chernyshevskii, "Otkupnaia sistema," in *Polnoe sobranie sochinenii v 10 tomakh* (St. Petersburg, 1906), 4:246.

9. Anonymous, "Pei da ne opokhmeliaisia. Pei da ne upivaisia," in *Sel'skie besedy dlia narodnogo chteniia: Pritchi i povesti* (St. Petersburg, 1843), 4:10.

10. Herlihy, *Alcoholic Empire,* 69.

11. See Gersevanov, *O p'ianstve;* S. Shipov, *O trezvosti v Rossii* (St. Petersburg, 1859); and M. Zablotskii, "O p'ianstve v Rossii," *Ekonomist, prilozheniia k ekonomicheskomu ukazateliu* 1 (1858): 109–50.

12. W. Arthur McKee, "Sobering Up the Soul of the People: The Politics of Popular Temperance in Late Imperial Russia," *Russian Review* 58 (April 1999): 225.

13. Ibid., 226.

14. For discussion of representations of peasants, see, for example, Donald Fanger, "The Peasant in Literature," in *The Peasant in Nineteenth Century Russia,* ed. Wayne Vucinich, 231–62 (Stanford, 1968); and Cathy Frierson, *Peasant Icons: Representations of Rural People in Late Nineteenth-Century Russia* (Oxford, 1993).

15. See, for example, Gleb Uspensky, *Rasskazy i ocherki* (Moscow, 1948); and M. D. Calvocoressi, *Modest Mussorgsky: His Life and Works* (Fair Lawn, 1956), 32–33.

16. On the major changes in censorship regulations, see Charles A. Ruud, *Fighting Words: Imperial Censorship and the Russian Press, 1804–1906* (Toronto, 1982), ch. 7; and Louise McReynolds, *The News Under Russia's Old Regime: The Development of a Mass Circulation Press* (Princeton, 1991).

17. See, for example, Patricia Herlihy, "The Russian Orthodox Church," paper presented at the annual meeting of the American Association for the Advancement of Slavic Studies, Honolulu, November, 1988; George Snow, "Temperance Education and Educational Temperance: Russian Temperance Groups' Efforts in Formal Education and Training, 1890–1914," paper presented at the annual meeting of the American Association for the Advancement of Slavic Studies, Honolulu, November 1988; Dixon, "Church's Social Role;" and Marc Lee Schulkin, "The Politics of Temperance: Nicholas II's Campaign against Alcohol Abuse" (Ph.D. diss., Harvard University, 1985).

18. See, for example, Roberta T. Manning, *The Crisis of the Old Order in Russia: Gentry and Government* (Princeton, 1982); and Neuberger, *Hooliganism.*

19. Patricia Herlihy convincingly argues that the issue of temperance was not lim-

ited to the educated elite but was taken up by all classes. She further argues that it was not just lower-class drinking that was the object of moral reform. It is not my intention to challenge this argument by focusing on the upper classes. However, the nature and goals of temperance differed between classes. See Herlihy, *Alcoholic Empire*, 11–12.

20. For discussion of fragmentation and cohesion among the educated elite, see William Wagner, "Ideology, Identity, and the Emergence of a Middle Class," in *Between Tsar and People: Educated Society and the Quest for Public Identity in Late Imperial Russia*, ed. Edith Clowes, Samuel Kassow, and James West, 149–63 (Princeton, 1991).

21. Here I am building on arguments put forth by Laura Engelstein in *Keys to Happiness*.

22. Aleksandr Pypin developed the first extensive scholarly idea of *obshchestvennost'* as the educated public and public opinion (*obshchestvennoe mnenie*) opposed to the autocracy. The core principles in defining the conception of an educated public are activism and reform-mindedness. See Aleksandr Pypin, *Moskovskoe masonstvo* (Petrograd, 1916); and Aleksandr Pypin, *Obshchestvennoe dvizhenie v Rossii pri Aleksandre I* (St. Petersburg, 1885).

23. Liberal reform is discussed in depth in Bradley, *Muzhik and Muscovite*, ch. 7.

24. See Segal, *Russian Drinking*, 341.

25. For discussion of the Guardianship, see Herlihy, *Alcoholic Empire*, 11–35.

26. *Popechitel'stva o narodnoi trezvosti v 1905 godu* (St. Petersburg, 1908), 4:8–9.

27. Cited in Kanel', *Alkogolizm*, 445.

28. *Tolkovyi ukazatel' knig dlia chteniia* (Moscow, 1907), 2:5.

29. A. M. Korovin, *Blagotvoritel'nost' i alkogolizm* (Moscow, 1901), 84–97.

30. A. R. Lednitskii, *Bor'ba s nishchenstvom* (Moscow, 1901), 82.

31. *Vos'moi godichnyi otchet' pervogo Moskovskogo obshchestva trezvosti za 1903 god* (Moscow, 1904), 11–16.

32. Ibid., 78–82.

33. Most detailed analyses of this stratum focus on the merchants. See, for example, Daniel Orlovsky, "The Lower Middle Strata," in *The City in Late Imperial Russia*, ed. Michael F. Hamm, 248–68 (Bloomington, 1986).

34. Jeffery Brooks, "Popular Philistinism and the Course of Russian Modernism," in *History and Literature: Theoretical Problems and Russian Case Studies*, ed. Gary Saul Morton, 90–91 (Stanford, 1986).

35. Here I am building on arguments put forth by Engelstein, *Keys to Happiness*, 17–55; and Neuberger, *Hooliganism*, 51–57.

36. This is a prevailing theme in Clowes, Kassow, and West, *Between Tsar and People*, 46–49, 146–48, 149–63, 248–68, 273–87, 288–307.

37. See, for example, Engelstein, *Keys to Happiness*, 17–55; Clowes, Kassow, and West, *Between Tsar and People*, esp. 183–99; John Hutchinson, *Politics and Public Health in Revolutionary Russia, 1890–1918* (Baltimore, 1990); and Nancy Frieden, *Russian Physicians in an Era of Reform and Revolution, 1856–1905* (Princeton, 1981).

38. A. M. Carr-Sanders and P. A. Wilson, *The Professions* (Oxford, 1933), 65–75, 289–318.

39. See, for example, Frieden, *Russian Physicians;* Ben Eklof, *Russian Peasant Schools: Officialdom, Village Culture, and Popular Pedagogy, 1861–1914* (Berkeley, 1986); N. M. Pirumova, *Zemskaia intelligentsiia i ee rol' v obshchestvennoi bor'be* (Moscow, 1986); and Jane Burbank, "Discipline and Punish in the Moscow Bar Association," *Russian Review* 54, no. 1 (January 1995): 44–64.

40. See A. V. Ushakov, *Revoliutsionnoe dvizhenie demokraticheskoi intelligentsii v Rossii, 1895–1904* (Moscow, 1976), 43–46.

41. John Hutchinson argues that physicians' attempts to make Russians healthy were a political struggle to control the place health was to play in Russia's political economy. See Hutchinson, *Politics and Public Health,* xv. Herlihy also discusses the political nature of public health. See Herlihy, *Alcoholic Empire,* 36.

42. See, for example, Kendall Bailes, *Science and Russian Culture in the Age of Revolution: V. I. Vernadsky and His Scientific School, 1863–1945* (Bloomington, 1990), esp. ch. 5.

43. Physicians were the first professionals allowed to engage in an unprecedented level of professional organization. See Frieden, *Russian Physicians.*

44. See, for example, *TPVS*, 1:250, 3:1254–95; and S. S. Korsakov, *Ob alkogol'nom paraliche* (Moscow, 1887). See also Segal, *Russian Drinking,* 320–23.

45. "Ot redaktsii," *Vrach'* no. 11 (1896): 326; "Ot redaktsii," *Nevrologicheskii vestnik* no. 4 (1896): 177. For discussion of Erisman's influence on zemstvo medicine, see Frieden, *Russian Physicians,* 99–104.

46. *Trudy pervogo s"ezda russkikh psikhiatrov* (Moscow, 1888), 7–10.

47. For discussion of the Kazan Temperance Society, see Herlihy, *Alcoholic Empire,* 30–32, 41–42, 100–101, 122–23.

48. *Trudy kommissii po voprosu ob alkogolizme* (St. Petersburg, 1899), 2.

49. For discussion of various medical remedies put forth by Russian health professionals, see Herlihy, *Alcoholic Empire,* 36–51.

50. See, for example, Patricia Herlihy, "Strategies of Sobriety: Temperance Movements in Russia, 1880–1914," Kennan Institute for Advanced Russian Studies Occasional Paper (Harvard, 1986); Dixon, "Church's Social Role."

51. The Holy Synod was a committee of twelve bishops or clerical leaders under a lay Ober-Procurator that replaced the Patriarchate in 1721.

52. Dixon, "Church's Social Role," 167. For details on the Alexander Nevskii Society, see Herlihy, *Alcoholic Empire,* 74–79.

53. Herlihy, *Alcoholic Empire.*

54. *Golos tserkvi* (June 1913): 19–33, as quoted in Herlihy, "Strategies of Sobriety," 10.

55. See Nadiezda Kizenko, *A Prodigal Saint: Father John of Kronstadt and the Russian People* (University Park, 2000).

56. Ibid.

57. McKee, "Sobering Up," 212.

58. E. I. Lotova, *Russkaia intelligentsiia i voprosy obshchestvennoi gigieny: Pervoe gigienicheskoe obshchestvo v Rossii* (Moscow, 1962), 15.

59. See, for example, Sharon Kowalsky, "Making Crime and Sex Soviet: Women, Deviance, and the Development of Criminology in Early Soviet Russia" (Ph.D. diss., University of North Carolina, Chapel Hill, 2004), esp. ch. 1.

60. *Trudy komissii po voprosu ob alkogolizme i merakh bor'by s nim,* 1:2–5.

61. G. I. Dembo, *Ocherki deiatel'nosti komissii po voprosu ob alkogolizme za 15 let, 1898–1913* (St. Petersburg, 1913), 5.

62. For fuller discussion of the commission, see John Hutchinson, "Medicine, Morality, and Social Policy in Imperial Russia: The Early Years of the Alcohol Commission," *Social History: A Canadian Review* no. 7 (1974): 202–26; Segal, *Russian Drinking,* 330–34. See also E. N. Fokina, "Iz istorii bor'by s alkogolizmom v Rossii (raboty A. M. Korovina 1864–1943)," *Sovetskoe zdravookhranenie* 21, no. 8 (1962): 60–64; Kh. I. Idel'chik, "Problema bor'by s alkogolizmom v nauchnoi i obshchestvennoi deiatel'nosti professora L. S. Minor," *Sovetskoe zdravookhranenie* 40, no. 3 (1981): 63–66.

63. D. A. Dril', "Nekotorye iz prichin massovogo alkogolizma i voprosy o sredstvakh bor'by s nim," *Trudy komissii,* vol. 2, pt. 2, 93–110.

64. Dembo, *Ocherki,* 86.

65. Takala, *Veselie Rusi,* 147. Other subcommittees were formed dealing with military affairs, the effects of the state liquor monopoly, the role of the clergy, statistics, medical matters, temperance societies, and research.

66. Dril', "Nekotorye," 95–100.

67. Ibid., 108–10.

68. N. I. Grigor'ev, "O p'ianstve sredi materovykh v S.-Peterburge," *Trudy komissii,* vol. 2, pt. 2, 111–19.

69. Ibid. See also Grigor'ev, *Alkogolizm.*

70. Grigor'ev, "O p'ianstve," 118–19.

71. D. G. Bulgakovskii, "Rol' pravoslavnogo dukhoventsva v bor'be s narodnym p'ianstvom," *Trudy komissii,* vol. 5, 309–16.

72. A. Vireneus, "Mery bor'by s alkogolizmom putem shkoly," *Trudy komissii,* vol. 6, 471–74.

73. Ibid. See also Dembo, *Ocherki,* 73–74.

74. For discussion of prostitution, see Engelstein, *Keys to Happiness,* 56–95. For debates within the commission linking alcoholism with prostitution and tuberculosis, see Dembo, *Ocherki,* 39–43; and *Trudy komissii,* vol. 9, pt. 1, 620, 634; pts. 7–8, 3, 59–61; and Hutchinson, "Medicine, Morality, and Social Policy," 212–14.

75. V. I. Lenin, *The Development of Capitalism in Russia,* 2nd ed. (Moscow, 1964), 579. See also V. I. Lenin, "New Economic Developments in Peasant Life," in *Collected Works,* 1:17.

76. Dembo, *Ocherki,* 55–56; G. I. Dembo, "Prichiny alkogolizma," *Trudy komissii,* vol. 10, "Prilozhenie."

77. "Prenie po obiom dokladom," *Trudy komissii,* vol. 2, pt. 2, 103.

78. A. M. Korovin, *Dipsomaniia kak ritm i istoshchenie* (Moscow, 1910).

79. A. M. Korovin, "Dvizhenie trezvosti v Rossii," *Trudy kommissii,* vol. 5, 335–41, 439–70.

80. See Segal, *Russian Drinking,* 340–42. See also note 6 above.

81. G. I. Dembo, *Alkogolizm i bor'ba s nim* (St. Petersburg, 1909), 34.

82. See, for example, G. I. Dembo, *Kratkii ocherki deiatel'nosti S-Peterburgskogo Popechitel'stva o narodnoi trezvosti, 1889–1908* (St. Petersburg, 1908); and M. I. Friedman, *Vinnaia monopoliia v Rossii* (Petrograd, 1916).

83. For discussion of radicalization of physicians, see, for example, Frieden, *Russian Physicians,* esp. chs. 10 and 11.

84. The call for a public forum on alcoholism came from many sectors, but the most sustained demands issued from socialist groups. See, for example, V. M. Bekhterev's speeches in *Trudy 2-go s"ezda otechestvennykh psikhiatrov* (Kiev, 1907), 28–52; Friedman, *Vinnaia monopoliia,* 596–608; and I. D. Strashun, *Russkaia obshchestvennaia meditsina v period mezhdu dvumia revoliutsiiami, 1907–1917 gg* (Moscow, 1964), 136–52.

85. Kh. I. Idel'chik, M. N. Aruin, and A. I. Nesterenko, "Vserossiiskii s"ezd po bor'be s p'ianstvom," *Sovetskoe zdravookhranenie* no. 2 (1972): 61. For further discussion of the congress, see Phillips, *Bolsheviks and the Bottle,* 12–17; and Snow, "Socialism," 243–64.

86. Anonymous, "Gorod i alkogolizm," *Peterburgskii listok,* August 5, 1906.

87. Gosudarstvennyi Arkhiv Rossiiskoi Federatsii (State Archive of the Russian Federation, GARF), f. 102, d. 14, chast' 210b., ll. 258–372.

88. "Obshchii plan organizatsii pervogo vserosiisskogo s"ezda po bor'be s p'ianstvom," *TPVS,* vol. 1, article 2, 7; and Borodin, *Itogi,* 3–5.

89. "K s"ezdu po bor'be s p'ianstvom," *Sotsial-demokrat* no. 9, November 13, 1909.

90. P. V. Barchugov, *Revoliutsionnaia rabota bol'shevikov v legal'nykh rabochikh organizatsiiakh (1907–1911)* (Rostov, 1963); I. Letunovskii, *Leninskaia taktika ispol'zovanie legal'nykh vserosiisskikh s"ezdov v bor'be za massy v 1908–1911* (Moscow, 1971), 38.

91. Reports compiled from these questionnaires are published in *TPVS,* 1:214, 230, 232–33, 2:799–833, 844–50.

92. Ibid., 1:116–17.

93. Ibid., 1:96; *Pechatnoe delo* no. 15 (January 12, 1910): 10; *Russkii vrach* no. 4. (January 23, 1910): 130.

94. *TPVS,* 1:74.

95. Ibid., 1:171, 156–57. See also *Trezvye vskhody* no. 1 (1910): 137.

96. Strashun, *Russkaia obshchestvennaia,* 144; Lotova, *Russkaia intelligentsiia,* 174.

97. *TPVS,* 1:156–57.

98. The most representative of these are Pervushin, *Opyt;* and A. Lositskii and I. Chernushev, *Alkogolizm peterburgskikh rabochikh* (St. Petersburg, 1913).

99. See, for example, James H. Bater, "Between Old and New: St. Petersburg in the Late Imperial Era," in Hamm, *City,* 201; and Bradley, *Muzhik and Muscovite,* 249–91.

For discussion of changing images of the poor in the press, see Neuberger, *Hooliganism*, 216–74.

Chapter 4: Sobering Up the Revolution

1. The word "*byt*" is extremely difficult to translate. Eric Naiman comes closest in referring to "what the Russians call *byt*: the category of nitty-gritty detail and everyday life." See Eric Naiman, *Sex in Public: The Incarnation of Early Soviet Ideology* (Princeton, 1997), 27.

2. For some of the best examples of early Bolshevik projects, see John E. Bowlt and Olga Mattich, eds., *Laboratory of Dreams: The Russia Avant-Garde and Cultural Experiment* (Stanford, 1996); Goldman, *Women, the State, and Revolution;* Husband, "*Godless Communists*"; Stites, *Revolutionary Dreams;* and Elizabeth Wood, *The Baba and the Comrade: Gender and Politics in Revolutionary Russia* (Bloomington, 1997).

3. GARF, f. 5515, op. 20, d. 7, l. 32.

4. *Pravda,* July 12, 1923, 1.

5. For a detailed discussion of prohibition in Russia, see David Christian, "Prohibition in Russia, 1914–1925," *Australian Slavonic and East European Studies* 9, no. 2 (1995): 90–118.

6. A. L. Sidorov, ed., *Ekonomicheskoe polozhenie Rossii nakanune Velikoi Oktiabr'skoi sotsialisticheskoi revoliutsii* (Leningrad, 1957–67), 2:432. For the law of March 27, 1917, see *Sobranie uzakonenii i rasporiazhenii rabochego i krest'ianskogo pravitel'stava,* 1917, 475, March 27, 1917.

7. *Sobranie uzakonenii,* 1918, 862–66, October 26, 1918.

8. Rossiiskii Gosudarstvennyi Arkhiv Ekonomiki (Russian State Archive of the Economy, RGAE), f. 7733, op. 1, d. 4433; *Sobranie uzakonenii,* 1920, nos. 1–2, 2; *Dekrety sovetskoi vlasti* (Moscow, 1957), 7:34–38.

9. Rossiiskii Tsentr Khraneniia i Izucheniia Dokumentov Noveishei Istorii (Russian Center for the Preservation and Study of Documents on Recent History, RTsKhIDNI), f. 17, op. 10, d. 139, l. 33.

10. A. G. Parkhomenko, "Gosudarstennvo-pravovye meropriiatiia v bor'be s p'ianstvom v pervye gody sovetskoi vlasti," *Sovetskoe gosudarstvo i pravo* no. 4 (1984), 114; *Dekrety sovetskoi vlasti,* 7:35.

11. D. N. Voronov, *O samogone* (Moscow, 1929), 6.

12. Takala, *Veselie Rusi,* 171.

13. Christian, "Prohibition in Russia," 106.

14. A. M. Bol'shakov, *Derevnia, 1917–1927* (Moscow, 1927), 338. See also A. M. Aronovich, "Samogonshchiki," in *Prestupnyi mir Moskvy,* ed. M. I. Gernet, 174–87 (Moscow, 1924); and Christian, "Prohibition in Russia," 108–9.

15. Bol'shakov, *Derevnia,* 338.

16. Ibid., 339.

17. V. M. Lavrov, ed., *Sibir' v 1923–24 godu* (Novonikolaevsk, 1925), 211–15.

18. A. A. Gurevich and A. Z. Zakevskii, *Alkogolizm: Sotsial'no-gigienicheskoe issledovanie* (Kharkov, 1930), 162–66.

19. Bol'shakov, *Derevnia,* 387–89.

20. Ibid., 341–42.

21. Ibid., 341.

22. Aronovich, "Samogonshchiki," 185.

23. G. Y. Sokolnikov, *Soviet Policy in Public Finance, 1917–1928* (Stanford, 1931), 39. These figures are difficult to verify. However, Sokolnikov, who headed the Commissariat of Finance in the early Soviet government and is credited with being the organizer of the State Bank in 1921–22 as well as the author of the currency reform of 1923–24, presents the most coherent and consistent figures for the period. His data correspond with data in Khromov, *Ekonomicheskoe.*

24. A. M. Michelson, *Russian Public Finance during the War* (New Haven, 1961), 45.

25. RTsKhiDNI, f. 17, op. 10, d. 139, ll. 6, 33, 66; "O bor'be s samogonovareniem i p'ianstvom," *Administrativnyi vestnik* no. 5 (May 1926): 13.

26. War Communism was the harsh policy adopted by the Bolsheviks during the civil war aimed at putting socialist principles into action and keeping the Red Army supplied. It included nationalization of industry, forced grain requisition, forced mobilization of labor, and rationing. It was quite brutal and created tremendous hardships for the population. When the Kronstadt sailors rebelled in 1921, Lenin backed away from the policy of War Communism and instituted the New Economic Policy geared toward economic recovery.

27. E. G. Gimpel'son, *Sovetskii rabochii klass, 1918–1920* (Moscow, 1974), 80.

28. A. G. Rashin, "Dinamika promyshlennykh kadrov SSSR v 1917–1958 gg.," in *Izmeneniia v chislennosti i sostave sovetskogo rabochego klassa* (Moscow, 1961), 9.

29. See, for example, Hoffman, *Peasant Metropolis;* Moshe Lewin, *The Making of the Soviet System* (New York, 1984); William Chase, *Workers, Society, and the Soviet State: Labor and Life in Moscow, 1918–1929* (Champaign-Urbana, 1987); and Hiroaki Kuromiya, "The Crisis of Proletarian Identity in the Soviet Factory, 1928–29," *Slavic Review* 44, no. 2 (Summer 1985): 280–97.

30. *Pravda,* January 31, 1926, 1.

31. L. S. Rogachevskaia, *Likvidatsiia bezrabotnitsy v SSSR (1917–1930 gg.)* (Moscow, 1973), 84.

32. For discussion of the importance of cultural transformation to the Bolshevik revolution, see Read, "Values, Substitutes, and Institutions," 298–319. For an interesting discussion of cultural revolution, see David-Fox, "What Is Cultural Revolution?" 181–201.

33. For elaboration on Bolshevik utopianism, see Stites, *Revolutionary Dreams.*

34. N. Bukharin and E. Preobrazhenskii, *The ABC of Communism* (Ann Arbor, 1966), 75.

35. Engels states that because workers had been objectified, they drank to escape their miserable lives. According to Engels, drinking was no longer a vice but a phenomenon arising out of capitalist exploitation. See Friedrich Engels, *The Condition of the Working Class in England* (London, 1891), esp. ch. 7.

36. Iu. Tokarev, "Dokumenty narodnykh sudov (1917–1922)," in *Voprosy istoriografii i istochnikovedeniia SSSR,* ed. S. N. Valk, 153 (Moscow, 1965).

37. From a speech delivered to the All-Russian Conference of Journalists, reprinted in *Rabochaia gazeta,* January 13, 1926.

38. Barchugov, *Revoliutsionnaia rabota bol'shevikov,* 277.

39. V. D. Bonch-Bruevich, *Na boevykh postakh fevral'skoi i oktiabr'skoi revoliutsii* (Moscow, 1931), 182–85; P. Ia. Kann, "Bor'ba rabochikh Petrograda s p'ianymi pogromami (noiabr'-dekabr' 1917 g.)" *Istoriia SSSR* no. 3 (1962): 133–36.

40. Deichman, *Alkogolizm,* 138–39.

41. *Pravda,* February 20, 1923, 3.

42. Ia. Iakovlev, *Derevnia kak ona est': Ocherki Nikol'skoi volosti* (Moscow, 1923), 106.

43. Ibid., 110.

44. Ibid., 109.

45. A. P. Kaplan, "Polovoi sostav naseleniia posle voiny," *Sotsial'naia gigiena Sbornik* (Moscow-Petrograd, 1923), pt. 2, 137. See also Wood, *Baba,* 123.

46. E. Z. Volkov, *Dinamika naseleniia SSSR za vosem'desiat let* (Moscow, 1930), 190.

47. *Kommunistka* no. 4 (April 1924): 45.

48. Wood, *Baba,* 153.

49. Ibid., 154.

50. Diane Koenker, "Urbanization and Deurbanization in the Russian Revolution and Civil War," in *Party, State, and Society in the Russian Civil War,* ed. Diane Koenker, 93 (Bloomington, 1989).

51. Ibid., 152.

52. Jane McDermid and Anna Hillyar, *Women and Work in Russia, 1880–1930* (New York, 1998), 195.

53. A. G. Rashin, *Zhenskii trud v SSSR* (Moscow, 1928), 48.

54. Ibid.

55. E. Ashmead-Bartlett, *The Riddle of Russia* (London, 1929), 207.

56. *Pravda,* October 6, 1922, 2; October 13, 1922, 1; January 5, 1923, 2; October 13, 1923, 5.

57. *Pravda,* February 19, 1923, 1.

58. For discussion of the regime's campaigns against *samogon,* see Helene Stone, "The Soviet Government and Moonshine, 1917–1929," in *Cahiers du Monde russe et sovietique* 27, nos. 3–4 (1986): 359–80; and Neil Weissman, "Prohibition and Alcohol Control in the USSR: The 1920s Campaign against Illegal Spirits," *Soviet Studies* 38, no. 3 (July 1986): 349–68.

59. *Ugolovnyi kodeks RSFSR* (1922), 24.

60. *Izvestiia,* October 8, 1922, 2.

61. Aronovich, "Samogonshchiki, 175.

62. *Pravda,* March 7, 1923, "Bor'ba s samogonshchinoi," 7.

63. Tsentralnii Derzhavnii Arkhiv Vishchikh Organov Vladi ta Upravliniia Ukraini

(Central State Archive of Organs of Higher Power and Administration of Ukraine, TsDAVOVTU), f. 6, op. 1, d. 1955, l. 13.

64. *Kommunist* no. 196 (August 13, 1923): 3.

65. Derzhavnii Arkhiv Kharkivskoi Oblasti (State Archive of Kharkov Oblast, DAKhO), f. R-203, op. 1, d. 1085, l. 83.

66. V. M. Chetyrin, "Tainoe vinokurenie v derevne," *Planovoe khoziastvo* 4–5 (1924): 89.

67. *Pravda,* February 20, 1923, "K voprosu o bor'be s samogonkoi," 2.

68. Weissman, "Prohibition," 363.

69. Gosudarstvennyi Arkhiv Tomskoi Oblasti (State Archive of Tomsk Oblast, GATO), f. R-279, op. 1, d. 127, ll. 29–37.

70. *Administrativnyi vestnik* no. 5 (1925): 8–12.

71. A. Uchevatov, "Tainoe vinokurenie v gorode i derevne," *Problemy prestupnosti* no. 2 (1927), 120, quoted in Kowalsky, "Making Crime and Sex Soviet," 215.

72. L. Rozenshtein, "Profilaktichesksaia psikhonevrologiia i bor'ba s alkogolizmom," *Voprosy zdravookhraneniia* no. 9 (1928): 11–14.

73. P. P. Brukhanskii, "Opyt lecheniia alkogolikov v psikhiatricheskikh bol'nitsakh," *Moskovskii meditsinskii zhurnal* no. 7 (1927): 15–25.

74. For discussion of the impact of the cultural revolution in psychiatry, see David Joravsky, "Construction of the Stalinist Psyche," in Fitzpatrick, *Cultural Revolution,* 105–28.

75. See, for example, *Zhurnal nevropatologiia i psikhatrii* no. 5 (1930): 123–30; and *Vrachebnaia gazeta* no. 2 (1931): 123.

76. *Gigiena i epidemiologiia* no. 11 (1928): 34.

77. Ibid., 2.

78. Ibid., 17–18.

79. *Voprosy zdravookhraneniia* no. 9 (1928): 11–14; *Voprosy narkologii* no. 2 (1928): 104–8.

80. *Sotsial'naia gigiena* no. 1 (1923): 8–9.

81. Ibid.

82. See Susan Gross Solomon, "Social Hygiene in Soviet Public Health, 1921–1930," in *Social Medicine in Revolutionary Russia,* ed. J. F. Hutchinson and Susan Gross Solomon, 175–99 (Bloomington, 1990).

83. I. V. Vengrova and Iu. A. Shilinis, *Sotsial'naia gigiena v SSSR (Ocherk istorii)* (Moscow, 1976), 115, 122–23.

84. *Administrativnyi vestnik* no. 3 (1926): 5; *Gigiena i epidemiologiia* nos. 7–8 (1926): 38–39; no. 9 (1926): 21–25.

85. "O blizhaishikh meropriiatiiakh po bor'be s alkogolizmom," in R. Vlassak, *Alkogolizm* (Moscow, 1928), 257. See, for example, E. I. Deichman, "Problema zasluzhivaiushchaia vnimaniia," *Bolshevik* nos. 19–20 (1927): 132–33.

86. *Biulleten' Narkomzdrava* no. 5 (1927): 56–58.

87. A. V. Mol'kov had been director of the prerevolutionary Commission on Sani-

tary Education of the Pirogov Society. In 1919 he was appointed director of the newly created State Museum of Social Hygiene that inherited the commission's exhibit.

88. A. V. Mol'kov, "Alkogolizm kak problema izucheniia," *Gigiena i epidemiologiia* nos. 7-8 (1926): 40–42.

89. "Alkogolizm," *Bol'shaia Meditsinskaia Entsiklopediia* (Moscow, 1928), 404.

90. Mol'kov, "Alkogolizm," 43, n. 1.

91. In 1922 empirical sociology ceased when the department of sociology in Leningrad was closed and some leading sociologists were exiled. See, for example, Elizabeth Ann Weinburg, *The Development of Sociology in the Soviet Union* (London, 1974).

92. RGAE f. 1562, op. 1, d. 490; op. 15, d. 607; op. 15, d. 594; f. 7971, op. 2, d. 662.

93. Questionnaire reproduced in A. V. Mol'kov, ed., *Alkogolizm kak nauchnaia i bytovaia problema* (Moscow-Leningrad, 1928), 263–67.

94. I. D. Strashun, "Bor'ba s alkogolizmom," in Mol'kov, *Alkogolizm kak nauchnaia,* 141–42.

95. GISG studies on alcoholism include N. I. Chuchelov, "Opyt izucheniia alkogolizma v fabrichno-zavodskom raione sredi muzhskoi molodezhi," *Sotsial'naia gigiena* no. 10 (1927): 38; and E. I. Deichman, "Opyt izucheniia alkogolizma sredi shkol'nikov," *Sotsial'naia gigiena* no. 10 (1927): 23–35.

96. Mol'kov, *Alkogolizm kak nauchnaia,* 260.

97. *Kul'tura i byt* no. 4 (May 1930): 18.

98. B. Didrikhson, "Voprosy alkogolizma v nauchnoi i populiarnoi meditsinskoi literature," *Zdravookhranenie* no. 1 (1928): 76–86.

99. For a fuller treatment of the conflict between social hygiene and psychiatry, see Susan Gross Solomon, "David and Goliath in Soviet Public Health: The Rivalry of Social Hygenists and Psychiatrists for Authority Over the *Bytovoi* Alcoholic," *Soviet Studies* 12, no. 2 (April 1989): 254–73.

100. Mol'kov, *Alkogolizm kak nauchnaia,* 2–9.

101. *Voprosy zdravookhranenii* no. 9 (1928): 7–9; see also A. S. Sholomovich, *Kak my boremsia s alkogolizmom* (Moscow, 1926).

102. See, for example, *Sotsial'naia gigiena* no. 10 (1927): 23–35; *Zdravookhranenie* no. 1 (1928): 76–86; *Voprosy zdravookhranenii* no. 9 (1928): 7–9, no. 10 (1928): 20–22; *Moskovskii meditsinskii zhurnal* no. 7 (1928): 15–25; and *Voprosy narkologii* no. 2 (1929): 104–8.

103. Solomon, "David and Goliath," 267.

104. Vengrova and Shilinis, *Sotsial'naia gigiena,* 170.

105. GARF, f. 9636, op. 5, d. 80, ll. 29–30.

106. *Moskovskii meditsinskii zhurnal* no. 2 (1928): 73–82.

107. See I. I. Rozenblum, "Kharakteristika alkogolizma rabochikh," *Sotsialisticheskoe zdravookhranenie* no. 7 (1928): 68–86; and Brukhanskii, "Opyt," 15–26.

108. Karl Marx and Friedrich Engels, *Works* (Moscow, 1962), 2:141.

109. The use of voluntary societies to mobilize the population for the public good was common throughout Europe at the turn of the century. In Great Britain, for

example, voluntary societies mushroomed: National League for Physical Education (1905), Food Education Society (1908), National League for Health and Child Welfare (1905), Eugenics Education Society (1908), and the like. Like their Soviet counterparts, these also had a political agenda.

110. For discussion of voluntary societies, see Dan Peris, *Storming the Heavens: The Soviet League of the Militant Godless* (Ithaca, 1998), 62–68.

111. GARF, f. 5465, op. 10, d. 189.

112. *Izvestiia,* February 18, 1928, 4.

113. Ibid.; Iu. Larin, *Alkogolizm promyshlennykh rabochikh i bor'ba s nim* (Moscow, 1929), 32–37.

114. The Right Opposition, sometimes called Right Deviation, represents a moderate strand of Bolshevism that urged moderation and cooperation with the peasantry to achieve socialism slowly. Until early 1928, the platform of the Right coincided with the policies of the Soviet government and the Politburo. This changed, however, toward the end of the 1920s, as Stalin increasingly secured control over the party apparatus. Having supported Bukharin and the Right's position on the cautious implementation of the NEP, Stalin in 1928 abruptly reversed his position and adopted the rapid industrialization program of the Left. Bukharin and the Right Opposition were subsequently denounced at the Central Committee plenum in January 1929. Bukharin ultimately was purged in 1936 and shot for crimes he could not have committed. For discussion of Bukharin and the Right Opposition, see Stephen Cohen, *Bukharin and the Bolshevik Revolution: A Political Biography 1888–1938* (Oxford, 1971), 270–337.

115. *Izvestiia,* February 18, 1928, 4; Larin, *Alkogolizm,* 32–37.

116. For an excellent discussion of the role of intellectuals in socialist societies, see Ivan Szelenyi, "The Intelligentsia in the Class Structure of State-Socialist Societies," *American Journal of Sociology* 88, supplement (1982): 287–326.

117. *Za novyi byt* nos. 7–8 (1928): 22.

118. GARF, f. 5467, op. 11, d. 179, l. 1.

119. Iu. Larin, *Novye zakony protiv alkogolizma* (Moscow, 1929), 3–7.

120. Deichman, *Alkogolizm,* 175–90.

121. Ibid.; Larin, *Novye zakony,* 36–41; GARF, f. 5467, op. 14, d. 108, l. 17.

122. GARF, f. 374, op. 15, d. 1291 (1), l. 22; f. 5467, op. 11, d. 179, l. 2.

123. Deichman, *Alkogolizm,* 185–90; Larin, *Alkogolizm,* 135–36.

124. *Put' k zdrov'iu* no. 3 (1929): 7.

125. GARF, f. 5467, op. 14, d. 108, l. 17; Deichman, *Alkogolizm,* 165–66.

126. RGAE, f. 733, op. 1, d. 144, ll. 1–9; op. 8, d. 69, l. 152; GATO, f. R-279, op. 1, d. 127, ll. 29–37.

127. Larin, *Alkogolizm,* 60–64.

128. RGAE, f. 733, op. 1, d. 144, l. 1.

129. RGAE, f. 733, op. 1, d. 144, ll. 1–9; op. 8, d. 69, l. 152; op. 8, d. 73, l. 27.

130. GARF, f. 374, op. 15, d. 1291(1), l. 11. See also *Statistika truda* nos. 5–6 (1929): 22–23.

131. RGAE, f. 733, op. 1, d. 144, ll. 1–9; op. 8, d. 69, l. 152.

132. *Pis'ma I. V. Stalina V. M. Molotovu, 1925–1936 gg.* (Moscow 1995), 209–10.

133. RGAE, f. 733, op. 8, d. 73, l. 24.

134. In 1932–33 an estimated seven million Ukrainian peasants starved to death in a famine that resulted from the excesses of collectivization and forced grain collections. Some of this grain went into alcohol production at precisely the time of the famine. See, for example, *Holod 1932–33 rokiv na Ukraini: Ochyma istorykiv, movoij dokumentiv* (Kyiv, 1990). See also Robert Conquest, *The Harvest of Sorrow: Soviet Collectivization and the Terror-Famine* (Edmonton, 1986).

135. Evginii Kruchina, *Vodka: Putevoditel* (Moscow, 2003), 162.

136. Kruchina, *Vodka*, 162.

137. Larin, *Alkogolizm*, 135–36; *Za novyi byt* nos. 1–2 (January 1929): 13.

138. RGAE, f. 1562, op. 15, d. 594, 595, 607, 675; op. 31, d. 343, 344, 461.

139. See, for example, *Metallistik* no. 2 (November 1928): 12–13.

140. Deichman, *Alkogolizm*, 165–66; Larin, *Alkogolizm*, 139–41; N. Tiapugin, *Narodnye zabliuzhdeniia i nauchnaia pravda ob alkogole* (Moscow, 1926), 105; *Trezvost' i kul'tura* no. 5 (1928): 1; no. 1 (1929): 13; no. 2 (1929): 9.

141. In a study on Komsomol activities, historian A. Bukharev concludes that antialcohol activities sponsored by the Komsomol were episodic actions taken by individual cells. See A. Bukharev, "Komsomol v bor'be za novyi byt (1926–1932 gg.)," in *Bor'ba partii za sotsialisticheskii byt (1921–1937 gg.): Sbornik nauchnykh trudov* (Volgograd, 1985), 82.

142. TsK LKSM-U, f. 7, op. 1, d. 426, l. 32; op. 12, d. 208, ll. 1–5.

143. Ibid.

144. B. F. Didrikhson, *P'ianku-'k stenke'* (Leningrad, 1929), 10.

145. Female membership estimates are based on the percentage of articles and testimonies by women in all issues of *Trezvost' i kul'tura* from 1928 to 1930 and *Kul'tura i byt* from 1930 to 1933, as well as the limited information on local membership rolls.

146. Larin, *Alkogolizm*, 135–36; N. A. Semashko, *Na bor'bu s p'ianstvom* (Moscow, 1926), 22; *Bor'ba s alkogolizmom v SSSR*, 72–75; *Rabotnitsa* no. 34 (September 1929): 19; *Rabotnitsa i krest'ianka* no. 15 (July 1928): 2; *Za novyi byt* nos. 1–2 (January 1929): 13.

147. See, for example, Lynn Abrams, *Workers' Culture in Imperial Germany: Leisure and Recreation in the Rhineland and Westphali* (New York, 1992); and Prestwich, *Drink and the Politics of Social Reform.*

148. See, for example, *Krasnyi treugol'nik* 8 (April 1929): 2; *Rabotnitsa i krest'ianka* no. 13 (June 1929): 6; and *Za novyi byt* nos. 1–2 (January 1929): 17–18.

149. Larin, *Alkogolizm*, 110.

150. Deichman, *Alkogolizm*, 174.

151. *Trezvost' i kul'tura* no. 12 (1929): 5; nos. 13–14 (1929): 15.

152. Larin, *Alkogolizm*, 33–34.

153. Ibid., 37, 110.

154. Ibid., 34–37. See also *Trezvost' i kul'tura* no. 5 (1929): 3; no. 8 (1929): 2; no. 12 (1929): 7.

155. Sheverdin, "Iz opyta bor'by protiv p'ianstva i alkogolizma," 112.

156. Gosudarstvennyi Arkhiv Saratovskoi Oblasti (State Archive of Saratov Oblast, GASO), f. 461, op. 2, d. 130, ll. 2–30.

157. I could find no documents in any archives in Tomsk relating to OBSA. This suggests that no OBSA cells existed in Tomsk.

158. T. P. Korzhikina, "Bor'ba s alkogolizmom v 1920-e-nachale 1930-x gg.," *Voprosy istorii* no. 9 (1985): 24–25.

159. RGAE, f. 8043, op. 11, d. 74, ll. 138–46. For information on food rationing in the First Five-Year Plan, see E. A. Osokina, *Ierarkhiia potrebleniia: O zhizni liudei v usloviakh stalinskogo snabzheniia, 1928–1935 gg.* (Moscow, 1993).

160. RGAE, f. 7622, op. 1, d. 1948, l. 38.

CHAPTER 5: DEMON VODKA

1. Peter Kenez, *The Birth of the Propaganda State: Soviet Methods of Mass Mobilization, 1917–1929* (Cambridge, 1985).

2. A few notable exceptions include Victoria Bonnell, *Iconography of Power: Soviet Political Posters under Lenin and Stalin* (Berkeley, 1997); Michaels, *Curative Powers;* and Peris, *Storming the Heavens.*

3. GARF, f. 9636, op. 1, d. 7, l. 1; op. 8, ll. 13–23; *Administrativnyi vestnik* no. 8 (1928): 57–58.

4. *Kul'turnaia revoliutsiia,* November 25, 1928, 40–42; *Trezvost' i kul'tura* no. 1 (1930): 17–19.

5. Larin, *Alkogolizm,* 80.

6. Ibid., 110.

7. See Mark von Hagen, *Soldiers in the Proletarian Dictatorship: The Red Army and the Soviet Socialist State* (Ithaca, 1990), 331–32.

8. *Trezvost' i kul'tura* no. 1 (1928): 4. A Ukrainian counterpart, *Za trezvisti,* was published beginning in 1929.

9. *Trezvost' i kul'tura* no. 12 (1929): 5; nos. 13–14 (1929): 15.

10. See, for example, S. D. Dreiden, *Za vashe zdrovie: Antialkogol'naia krestomatiia* (Leningrad, 1929); and A. S. Berliand, *Alkogolizm i bor'ba s nim* (Moscow, 1929).

11. For discussion of Manichean rhetoric in the 1930s, see Jeffery Brooks, *Thank You Comrade Stalin! Soviet Public Culture from Revolution to Cold War* (Newark, 2000), 139–49.

12. For a discussion of the status politics of temperance, see Joseph Gusfield, *Symbolic Crusade: Status Politics and the American Temperance Movement* (Urbana, 1963).

13. Quoted in A. L. Mendel'son, *Nervno-psikhicheskaia gigiena i profilaktika* (Leningrad, 1927), 202.

14. See N. A. Dobroliubov, *Sobranie sochinenii,* vol. 5 (Moscow, 1962), for essays "Temnoe tsarstvo" and "Luch sveta v temnom tsarstve."

15. D. Bednyi, "Chortova Sklianitsa i Lipetskii P'ianitsa," GARF, f. 9636, op. 5, d. 80, l. 17.

16. Kadets, or Constitutional Democrats, were a nonrevolutionary liberal political party that opposed the socialist parties prior to 1917, calling instead for a constitutional monarchy.

17. From the journal *Begemot* (1924), cited in Tiapugin, *Narodnye zabluzhdeniia*, 88.

18. Bukharin and Preobrazhenskii, *ABC of Communism*, 76–77.

19. See Gusfield, *Symbolic Crusade*, 87–110.

20. RTsKhIDNI, f. 17, op. 85, d. 307, l. 10.

21. Iu. Larin, *Alkogolizm promyshlennykh rabochikh i bor'ba s nim* (Moscow, 1929), 19–20.

22. Deichman, *Alcoholism*, 127.

23. "Instruktsiia po primeneniiu prinuditel'nogo lecheniia alkogolikov, predstavliaiushchikh sotsial'nuiu opasnost'," reprinted in Mol'kov, *Alkogolizm kak nauchnaia*, 262–63.

24. See, for example, A. L. Oprishchenko, *Istoriografiia sotsialisticheskogo sorevnovaniia rabochego klassa SSSR* (Kharkov, 1975), 62–71; and I. N. Mikhailovskii, *Komsomol ukrainy v bor'be za postroenie sotsializma v SSSR (1925–1937 gg.)* (Lvov, 1966), 82.

25. See, for example, Hiroaki Kuromiya, *Stalin's Industrial Revolution: Politics and Workers, 1928-1932* (Cambridge, 1988), 128–35, 235–38; and *Proizvodstvennyi zhurnal* no. 14 (1929): 8.

26. "P'iushchii—vrag sotsialisticheskogo stroitel'stva," *Kul'tura i byt* no. 9 (June 1930): 18.

27. *Kul'tura i byt* no. 1 (April 1930): 16.

28. This was according to a law against absenteeism. See *Sobranie zakonov i rasporiazhenii raboche-krest'ianskogo pravitel'stva RSFSR* no. 78, art. 475.

29. *Kul'tura i byt* no. 5 (May 1930): 17.

30. Tsentralnii Derzhavnii Arkhiv Zhovtnevoi Revoliutsii, Vyshchykh Organov Derzhavnoi Vlady i Organiv Derzhavnogo Upravlinni Ukrainskoi RSR (Central State Archive of the October Revolution, Highest Organs of State Government and Organs of State Administration of the Ukrainian RSR, TsDAZhR URSR), f. 342, op. 3 d. 3080, l. 50; TsK LKSM U, f. 7, op. 71, d. 668, ll. 13–14; RTsKhIDNI, f. 17, op. 7, d. 160, l. 6.

31. See, for example, T. H. Rigby, *Communist Party Membership in the USSR, 1917–1967* (Princeton, 1968), 121–25, 166–67.

32. Lewis Siegelbaum, *Soviet State and Society between Revolutions, 1918–1929* (Cambridge, 1992), 181.

33. Ibid., 181–82.

34. RTsKhIDNI, f. 17, op. 26, d. 883, ll. 16, 32–35; d. 871, ll. 40–41.

35. RTsKhIDNI, f. 17, op. 26, d. 885, l. 11.

36. RTsKhIDNI, f. 17, op. 25, d. 259, l. 178.

37. There are at least fifty-six such cases in Moscow in 1929 alone. See RTsKhIDNI, f. 17, op. 26, d. 884, ll. 1–38.

38. GARF, f. 5469, op. 13, d. 419, ll. 1–5.

39. GARF, f. 9636, op. 5, d. 80, l. 14.

40. GARF, f. 9636, op. 5, d. 80, l. 47.

41. See Elizabeth Wood, "The Trial of Lenin: Legitimizing the Revolution through Political Theater, 1920–23," *Russian Review* 61 (April 2002): 235–48. For broader studies of the *agitsudy* as propagandistic theater, see Julie A. Cassidy, *The Enemy on Trial: Early Soviet Courts on Stage and Screen* (DeKalb, 2000), esp. ch. 3.

42. Wood, "Trial of Lenin," 236.

43. Ibid., 237.

44. Julie A. Cassidy, "Alcohol Is Our Enemy! Soviet Temperance Melodrama of the 1920s," in *Imitations of Life: Two Centuries of Melodrama in Russia,* ed. Louise McReynolds and Joan Neuberger, 160 (Durham, 2002).

45. Boris Sigal was one of the genre's most prolific authors, writing thirteen such dramas dealing with various questions of *byt*. Boris Sigal, *Sud nad p'ianitsei* (Leningrad, 1929).

46. Sigal, *Sud nad p'ianitsei,* 5.

47. Cassidy, "Alcohol Is Our Enemy," 160.

48. For an interesting discussion of the merging of agitational plays with the shock-worker movement, see Lynn Mally, *Revolutionary Acts: Amateur Theater and the Soviet State, 1917–1938* (Ithaca, 2000), esp. ch. 5.

49. For the plays and their *anketi,* see GARF f. 9639, op. 5, d. 3, 4, 10, 11, 24, 32, 45, 63, 80, 91.

50. GARF, f. 9635, op. 5, d. 80.

51. *Rabotnitsa i krest'ianka* no. 24 (December 1928): 27.

52. *Zorkii glaz,* March 8, 1929, 1.

53. See Kowalski, "Making Crime and Sex Soviet."

54. Here I am building on ideas put forth by Lars T. Lih, "Melodrama and the Myth of the Soviet Union," in McReynolds and Neuberger, *Imitations of Life,* 178–207.

55. Lih, "Melodrama," 178–207.

56. Mikhail Verestinskyi, *Pautina* (Moscow, 1927), 48.

57. Ibid., 9.

58. GARF f. 9639, op. 5 d. 3, 4, 10, 11, 24, 45, 80.

59. TsDAVOVTU f. 342, op. 3, d. 3096, ll. 1–15; GARF f. 9636, op. 5, d. 10, 11.

60. GARF f. 9639, op. 5 d. 3, 4, 10, 11, 24, 32. Judging from *anketi* and various other documents, hundreds of workers attended each play.

61. Lih, "Melodrama," 203.

62. Partiinyi Archiv Instytutu Istorii Partii pry Tsentralnomu Komiteti Komunisty-chnoi Partii Ukrainy (Party Archive of the Institute of the History of the Central Committee of the Ukrainian Communist Party, PA KPU), f. 1, op. 20, d. 2828, l. 1.

63. *Smychka* was probably seen by thousands of workers. GARF. f. 9636, op. 5, d. 26.

Chapter 6: Liquid Assets

1. See, for example, John Hatch, "Labor Conflict in Moscow, 1921–1925," in *Russia in the Era of NEP: Explorations in Soviet Society and Culture,* ed. Sheila Fitzpatrick, Alexander Rabinowitch, and Richard Stites, 58–71 (Bloomington, 1991); Douglas R.

Weiner, "'Razmychka?' Urban Unemployment and Peasant In-migration as Sources of Social Conflict," in ibid., 144–55; Donald Filtzer, *Soviet Workers and Stalinist Industrialization* (New York, 1986), 25–33; and Chase, *Workers,* 136–72.

2. Quoted in E. H. Carr, *Socialism in One Country, 1924–1926* (London, 1973), 1:390.

3. Wendy Goldman, *Women at the Gates: Gender and Industry in Stalin's Russia* (New York, 2002), 14–15.

4. K. I. Suvorov, *Istoricheskii opyt KPSS po likvidatsii bezrabotnitsy (1917–1930 gg.)* (Moscow, 1968), 82–83.

5. Because women did not factor significantly in the industries under study, the following discussion focuses primarily on male workers.

6. See, for example, Alexander Erlich, *The Soviet Industrialization Debate, 1924–1928* (Cambridge, 1960); Stephen Cohen, *Bukharin and the Bolshevik Revolution: A Political Biography, 1888–1938* (Oxford, 1971); Lewin, *Making of the Soviet System;* Moshe Lewin, *Russian Peasants and Soviet Power: A Study of Collectivization* (New York, 1968); and Robert Tucker, ed., *Stalinism: Essays in Historical Interpretation* (New York, 1977).

7. For discussion on social mobility and the formation of a technical intelligentsia in 1928–32, see K. E. Bailes, *Technology and Society under Lenin and Stalin: Origins of the Soviet Technical Intelligentsia, 1917–41* (Bloomington, 1978); and Sheila Fitzpatrick, "Stalin and the Making of a New Elite, 1928–39," *Slavic Review* (September 1979): 377–402.

8. See, for example, Chase, *Workers,* 103–35; Filtzer, *Soviet Workers;* Gabor T. Rittersporn, "From Working Class to Urban Laboring Mass: On Politics and Social Categories in the Formative Years of the Soviet System," in *Making Workers Soviet: Power, Class, and Identity,* ed. Lewis Siegelbaum and Ronald Suny, 253–73 (Ithaca, 1994); and William Rosenberg and Lewis Siegelbaum, eds., *Social Dimensions of Soviet Industrialization* (Bloomington, 1993). On industrial policy and social conflicts, see David Shearer, "The Language and Politics of Socialist Rationalization," *Cahiers du Monde russe et sovietique* 32, no. 4 (October–December 1991): 581–608.

9. Vladimir Andrle, *Workers in Stalin's Russia* (New York, 1988), 32.

10. Ibid., 33.

11. For discussion of the transformation of the working class, see Lewin, *Making of the Soviet System,* 218–57.

12. Filtzer, *Soviet Workers,* 45.

13. Ibid., 49.

14. Z. G. Likholobova, *Rabochie Donbassa v period sotsialisticheskoi rekonstruktsii narodnogo khoziaistva (1926–1937 gg.)* (Kiev, 1974), 160; RTsKhIDNI, f. 17, op. 26, d. 31, ll. 55–63.

15. *Statistika truda* nos. 2–3 (1929): 18. See also Kenneth M. Straus, *Factory and Community in Stalin's Russia: The Making of an Industrial Working Class* (Pittsburgh, 1997), 198–205; and Filtzer, *Soviet Workers,* 57–60.

16. Straus, *Factory and Community,* 69.

17. See, for example, Sheila Fitzpatrick, "The Bolsheviks' Dilemma: Class, Culture, and Politics in Early Soviet Years," *Slavic Review* 47, no. 4 (1988): 599–613.

18. GARF, f. 5469, op. 15, d. 4, l. 45.

19. Stories and articles centered on this image are too numerous to list here. See, for example, *Voprosy truda* no. 7 (1929): 95–99; *Za industrialisatsiiu,* August 14, 1930, 3; February 19, 1931, 2; *Pravda,* January 17, 1929, 2, 3; February 5, 1929, 1.

20. *Molodaia gvardiia* no. 14 (1929): 58–68; no. 16 (1920): 53; *Pravda,* April 9, 1929, 1. See also Kuromiya, *Stalin's Industrial Revolution,* 88–100.

21. This image was continually repeated in the press, the sources too numerous to list. See, for example, *Predpriiatie* no. 4 (1928): 11–13; no. 1 (1929): 23–25; *Voprosy profdvizheniia* no. 9 (1933): 48; *Pravda,* January 3, 1929, 5; February 5, 1929, 5; February 7, 1929, 2.

22. *Voprosy truda* nos. 3–4 (1929): 9–13; no. 7 (1929): 95–99; *Za industrializatsiiu,* August 14, 1930, 3; September 28, 1932, 3; RTsKhIDNI, f. 17, op. 85, d. 347, ll. 1–5.

23. James C. Scott, *Domination and the Arts of Resistance: Hidden Transcripts* (New Haven, 1990), 27.

24. Moskovskii Oblastnoi Tsentr Dokumentatsii Noveishei Istorii (Moscow Oblast Center for the Documentation of Recent History, MOTsDNI), f. 635, op. 1, d. 69, l. 16.

25. GARF, f. 5451, op. 13, d. 76, ll. 36, 66.

26. Kuromiya, "Crisis of Proletarian Identity," 280–97.

27. GARF, f. 518, op. 1, d. 85a, ll. 142–43.

28. See Phillips, *Bolsheviks and the Bottle,* ch. 6.

29. Much time and debate went into formulating the wording of the questionnaires and how the surveys would be conducted. See RGAE, f. 1562, op. 1, d. 490, ll. 1–194.

30. RGAE, f. 1562, op. 15, d. 607; d. 594.

31. Ibid. For per capita consumption of all alcoholic drinks by village and city, see RGAE, f. 7971, op. 2, d. 662.

32. GARF, f. 5515, op. 20, d. 7, l. 43.

33. GARF, f. 5515, op. 20, d. 28b, l. 10.

34. GARF, f. 5469, op. 13, d. 419, l. 31.

35. RTsKhIDNI, f. 17, op. 26, d. 873, l. 89; d. 878, l. 6; d. 860, l. 33.

36. RTsKhIDNI, f. 17, op, 26, d. 873, l. 89; d. 878, l. 6; d. 860, l. 33; GARF, f. 5515, op. 20, d. 7, ll. 19–20.

37. GARF, f. 5469, op. 13, d. 419, l. 31; f. 5515, op. 20, d. 7, ll. 19–20, 27; f. 374, op. 15, d. 58 (2), ll. 83–84; RTsKhIDNI, f. 17, op. 85, d. 307, ll. 85–86.

38. PA KPU, f. 1, op. 20, d. 2828, l. 55.

39. PA KPU, f. 1, op. 20, d. 2828, l. 1.

40. *Komsomol'skaia pravda,* February 27, 1927, 3.

41. *Rabochii krai,* March 11, 1927, 7.

42. *Komsomol'skaia pravda,* February 27, 1927, 3.

43. GARF, f. 5515, op. 20, d. 7, ll. 19–20.

44. GASO, f. 616, op. 1, d. 222, l. 3.

45. *Golos tekstilei,* May 19, 1928, 1.

46. GARF, f. 5469, op. 14, d. 313, l. 17; f. 5475, op. 13, d. 160, l. 62.

47. For discussion of the symbolic nature of a shared drink in Western working-class culture, see Marianna Adler, "From Symbolic Exchange to Commodity Consumption: Anthropological Notes on Drinking as a Symbolic Practice," in Barrows and Room, *Drinking Behavior,* 376–98; Thomas Brennan, "Social Drinking in Old Regime Paris," in ibid., 61–86; and Brian Harrison, *Drink and the Victorians* (Pittsburgh, 1971), ch. 2.

48. Scott, *Domination,* 45.

49. GARF, f. 5515, op. 20, d. 7, l. 43; f. 5469, op. 13, d. 419, l. 31; GASO, f. 616, op. 1, d. 226, l. 7; Gosudarstvennyi Arkhiv Kharkovskoi Oblasti (State Archive of Kharkov Oblast, GAKhO), f. 1010, op. 1, d. 1862, l. 2; RTsKhIDNI, f. 17, op. 26, d. 885, l. 9. For further discussion on divisions between skilled and unskilled workers in Moscow, see Hoffmann, *Peasant Metropolis,* 108–15.

50. GARF, f. 7952, op. 3, d. 214, l. 1.

51. MOTsDNI, f. 432, op. 1, d. 178, l. 174.

52. V. V. Kolotov, *Nikolai Alekseevich Voznesenskii* (Moscow, 1974), 101–7.

53. One such specialization was semiartisanal labor done on universal machines. See David Shearer, "Rationalization and Reconstruction in the Soviet Machine Building Industry, 1926–1934" (Ph.D. diss., University of Pennsylvania, 1988), 232–33.

54. Hoffmann, *Peasant Metropolis,* 113.

55. GARF, f. 7952, op. 3, d. 214, l. 1.

56. In 1935 Alexei Stakhanov, a Donbass coal miner, set a record by producing fourteen times more coal than the norm. The regime immediately initiated a movement—partially faked—in which selected "Stakhanovite" workers far outnumbered industry norms and were mythologized in the press for doing so. For details of the various labor movements, see, for example, Andrle, *Workers,* 105–80; Chase, *Workers,* 214–92; Hiroaki Kuromyia, *Stalin's Industrial Revolution: Politics and Workers* (Cambridge, 1988), 115–27; and Lewis Siegelbaum, *Stakhanovism and the Politics of Productivity in the USSR, 1935–1941* (New York, 1988), 16–98.

57. James C. Scott, *Weapons of the Weak: Everyday Forms of Peasant Resistance* (New Haven, 1985), xvi.

58. Michel Foucault, *The History of Sexuality,* vol. 1, *An Introduction* (New York, 1978), 95. Scott makes the point that the reverse is just as plausible, that "power is never in a position of exteriority in relation to resistance." See Scott, *Domination,* 111 n. 5.

59. For very thoughtful discussion of resistance in Russian and Soviet history, see Lynne Viola, "Popular Resistance in the Stalinist 1930s: Soliloquy of a Devil's Advocate," *Kritika* 1, no. 1 (Winter 2000): 45–71.

60. For discussion of worker iconography, see Victoria Bonnell, "The Iconography of the Worker in Soviet Political Art," in Siegelbaum and Suny, *Making Workers Soviet,* 341–75.

61. Scott, *Domination,* 213.

62. Although foremen at this time appeared to be a law unto themselves, they in fact were restrained by party cells and trade union committees. One of the functions of these two bodies was to head off trouble between workers and line supervisors by inviting and investigating complaints. There were also numerous other channels through which grievances could be aired. See *Trud,* January 14, 1928, 2.

63. GARF, f. 374, op. 15, d. 58 (II), l. 83.

64. GARF, f. 5515, op. 20, d. 7, l. 54.

65. Ibid.

66. *Khvostizm* meant hanging on to the tail of the workers' movement rather than leading it.

67. For discussion of village networks adapted or re-created in Moscow, see Hoffmann, *Peasant Metropolis,* 86–91, 107–13

68. Scott, *Domination,* 114.

69. RGAE, f. 1562, op. 31, d. 461, ll. 31–181; d. 343, ll. 38–44; ll. 225–36; d. 344, l. 33; RTsKhIDNI, f. 17, op. 26, d. 864, l. 83; op. 10, d. 139, ll. 1–5; PA KPU, f. 1, op. 20, d. 2828, l. 52; GARF, f. 5515, op. 20. d. 7, ll. 27, 66, 117; f. 5469, op. 13, d. 419, l. 120; GASO, f. 1295, op. 1, d. 33, l. 77.

70. GARF, f. 5515, op. 20 d. 7, l. 51.

71. GARF, f. 5515, op. 20 d. 7, l. 54.

72. *Kharkovskyi proletarii,* October 2, 1928, 8.

73. See Phillips, *Bolsheviks and the Bottle,* 84–86.

74. For discussion of taverns as centers of sociability and organizing locales among prerevolutionary printers, see Steinberg, *Moral Communities,* 128, 129, 131, 153.

75. *Stroitel'* no. 6 (1925): 41–44. See also G. B. Getsov, *Zhenshchina, na bor'bu s alkogolizmom!* (Moscow, 1929), 43.

76. *Moskovskii proletarii,* February 28, 1928, 14–15.

77. *Kharkovskyi proletarii,* October 2, 1928, 8.

78. Tsentralnyi Gosudarstvennyi Arkhiv Oktiabrskoi Revoliutsii i Sotsialistichesko-go Stroitelstva g. Moskvy (Central State Archive of the October Revolution and Socialist Construction of the City of Moscow, TsGAORSSgM), f. 168, op. 3, d. 7, l. 29; GARF f. 5515, op. 15, d. 410, l. 55.

79. MOTsDNI, f. 432, op. 1, d. 176, l. 137. For discussion of settlement patterns in Moscow, see Hoffmann, *Peasant Metropolis,* 128–35.

80. *Trud,* September 11, 1931, 3.

81. James Scott argues that the hidden transcript will be uninhibited when two conditions are met: when there is a sequestered social site far from the control or surveillance of the dominant and when the social milieu is composed of those who share similar experiences of domination. See Scott, *Domination,* 120.

82. Scott, *Domination,* 122. For discussion of taverns as a place for secret assembly and antihegemonic discourse, see E. P. Thompson, *The Making of the English Working Class* (New York, 1963).

83. *Povolzhskaia Pravda,* July 24, 1928, 6.

84. *Saratovskie izvestiia,* January 28, 1928, 3; *Povolzhskaia Pravda,* July 24, 1928, 6; *Trezvost' i kul'tura* no. 1 (July 1928): 11; *Krasnyi treugol'nik,* December 21, 1929, 4. See also Phillips, *Bolsheviks and the Bottle,* 88–91; and John Hatch, "Hangouts and Hangovers: Workers' Clubs during NEP," unpublished paper for the Workshop on Soviet Popular Culture.

85. *Trezvost' i kul'tura* no. 1 (July 1928): 11.

86. *Krasnyi treugol'nik,* December 21, 1929, 4.

87. *Kharkovskyi proletarii,* July 14, 1929, 6.

88. Ibid., 7.

Chapter 7: Giddy with Success

1. Tsentralnyi Gosudarstvennyi Arkhiv RSFSR (Central State Archive of the RSFSR, TsGA), f. 482, op. 24, d. 3, ll. 301–22.

2. I could find no evidence of social hygienists conducting research in any other institutional setting after 1930. See also T. S. Prot'ko, *V bor'be za trezvost': Stranitsy istorii* (Minsk, 1988), 126–28.

3. *Trezvost' i kul'tura* no. 1 (1930): 4.

4. Ibid.

5. Larin, *Alkogolizm,* 35.

6. *Kul'tura i byt* no. 8 (1930): 4.

7. Ibid., no. 9 (1930): 19.

8. Ibid., no. 1 (1989): 19. In 1989 the journal was revived as part of Gorbachev's anti-alcohol campaign.

9. No mention of any of these measures, which were central to OBSA's initial platform, appeared in the pages of *Kul'tura i byt.*

10. *Pis'ma I. V. Stalina,* 209–10.

11. *Kul'tura i byt* no. 1 (1930): 4.

12. Ibid., no. 20 (1930): 15

13. Ibid., no. 7 (1930): 18.

14. Examination of four national, one republican, and nine regional newspapers and journals for the years 1931–34 turned up no mention of OBSA or alcoholism: *Administrativnyi vestnik, Biulleten' narodnogo komissariata zdravookhraneniia, Izvestiia, Pravda, Komsomolets' Ukraini, Khar'kovskaia pravda, Khar'kovskii proletarii, Molodoi bol'shevik, Molodoi Leninets, Moskovskii proletarii, Povolzhskaia pravda, Proletarii, Rabochaia Moskva, Saratovskie izvestiia, Serp i molot.*

15. *KPSS v rezoliutsiiakh i resheniiakh s"ezdov, konferentsii i plenumov TsK* (Moscow, 1983), 2:92.

16. V. I. Lenin, *Polnoe sobranie sochinenii* (Moscow, 1958–65), 43:326.

17. Ibid., 45:120.

18. I. V. Stalin, *Sochineniia* (Moscow, 1946–51), 9:192.

19. *Piatnadtsatyi s"ezd VKP(b): Stenograficheskii otchet* (Moscow, 1961), 1:67

20. RGAE, f. 733, op. 1, d. 144, ll. 23–30; d. 200, l. 7; op. 8, d. 1166, ll. 146–52.

21. White, *Russia Goes Dry*, 27.

22. *Kniga o vkusnoi i zdorovoi pishche* (Moscow, 1936), 79–80.

23. See Phillips, *Bolsheviks and the Bottle*, 143.

24. RGAE, f. 1562, op. 15, d. 607; d. 594.

25. GARF, f. 374, op. 15, d. 1291(1), l. 11; RGAE, f. 733, op. 8, d. 73, l.24. See also *Statistika truda* nos. 5–6 (1929): 22–23.

26. See Hoffmann, *Stalinist Values*, 37.

27. Clark, *Petersburg*, 297.

28. Elena Osokina, *Our Daily Bread: Socialist Distribution and the Art of Survival in Stalin's Russia, 1927–1941* (New York, 1999).

29. I. V. Stalin, "Otchetnyi doklad XVII s"ezdu partii o rabote TsK VKP(b)" (January 26, 1934), in *Sochineniia* (Moscow, 1946–52), 13:308–9.

30. "Alkogolizm," *Bol'shaia Sovetskaia Entsiklopediia*, 2–e izd. T.2 (Moscow, 1950), 119.

31. Kruchina, *Vodka*, 162.

32. Takala, *Veselie Rusi*, 215–16.

33. Ibid., 250–51.

34. For an excellent history of Gorbachev's temperance campaign, see White, *Russia Goes Dry*.

35. Kruchina, *Vodka*, 182.

36. Ibid.

37. Ibid., 183.

38. Ibid., 56.

39. Ibid., 58.

SELECT BIBLIOGRAPHY

PRIMARY SOURCES

Archival Sources

Central Russian Archives

Gosudarstvennyi Arkhiv Rossiiskoi Federatsii (State Archive of the Russian Federation, GARF)

f. 374 Narodnyi komissariat raboche-krest'ianskoi inspektsii

f. 382 Narkomat truda RSFSR

f. 393 NKVD

f. 5451 Vsesoiuznyi tsentral'nyi sovet profsoiuzov

f. 5452 TsK soiuza gornorabochikh

f. 5453 TsK soiuza kozhevnikov

f. 5466 TsK soiuza sel'skhoziaistvennykh i lesnykh rabochikh

f. 5467 TsK soiuza derevoobdeloinikov

f. 5469 TsK soiuza rabochikh metallistov

f. 5475 TsK soiuza stroitelei

f. 5515 Narkomat truda

f. 5525 TsK soiuza pechatnikov

f. 6983 Narkomzdrav

f. 7676 TsK soiuza rabochikh obshchego mashinostroeniia

f. 7952 Gosudarstvennoe izdatel'stvo

f. 9636 Institut sanitarnoi kul'tury

Rossiiskii Gosudarstvennyi Arkhiv Ekonomiki (Russian State Archive of the Economy, RGAE)

f. 733 Tsentral'noe pravlenie gosudarstvennoi spirtovoi monopolii TsUGProma VSNKh SSSR (1925–31), Soiuzsprit SSSR (1931–32)

f. 1562 Tsentral'noe statisticheskoe upravlenie

f. 3429 Vysshii Sovet Narodnogo Khoziaistva SSSR

f. 4372 Gosplan SSSR

f. 5240 Narkomtorg SSSR

f. 7604 Narkomat legkoi promyshlennosti SSSR

f. 7995 Narkomat tiazheloi promyshlennosti

f. 8043 Narkomsnab SSSR

f. 9305 Glavspirt SSSR

Rossiskii Tsentr Khraneniia i Izucheniia Dokumentov Noveishei Istorii (Russian Center for the Preservation and Study of Documents on Recent History, RTsKhIDNI)

f. 17 Tsentral'nyi komitet

Tsentral'nyi Gosudarstvennyi Arkhiv RSFSR (Central State Archive RSFSR, TsGA RSFSR)

f. 386 Ekonomicheskii sovet pri sovete narodnykh komissarov RSFSR

f. 406 Narodnyi komissariat raboche-krest'ianskoi inspektsii

f. 482 Narodnyi komissariat zdravookhraneniia RSFSR

f. 2306 Ministerstvo prosveshcheniia RSFSR

Moscow Archives

Moskovskii Oblastnoi Tsentr Dokumentatsii Noveishei Istorii (Moscow Oblast Center for the Documentation of Recent History, MOTsDNI)

f. 3 Moskovskii oblastnoi komitet VKP(b)

f. 4 Moskovskii gorodskoi komitet VKP(b)

f. 429 Partiinaia organizatsiia zavoda Serpa i Molota

f. 432 Partiinaia organizatsiia zavoda Dinamo

f. 433 Partiinaia organizatsiia Pervogo gosudarstvennogo avtomobil'nogo zavoda (im. Stalina)

f. 634 Moskovskii oblastnoi komitet VLKSM

Tsentral'nyi Gosudarstvennyi Arkhiv Moskovskoi Oblasti (Central State Archive of Moscow Oblast, TsGAMO)

f. 1921 Upravlenie rabochego snabzheniia Moskovskogo oblastnogo otdela snabzheniia

f. 4775 Moskovskoi oblastnoi statisticheskii otdel

Tsentral'nyi Gosudarstvennyi Arkhiv Oktiabr'skoi Revoliutsii i Sotsialisticheskogo Stroitel'stva g. Moskvy (Central State Archive of the October Revolution and Socialist Construction of the City of Moscow, TsGAORSS g. Moskvy)

f. 100 Zavod "Dinamo" (im. Kirova)

f. 176 Zavod "Serp i Molot"

f. 370 Zavod "Krasnaia roza"

f. 415 Avtozavod (im. Stalina)

f. 1289 Moskovskii komitet raboche-krest'ianskoi inspektsii

Saratov Archives

Gosudarstvennyi Arkhiv Saratovskoi Oblasti (State Archive of Saratov Oblast, GASO)

f. 19 Zavod "Zhest'"

f. 99

f. 274 Zavod im. V. I. Lenina

f. 229 Otdel zdravookhraneniia Saratovskogo gubispolkoma

f. 338 Saratovskii komitet raboche-krest'ianskoi inspektsii

f. 352 Zavod "Universal"

f. 356 Zavod "Sotrudnik revoliutsii"

f. 461 Ispolnitel'nyi komitet Saratovskogo gorodskogo Soveta

f. 521 Ispolnitel'nyi komitet Saratovskogo gubernskogo Soveta

f. 1295 Komissii po chistke sovetskogo apparata

Saratovskii Oblastnoi Tsentr Dokumentatsii Noveishei Istorii (Saratov Oblast Center
    for the Documentation of Recent History, SOTsDNI)

f. 27 Saratovskii gubernskii komitet VKP(b)

f. 28 Saratovskaia organizatsiia VLKSM

f. 81 1-i Raikom VKP(b) g. Saratova

f. 136 2-i Raikom VKP(b) g. Saratova

f. 138 3-i Raikom VKP(b) g. Saratova

Tomsk Archives

Gosudarstvennyi Arkhiv Tomskoi Oblasti (State Archive of Tomsk Oblast, GATO)

f. R-163 Tomskii komitet raboche-krest'ianskoi inspektsii

f. R-279 Tomskii gubernii militsii

Tomskii Oblastnoi Tsentr Dokumentatsii Noveishei Istorii (Tomsk Oblast Center for
    the Documentation of Recent History, TOTsDNI)

f. 76 Tomskii uezd TsK RKP statistichiskii otdel

Central Ukrainian Archives

Tsentral'nii Derzhavnii Arkhiv Zhovtnevoi Revoliutsii, Vyshchykh Orhaniv Derzhavnoi
    Vlady i Orhaniv Derzhavnoho Upravlinni Ukrainskoi RSR (Central State Archive
    of the October Revolution, Highest Organs of State Government, and Organs of
    State Administration of the Ukrainian RSR, TsDAZhR URSR)

f. 6 Golovne upravlinnia selianskoi militsii

f. 44 Tsentrosprit

f. 342 Narkomzdrav

f. 2605 Vseukrainskii tsentral'nyi sovet profsoiuzov

Partiinyi Arkhiv Instytutu Istorii Partii pry Tsentral'nomu Komiteti Komunistychnoi
    Partii Ukrainy (Party Archive of the Institute of History of the Central Committee
    of the Ukrainian Communist Party, PA KPU)

f. 1 Tsentral'ny komitet kommunisticheskoi partii Ukrainy

f. 7 Tsentral'ny komitet leninskogo kommunisticheskogo soiuza molodezhi

Khar'kov Archives

Gosudarstvennyi Arkhiv Khar'kovskoi Oblasti (State Archive of Khar'kov Oblast,
    GAKhO)

f. 408

f. 845 Spirotresta

f. 855 Khar'kovskii otdel zdravookhraneniia

f. 948 Zavod "Serp i Molot"

f. 1010 Khar'kovskii raikom profsoiuza metallistov

Khar'kovskii Oblastnoi Tsentr Dokumentatsii Noveishei Istorii (Khar'kov Oblast Center for the Documentation of Recent History, KhOTsDNI)

f. 3

f. 27

JOURNALS AND NEWSPAPERS

Administrativnyi vestnik. Commissariat of Internal Affairs.

Bezbozhnik i stanka. Society of the Godless.

Biulleten' narodn'ogo komissariiatu zdarov'ia. Kar'kov, Ukrainian Commissariat of Public Health.

Biulleten' narodn'ogo komissariata zdravookhraneniia. Commissariat of Public Health.

Biulleten' tsentrospirta. State Alcohol Monopoly.

Ezhenedel'nik sovetskoi iustitsii. Commissariat of Justice.

Gazeta Kopeika. Kopeika Publishing House.

Gigiena i epidemiologiia. Commissariat of Public Health.

Gigiena i populiarnoi meditsiny. Commissariat of Public Health.

Gigiena i sanitariia. Commissariat of Public Health.

Gigiena i zdorov'e rabochei i krest'ianskoi sem'i. Institute of Sanitary Culture.

Izvestiia. Official organ of the government.

Izvestiia tekstil'noi promyshlennosti i torgovli. Textile Workers Union.

Khar'kovskaia pravda. Khar'kov Committee of the Communist Party.

Khar'kovskii parovozostroitel'nyi zavod. Khar'kov locomotive factory.

Khar'kovskii proletarii. Khar'kov Oblast Council of Trade Unions.

Klub. All-Union Central Council of Trade Unions.

Kommuna. Tomsk Committee of the Communist Party.

Komsomolets' Ukraini. Central Committee of the Ukrainian Komsomol.

Komsomol'skaia pravda. Central Committee of the Komsomol.

Krasnaia Sibirianka. Tomsk Communist Party.

Krasnyi putlivots. Putilov metalworks.

Krasnyi treugol'nik. Krasnyi Treugol'nik rubber works.

Kul'tura i byt. Official OBSA journal.

Kul'turnaia revoliutsiia. All-Union Central Council of Trade Unions.

Legkaia industriia. Commissariat of Light Industry.

Leningradskii meditsinskii zhurnal. Leningrad Department of Health.

Literaturnaia gazeta. Writers' Union.

Metallist. Metalworkers' Union.

Molodaia gvardiia. Central Committee of the Komsomol.

Molodoi bol'shevik. Moscow city Komsomol.

Molodoi Leninets. Saratov Komsomol.

Moskovskii meditsinskii zhurnal. Moscow Department of Health.

Moskovskii proletarii. Moscow Oblast Council of Trade Unions.

Nevrologicheskii vestnik. Moscow Congress of Physicians.

Nizhnee Povolzh'e. Journal of Saratov Planning Commission.

Obozrenie psikhiatr. St. Petersburg Society of Psychiatrists.

Pechatnik. Printers' Union.

Planovoe khoziaistvo. Journal of Gosplan.

Povolzhskaia pravda. Saratov Committee of the Communist Party.

Pravda. Central Committee of the Communist Party.

Proletarii. Ukrainian Council of Trade Unions.

Puti industrializatsii. All-Union Economic Council.

Put' k zdorov'iu. Khar'kov branch of OBSA.

Rabochaia gazeta. Central Committee of the Communist Party.

Rabochaia Moskva. Moscow City Council.

Rabochii bumazhnik. Papermakers' Union.

Rabochii golos. Social Democrats.

Rabotnitsa. Pravda Publishing House.

Rabotnitsa i domashniaia khoziaika. Pravda Publishing.

Rabotnitsa i krest'ianka. Leningrad Communist Party.

Russkii vrach. St. Petersburg medical journal.

Saratovskie izvestiia. Saratov City Soviet.

Serp i molot. Ukrainian Metalworkers' Union.

Shliakh do zdorov'ia. All-Ukrainian branch of OBSA.

Sibir. Prerevolutionary popular journal.

Sibirskii meditsinskii zhurnal. Tomsk Department of Health.

Sotsial'naia gigiena. Institute of Social Hygiene.

Sovetskoe zdravookhranenie. Commissariat of Public Health.

Statistika truda. Central Bureau of Labor Statistics.

Statisticheskoe obozrenie. Central Statistical Administration.

Stroitel'. Construction Workers' Union.

Trezvaia zhizn'. Aleksandr Nevskii Temperance Society.

Trezvost i kul'tura. OBSA.

Trud. Central Council of Trade Unions.

Udarnik. Central Council of Trade Unions.

Vestnik truda. Commissariat of Labor.

Visnik statistiki Ukraini. Ukrainian Statistical Administration.

Voprosy narkologii. Moscow Psycho-neurological Institute.

Voprosy zdravookhraneniia. Commissariat of Public Health.

Za novyi byt. Moscow Department of Public Health.

Za trezvisti. Khar'kov branch of OBSA.

Za zdorovyi truda i byt. Commissariat of Health.

Zdorov'e. Prerevolutionary popular medical journal, St. Petersburg.

PUBLISHED SOURCES

Alkogolizm promyshlennykh rabochikh i bor'ba s nim. Moscow, 1920.

Alkogolizm v sovremennoi derevne. Moscow, 1929.

Alpatov, D. M. *Alkogolizm sredi shkol'nikov i mery bor'by s nim.* Voronezh, 1929.

Amosov, N. K. *O p'ianykh prazdnikakh.* Moscow, 1929.

"Ankety Gosspirta po 48 guberniiam (obrabotka Gosplana)." *Planovoe khoziaistvo* nos. 4–5 (1924).

Bednyi, D. *P'ianka.* Moscow, 1928.

Belliustin, I. S. *Description of the Parish Clergy in Rural Russia: The Memoir of a Nineteenth-Century Priest.* Trans. and with an introductory essay by Gregory L. Freeze. Ithaca, 1985.

Berliand, A. S. *Alkogolizm i bor'ba s nim.* Moscow, 1927.

———. *Alkogolizm v khudozhestvennoi literatury: Khrestomatie.* Moscow, 1930.

Berliand, A. S., and Ia. Strashun, eds. *Sanitarnoe prosveshchenie v rabochet klube.* Moscow, 1925.

Bol'shaia Sovetskaia Entsiklopediia. 1st ed. Moscow, 1926. S.v. "Alkogolizm."

Bol'shakov, A. M. *Sovetskaia derevnia (1917–1924 gg).* Leningrad, 1924.

Bor'ba s alkogolizmom v SSSR. Pervyi plenum Vsesoiuznogo Soveta protivoalkogolnykh obshchestv v SSSR (30/V–1/VI 1929). Moscow-Leningrad, 1929.

Borodin, D. N. *Itogi vinnoi monopolii i zadachi budushchego.* St. Petersburg, 1908.

———. *Itogi rabot pervogo vserossiiskogo s"ezda po bor'be s p'ianstvom.* St. Petersburg, 1910.

Bugaiskii, Ia. *Khuliganstvo kak sotsial'no-patologigeskoe iavlenie.* Moscow, 1927.

Burak, Iu. Ia. *Kak i pochemu Sovetskaia vlast' boretsia s alkogolizmom.* Moscow, 1925.

Buzinov, A. *Za Nevskoi zastavoi: Zapiski rabochego.* Moscow, 1930.

Chebysheva-Dmitrieva, E. A. *Rol' zhenshchiny v bor'be s alkogolizmom.* St. Petersburg, 1904.

Cherliunchakaevich, N., ed. *Alkogolizm v sovremennoi derevne.* Moscow, 1929.

Deichman, E. I. *Alkogolizm i bor'ba s nim.* Moscow, 1929.

Dembo, G. I. *Ocherki deiatel'nosti kommissii po voprosu ob alkogolizme za 15 let, 1898–1913.* St. Petersburg, 1913.

Didrikhson, B. F. *Alkogolizm i proizvoditel'nost' truda.* Leningrad, 1931.

Dmitriev, V. K. *Kriticheskie issledovaniia o potreblenii alkogolia v Rossii.* Moscow, 1911.

Dreiden, S. D. *Antialkogol'naia pabota v klube.* Leningrad, 1930.

———. *Za vashe zdorove: Antialkogol'naia krestomatiia.* Leningrad, 1929.

Druzhinin, N. M. *Gosudarstvennye krest'iane i reforma P. D. Kiseleva.* Moscow, 1946.

"Ekonomicheskoe polozhenie Rossii pered revoliutsei." *Russkii arkhiv* 10, no. 3 (1925): 67–94.

Emel'ianov, A. V. *P'ianitsa-soiuznik klassogo vraga.* Moscow-Leningrad, 1930.

Etnograficheskii sbornik izd. Imperatorskim Russkim geograficheskim obshchestvom. 2 vols. St. Petersburg, 1830–34.

Fabriki i zavody Moskovskoi oblasti na 1928–29 god. Moscow, 1929.

4th *Eniseiskii gubernskii s"ezd sovetov rabochikh, krestianskikh i krasnoarmeiskikh deputatov. 5–9 Dekabria, 1922.* Krasnoiarsk, 1923.

Frenkel, Z. G. *Obshchestvennaia meditsina i sotsial'naia gigiena.* Leningrad, 1926.

Fridman, M. I. *Vinnaia monopliia.* 2 vols. St. Petersburg, 1914–16.

Gabinov, L. A. *Pochemu v Sovetskom Soiuze razreshena prodazha spirtynykh napitkov?* Khar'kov, 1927.

Gernet, M. N. *Prestupnost' za granitsei i v SSSR.* Moscow, 1931.

Gersevanov, N. *O p'ianstve v Rossii i sredstvakh istrebleniia ego.* Odessa, 1845.

_____. *Prestupnni mir Moskvu.* Moscow, 1924.

Gertsenzon, A. A. *Bor'ba s prestupnost'iu v RSFSR.* Moscow, 1928.

_____. *Prestupnost' i alkogolizm v RSFSR.* Moscow, 1930.

Getsov, G. B. *Zhenshchina na bor'bu s alkogolizmom.* Moscow, 1929.

Golant, P. Ia. *Alkogolizm i narkotizm na osnovanii opyta Leningrada. Trudy 1-go Vsesoiuznogo soveshchaniia po psikhiatrii i nevrologii i gosudarstvennogo nevropsikhiatricheskogo dispansera.* Ul'ianovsk, 1926.

Gregor'iev, N. I. *Alkogolizm i prestupleniia v Peterburge.* St. Petersburg, 1900.

Gurevich, Z. A., and A. Z. Zalevskii. *Alkogolizm: Sotsial'no-gigienicheskoe issledovanie.* Khar'kov, 1930.

Iakovlev, Ia. *Derevnia kak ona est': Ocherki Nikol'skoi volosti.* Moscow, 1923.

Kabo, E. O. *Ocherki rabochego byta.* Moscow, 1928.

Kanel', V. Ia. *Alkogolizm i bor'ba s nim.* Moscow, 1914.

Kaplun, S. I. *Obshchaia gigiena truda.* Moscow, 1940.

Kapustin, A. I. *Udarniki: Praktika raboty udarnykh brigad.* Moscow, 1930.

Khar'kovshchina v tsifrakh i faktakh (materialy k otchetnoi kampanii sovetov). Khar'kov, 1929.

Kniga o vkusnoi i zdorovoi pishche. Moscow, 1936.

Kolontai, A. *Rabotnitsa-mat'.* Omsk, 1920.

Kolpakov, M. N. *K voprosu ob alkogolizme v S. Peterburge i o merakh obshchestvennoi bor'by s nim.* St. Petersburg, 1896.

Korovin, A. M. *Blagotvoritel'nost' i alkogolizm.* Moscow, 1901.

Kovgankin, B. S. *Alkogol', alkogolizm i bor'ba s nim: Konspekt dlia vystuplenii vrachov, sester, agitatorov i propagandistov.* Moscow, 1927.

Lapitskaia, S. *Byt rabochikh Trekhgornoi manufaktury.* Moscow, 1935.

Larin, Iu. *Alkogolizm i sotsializm.* Moscow, 1929.

_____. *Alkogolizm promyshlennykh rabochikh i bor'ba s nim.* Moscow, 1929.

_____. *Novye zakony protiv alkogolizma i protivoalkogol'noe dvizhenie.* Moscow, 1929.

Lavrov, V. M., ed. *Sibir' v 1923–24g.* Tomsk, 1925.

Lebedev, S. V. *Potreblenie alkogolnyikh napitkov.* Tomsk, 1923.

Leninskoe pokolenie: Stat'i, vospominanie. Leningrad, 1925.

Lifshits, Ia. I. *Alkogol' i trud.* Khar'kov, 1929.

_____. *Bor'ba s p'ianstvom.* Khar'kov, 1929.

Materialy po istorii sovremennogo protivoalkogol'nogo dvizheniia v Rossii. St. Petersburg, 1913.

Ministerstvo finansov, 1802–1902. 2 vols. St. Petersburg, 1904.

Minor, L. S. *Chisla i nabliudeniia iz oblasti alkogolizma.* Moscow, 1910.

Mints, L. E., ed. *Voprosy truda v tsifrakh: Statisticheski spravochnik za 1927–39gg. (k XVI s"ezdu VKP[b]).* Moscow, 1930.

Mol'kov, A. V., ed. *Alkogolizm kak nauchnaia i bytovaia problema.* Moscow-Leningrad, 1928.

_____. "Alkogolizm kak problema izucheniia." *Gigiena i epidemiologiia* nos. 7–8 (1926): 37–46.

Nizhegorodtsev, M. N., ed. *Alkogolizm i bor'ba s nim.* St. Petersburg, 1909.

Oktiabr'skie dni v Tomske: Opasanie krovavykh' sobytii 20–23 Oktiab'ria. Tomsk, 1905.

Otchet Moskovskogo stolichnogo popechitel'stva o narodnoi trezvosti. Moscow, 1906.

Ozerv', I. Kh. *Alkogolizm i bor'ba s nim.* Moscow, 1914.

Pazhitnov, K. A. *Polozhenie rabochego klassa v Rossii.* Leningrad, 1925.

Pervushin, S. A. *Opyt' teorii massovogo alkogolizma v sviazi s teoriei potrebnostei.* St. Petersburg, 1912.

_____. *Vliianie urozhaev na potreblenie spirtnykh napitkov v Rossii.* St. Petersburg, 1909.

Pis'ma I. V. Stalina V. M. Molotovu, 1925–1936 gg. Moscow, 1995.

Popechitel'stva o narodnoi trezvosti v 1905 godu. 4 vols. St. Petersburg, 1908.

Prikhod'ko, P. T. *Fizicheskoe razvitie i zdorov'e gorno-rabochikh.* Tomsk, 1928.

_____. *Okhrana zdorov'ia, trud, i byt trudiashchikhsia.* Tomsk, 1930.

Pryzhov, I. T. *Istoriia kabakov v Rossii (v sviazi s istoriei russkogo naroda).* 1868. Reprint, Moscow, 1991.

Rashin, A. G. *Sostav fabrichno-zavodskogo proletariata SSSR: Predvaritel'nye itogi perepisi metalistov, gornorabochikh i tekstil'shchikov v 1929 g.* Moscow, 1930.

Rasskazy o Zapadnoi Sibiri ili o guberniiakh Tobol'skoi i Tomskoi. Moscow, 1898.

Rokhlin, I. *Trud, byt i zdorov'e partiinogo aktiva.* Dvou, 1931.

Rubakin, N. *Rasskazy o Zapadnoi Sibiri.* Moscow, 1908.

Sazhin, I. V. *Alkogolizm v armii.* St. Petersburg, 1907.

Semashko, N. A. *Kul'turnaia revoliutsiia i ozdorovlenie byta.* Moscow, 1929.

_____. *Na borbu s p'ianstvom.* Moscow, 1926.

Shipov, N. N. *Alkogolizm i revoliutsiia.* St. Petersburg, 1908.

Sholomovich, A. S. *Kak my boremsia s alkogolizmom.* Moscow, 1926.

Sigal, B. *Sud nad mater'iu, vinovnoi v plokhom ukhode za det'mi, povlekshem za soboi smert rebenka.* Moscow, 1926.

_____. *Sud nad p'ianitsei.* Moscow, 1929.

Slepkov, A., ed. *Byt i molodezh'.* Moscow, 1926.

Smirnov, I. N., ed. *Bor'ba za Ural i Sibir': Vospominaniia i stat'i.* Moscow, 1926.

Sobranie uzakonenii i rasporiazhenii rabochego i krestianskogo pravitel'stva, 1917–1938. Moscow, 1938.

Statistika po kazennoi prodazhe pitei, 1912–1914. Vyp III (Materialy o chisle mest prodazhi spirtnyikh napitkov). St. Petersburg, 1914.

Statistika proizvodstve aktsizom: Potreblenie 40% vina v 1913. St. Petersburg, 1913.

Statistka proizvodstve oblagaemyikh aktsizom' (s predvaritel'nymi dannymi za 1913 po vinokurennoi promyshlennosti). Vyp. II, chast I. St. Petersburg, 1914.

Stenogrammy dokladov Tsentrosoiuza SSSR, VSNKh SSSR, Narkomzdrovov RSFSR i SSSR na zasedanii protivoalkogol'nykh obshchestv v SSSR. Moscow-Leningrad, 1929.

Svedieniia piteinykh sborakh v Rossii. St. Petersburg, 1860.

Tian-Shanskaia, O. S. *Village Life in Late Tsarist Russia.* Trans. and ed. David L. Ransel. Bloomington, 1993.

Tiapugin, N. *Narodnye zabluzhdeniia i nauchnaia pravda ob alkogole.* Moscow, 1926.

Tomilin, S. A. "Rasprostranenie samogona sredi sel'skogo naseleniia Ukrainy." *Profilaktika meditsina* nos. 11–12 (1924).

TsU RSFSR. *Alkogolizm v sovremennoi derevne.* Moscow, 1929.

Trakhtman, Ia., ed. *Sanitarnoe prosveshchenie v otryvkakh khudozhestvennoi literatury: Krestomatiia.* Moscow, 1928.

Trudy kommissii po voprosam ob alkogolizme, merakh bor'by s nim, i dlia vyrabotki normal'nago ustava zavedenii dlia alkigolikov. Vyp. VII i VIII. St. Petersburg, 1905.

Trudy kommissii po voprosam ob alkogolizme i merakh bor'by s nim. 4 vols. St. Petersburg, 1900.

Trudy kommissii po voprosu ob alkogolizme. St. Petersburg, 1899.

Trudy pervogo vserossiiskogo s"ezda po bor'be s p'ianstvom. 3 vols. St. Petersburg, 1910.

Trudy postoiannoi kommissii po voprosu ob alkogolizme. 14 vols. St. Petersburg, 1913.

"'Vos'moi godichnyi otchet' pervogo Moskovskogo obshchestva trezvosti za 1903 god.* Moscow, 1904.

Vlassak, R. *Alkogolizm.* Moscow, 1928.

Voronov, D. N. *Alkogolizm v sovremennom bytu.* Moscow, 1930.

____. "Analiz derevenskogo alkogolizma i samogonnogo promysla." *Voprosy Narkologii* no. 3 (1926): 51–70.

VTs SPS. *Trud v SSSR, 1926–30gg: Spravochik.* Moscow, 1930.

SECONDARY SOURCES

Abrams, Lynn. *Workers' Culture in Imperial Germany: Leisure and Recreation in the Rhineland and Westphalia.* New York, 1992.

Ambler, Charles, and Jonathan Crush, eds. *Liquor and Labor in South Africa.* Athens, 1992.

Anderle, Vladimir. *Workers in Stalin's Russia.* New York, 1988.

Antonov-Romanovskii, G. V. *P'ianstvo pod zapretom zakona.* Moscow, 1985.

Babayan, E. A., and M. H. Gonopolsky. *Textbook on Alcoholism and Drug Abuse in the Soviet Union.* New York, 1985.

Balzer, Marjorie Mandelstain. *Russian Traditional Culture: Religion, Gender, and Customary Law.* New York, 1992.

Barrows, Susanna, and Robin Room, eds. *Drinking: Behavior and Belief in Modern History.* Berkeley, 1991.

Bauer, Raymond A. *The New Man in Soviet Psychology.* Cambridge, 1959.

Birman, R. S. *Moskovskii metallurgicheskii zavod "Serp i molot."* Moscow, 1967.

Bor'ba trudiashchikhsia Khar'kovshchiny za sozdanie fundamenta sotsialisticheskoi ekonomiki (1926–32). Khar'kov, 1960.

Bordiugov, G. A. "Problemy bor'by s sotsial'nymi anomaliiami v pervom piatiletnem plane." In *Opyt planirovaniia kul'turnogo stroitel'stva v SSSR.* Moscow, 1988.

———. "Sotsial'nyi parazitizm ili sotsial'nye anomalii? (Iz istorii bor'by s alkogoliz-mom, nishchenstvom, prostitutsiei, brodiazhnichestvom v 20–30-e gody)." *Istoriia SSSR* no. 1 (1989): 60–74.

Borzek, Josef, and Dan Slobin. *Psychology in the USSR: An Historical Perspective.* White Plains, 1972.

Bourdieu, Pierre. *Language and Symbolic Power.* Cambridge, 1991.

Bradley, Joseph. *Muzhik and Muscovite: Urbanization in Late Imperial Russia.* Berkeley, 1985.

Brennan, Thomas. *Public Drinking and Popular Culture in Eighteenth-Century France.* Princeton, 1988.

Brooks, Jeffrey. *Thank You Comrade Stalin! Soviet Public Culture from Revolution to Cold War.* Newark, 2000.

———. *When Russia Learned to Read: Literacy and Popular Literature, 1861–1917.* Princeton, 1985.

Brown, Julie V. "Revolution and Psychosis: The Mixing of Science and Politics in Russian Psychiatric Medicine, 1905–1913." *Russian Review* 46, no. 3 (1987): 283–302.

Cassidy, Julie. "Alcohol Is Our Enemy! Soviet Temperance Melodrama of the 1920s." In *Two Centuries of Melodrama in Russia,* ed. L. McReynolds and J. Neuberger, 152–77. Durham, 2002.

———. *The Enemy on Trial: Early Soviet Courts on Stage and Screen.* DeKalb, 2000.

Chase, William. *Workers, Society, and the Soviet State: Labor and Life in Moscow, 1918–1929.* Champaign-Urbana, 1987.

Chase, William, and Lewis Siegelbaum. "Worktime and Industrialization in the USSR, 1917–1941." In *Work and Industrialization: An International History,* ed. Gary Cross, 183–216. Philadelphia, 1988.

Christian, David. *"Living Water": Vodka and Russian Society on the Eve of Emancipation.* Oxford, 1990.

———. "Prohibition in Russia, 1914–1925." *Australian Slavonic and East European Studies* 9, no. 2 (1995): 89–118.

Christian, David, and R. E. F. Smith. *Bread and Salt: A Social and Economic History of Food and Drink in Russia.* Cambridge, 1984.

Clark, Katerina. *Petersburg, Crucible of Cultural Revolution.* Cambridge, 1995.

Clements, Barbara Evans, Rebecca Friedman, and Dan Healy, eds. *Russian Masculinities in History and Culture.* London, 2002.

Clowes, Edith W., Samuel Kassow, and James West, eds. *Between Tsar and People: Educated Society and the Quest for Public Identity in Late Imperial Russia.* Princeton, 1991.

Connor, Walter D. "Alcohol and Soviet Society." *Slavic Review* 30, no. 3 (September 1971): 570–88.

_____. *Deviance in Soviet Society: Crime, Delinquency and Alcoholism.* New York, 1972.

Conrad, Peter, and Joseph W. Schneider. *Deviance and Medicalization: From Badness to Sickness.* Philadelphia, 1992.

Conroy, David W. *In Public Houses: Drink and the Revolution of Authority in Colonial Massachusetts.* Chapel Hill, 1995.

Crisp, Olga, and Linda Edmondson, eds. *Civil Rights in Imperial Russia.* Oxford, 1989.

David-Fox, Michael. "What Is Cultural Revolution?" *Russian Review* 58 (April 1999): 181–201.

Davies, R. W. *The Development of the Soviet Budgetary System.* Cambridge, 1958.

Dixon, Simon. "The Church's Social Role in St. Petersburg, 1880–1914." In *Church, Nation, and State in Russia and Ukraine,* ed. G. Hosking, 167–92. New York, 1991.

Dlia chego liudi odurmanivaliutsia. Moscow, 1988.

Eklof, Ben, John Bushnell, and Larissa Zakharova, eds. *Russia's Great Reforms, 1855–1881.* Bloomington, 1994.

Engelstein, Laura. *The Keys to Happiness: Sex and the Search for Modernity in Fin-de-siècle Russia.* Ithaca, 1992.

Eriksen, Sidsel. "Alcohol as a Gender Symbol." *Scandinavian Journal of History* 24 (1999): 45–73.

Erlich, Alexander. *The Soviet Industrialization Debate, 1924–1928.* Cambridge, 1960.

Fedorov, V. A. "Krest'ianskoe trezvennoe dvizhenie, 1858–1860 gg." In *Revoliutsionnaia situatsiia v Rossii v 1859–1861 gg.,* ed. M. V. Netchkina. Moscow, 1962.

Filtzer, Donald. *Soviet Workers and Stalinist Industrialization.* New York, 1986.

Fitzpatrick, Sheila, *Cultural Revolution in Russia, 1928–1931.* Bloomington, 1978.

_____, ed. *Stalinism: New Directions.* London, 2000.

Fitzpatrick, Sheila, Alexander Rabinowitch, and Richard Stites, eds. *Russia in the Era of NEP: Explorations in Soviet Society and Culture.* Bloomington, 1991.

Frank, Stephen P. *Crime, Cultural Conflict, and Justice in Rural Russia, 1856–1914.* Berkeley, 1999.

Frank, Stephen P., and Mark D. Steinberg, eds. *Cultures in Flux: Lower-Class Values, Practices, and Resistance in Late Imperial Russia.* Princeton, 1994.

Frieden, Nancy Mandelker. *Russian Physicians in an Era of Reform and Revolution, 1856–1905.* Princeton, 1981.

Gilman, Sander. *Picturing Health and Illness: Images of Identity and Difference.* Baltimore, 1995.

Goldman, Wendy. *Women at the Gates: Gender and Industry in Stalin's Russia.* New York, 2002.

Gorsuch, Anne E. *Youth in Revolutionary Russia: Enthusiasts, Bohemians, Delinquents.* Bloomington, 2000.

Gusfield, Joseph R. *Contested Meanings: The Construction of Alcohol Problems.* Madison, 1996.

Haine, W. Scott. *The World of the Paris Cafe: Sociability among the French Working Class, 1789–1914*. Baltimore, 1996.

Hamm, Michael F., ed. *The City in Late Imperial Russia*. Bloomington, 1986.

Herlihy, Patricia. *The Alcoholic Empire: Vodka and Politics in Late Imperial Russia*. New York, 2002.

_____. "The Joy of Rus': Rites and Rituals of Russian Drinking." *Russian Review* 50, no. 2 (April 1991): 131–47.

_____. "The Russian Orthodox Church and Alcoholism." Paper presented at the annual meeting of the American Association for the Advancement of Slavic Studies, Honolulu, November, 1988.

Hoffman, David L. *Peasant Metropolis: Social Identities in Moscow, 1929–1941*. Ithaca, 1994.

_____. *Stalinist Values: The Cultural Norms of Soviet Modernity, 1917–1941*. Ithaca, 2003.

Husband, William B. *"Godless Communists": Atheism and Society in Soviet Russia, 1917–1932*. DeKalb, 2000.

Hutchinson, J. F. *Politics and Public Health in Revolutionary Russia, 1890–1918*. Baltimore, 1990.

_____. "Science, Politics and the Alcohol Problem in post-1905 Russia." *Slavonic and East European Review* 58, no. 2 (April 1980): 232–54.

Hutchinson, J. F., and Susan Gross Solomon, eds. *Health and Society in Revolutionary Russia*. Bloomington, 1990.

Istoriia fabrik i zavodov SSSR. Moscow, 1956.

Iz istorii bor'by trudiashchikhsia Moskvy i Moskovskoi oblasti za ustanovlenie Sovetskoi vlasti i sotsialisticheskow stroitel'stvo: Sbornik trudov. Moscow, 1977.

Izmeneniia sotsial'noi struktury sovetskogo obshchestva, 1921–seredina '30-kh godov. Moscow, 1979.

Khromov, P. A. *Ekonomicheskoe razvitie Rossii v XIX–XX vekakh, 1800–1917*. Moscow, 1950.

Kingston-Mann, Esther, and Timothy Mixter, eds. *Peasant Economy, Culture, and Politics of European Russia, 1800–1921*. Princeton, 1991.

Korzhikhina, T. P. "Bor'ba s alkogolizmom v 1920-e—nachale 1930-kh godov." *Voprosy istorii* no. 9 (1985): 20–32.

Kotkin, Stephen. *Magnetic Mountain: Stalinism as a Civilization*. Berkeley, 1995.

Kovrigina, Mariia D., ed. *Forty Years of Soviet Public Health*. New York, 1959.

KPSS v rezoliutsiiakh i resheniiakh s"ezdov, konferentsii i plenumov TsK. Vol. 2. Moscow, 1983.

Krasnov-Levitin, A. *Likhie gody, 1925–41*. Paris, 1977.

Krawchenko, B. *Social Change and National Consciousness in Twentieth-Century Ukraine*. New York, 1985.

Kruchina, Evgenii. *Vodka: Putevoditel'*. Moscow, 2003.

Kuromiya, Hiroaki. *Stalin's Industrial Revolution: Politics and Workers, 1928–1932*. Cambridge, 1988.

Lebina, Natalia. "The Crisis of Proletarian Identity in the Soviet Factory, 1928–29." *Slavic Review* 44, no. 2 (1985): 280–97.

_____. "'Papa, otdai den'gi mame. . . .'" *Rodina* no. 12 (Winter 1996): 69–75.

Lewin, Moshe. *The Making of the Soviet System: Essays in the Social History of Interwar Russia.* New York, 1985.

Lotova, E. I. "Opyt antialkogol'nogo vospitaniia v shkole v 20–30kh godakh." *Sovetskoe zdravookhranenie* no. 9 (1976): 76–79.

_____. *Russkaia intelligentsiia i voprosy obshchestvennoi gigieny: Pervie gigienicheskoe obshchestvo v Rossii.* Moscow, 1962.

Lotova, E. I., and A. V. K. Pavluchkova. "K istorii sozdaniia i deiatel'nosti Vsesoiuznogo obshchestva bor'by s alkogolizmom." *Sovetskoe zdravookhranenie* no. 2 (1972): 65–69.

Mally, Lynn. *Revolutionary Acts: Amateur Theater and the Soviet State, 1917–1938.* Ithaca, 2000.

McKee, Arthur W. "Sobering Up the Soul of the People: The Politics of Popular Temperance in Late Imperial Russia." *Russian Review* 58 (April 1999): 212–43.

_____. "Taming the Green Serpent: Alcoholism, Autocracy, and Russian Society, 1890–1917." Ph.D. diss., University of California, Berkeley, 1997.

Michaels, Paula A. *Curative Powers: Medicine and Empire in Stalin's Central Asia.* Pittsburgh, 2003.

Mikhailovskii, I. N. *Komsomol Ukrainy v bor'be za postroenie sotsializma v SSSR (1925–37 gg).* L'vov, 1966.

Miller, Martin. "Freudian Theory under Bolshevik Rule: The Theoretical Controversy during the 1920s." *Slavic Review* 44, no. 4 (Winter 1985): 625–46.

Murdock, Catherine Gilbert. *Domesticating Drink: Women, Men, and Alcohol in America, 1870–1940.* Baltimore, 1998.

Neuberger, Joan. *Hooliganism: Crime, Culture, and Power in St. Petersburg, 1900–1914.* Berkeley, 1993.

Novikov, S. *Bor'ba VLKSM s p'ianstvom (1926–29).* Moscow, 1986.

Pervye shagi industrializatsii SSSR 1926–27. Moscow, 1959.

Petrochenko, P., and K. Kuznetsova. *Organizatsiia i normirovanie truda v promyshlennosti SSSR.* Moscow, 1971.

Phillips, Laura L. *The Bolsheviks and the Bottle: Drink and Worker Culture in St. Petersburg, 1900–1929.* DeKalb, 2000.

_____. "Everyday Life in Revolutionary Russia: Working-Class Drinking in Taverns in St. Petersburg, 1900–1929." Ph.D. diss., University of Illinois at Urbana-Champaign, 1993.

_____. "In Defense of Their Families: Working-Class Women, Alcohol, and Politics in Revolutionary Russia." *Journal of Women's History* 11, no. 2 (Spring 1999): 97–120.

Piatnadtsatyi s"ezd VKP(b). *Piatnadtsatyi s"ezd VKP(b): Stenograficheskii otchet (Dekabr' 1927 goda).* 2 vols. Moscow, 1961.

Plotnikov, K. N. *Biudzhet sotsialisticheskogo gosudarstva.* Moscow, 1948.

Prestwich, Patricia E. *Drink and the Politics of Social Reform: Antialcoholism in France since 1870.* Palo Alto, 1988.

_____. "French Workers and the Temperance Movement." *International Review of Social History* 25 (1980): 35–52.

Proceedings of the Fifteenth International Congress against Alcoholism, Washington, D.C., Sept. 21–26, 1920. Washington, D.C., 1921.

Promyshlennost' i rabochii klass Ukrainskoi SSR v period postroeniia fundamenta sotsialisticheskoi ekonomiki (1926–32 gody). Sbornik dokumentov i materialov. Kiev, 1966.

Roberts, James. *Drink, Temperance, and the Working Class in Nineteenth-Century Germany.* Boston, 1984.

Rosenberg, William G., and Lewis H. Siegelbaum, eds. *Social Dimensions of Soviet Industrialization.* Bloomington, 1993.

Rosenzweig, Roy. *Eight Hours for What We Will: Workers and Leisure in an Industrial City, 1870–1920.* Cambridge, 1983.

Rossman, Jeffery J. "The Teikovo Cotton Workers' Strike of April, 1932: Class, Gender, and Identity Politics in Stalin's Russia." *Russian Review* 56 (January 1997): 44–69.

Scott, James C. *Domination and the Arts of Resistance: Hidden Transcripts.* New Haven, 1990.

Segal, Boris. *Alkogolizm: Klinicheskie sotsial'no psikhologicheskie i biologicheskie problemy.* Moscow, 1967.

_____. *The Drunken Society: Alcohol Abuse and Alcoholism in the Soviet Union.* New York, 1990.

_____. *Russian Drinking: Use and Abuse of Alcohol in Prerevolutionary Russia.* New Brunswick, 1987.

Shakhmaev, Sergei, and Igor Korokin. *Kabak na Rusi: Pervaia pravidivaia istoriia rossiiskogo p'ianstvo.* New York, 1996.

Shearer, David R. "Crime and Social Disorder in Stalin's Russia: A Reassessment of the Great Retreat and the Origins of Mass Repression." *Cahiers du Monde russe* 39, nos. 1–2 (1998): 119–48.

Sheverdin, S. N. "Aktivizatsiia chelovecheskogo faktora i bor'ba za trezvyi obraz zhizni." *Kommunist* no. 12 (1985): 65.

_____. "God neznamenitogo pereloma +/-1." *Trezvost' i kul'tura* no. 9 (1989): 17–38.

_____. "Iz opyta bor'by protiv p'ianstva i alkogolizma." *Voprosy istorii KPSS* no. 9 (1985): 103–17.

Shlapentokh, Dmitry. "Drunkenness and Anarchy in Russia: A Case of Political Culture." *Russian History/Histoire russe* 18, no. 4 (1991): 457–500.

Siegelbaum, Lewis. "Socialist Competition and Socialist Construction in the USSR: The Experience of the First Five-Year Plan (1928–32)." *Thesis Eleven* no. 4 (1982): 48–67.

_____. *Soviet State and Society between Revolutions, 1918–1929.* Cambridge, 1992.

Siegelbaum, Lewis, and Ronald Grigor Suny, eds. *Making Workers Soviet: Power, Class and Identity.* Ithaca, 1994.

Smith, Steve A. "Russian Workers and the Politics of Social Identity." *Russian Review* 56 (January 1997): 1–7.

Solomon, Susan Gross. "David and Goliath in Soviet Public Health: The Rivalry of Social Hygienists and Psychiatrists for Authority Over the *Bytovoi* Alcoholic." *Soviet Studies* 12, no. 2 (April 1989): 254–75.

Strashun, I. D. *Russkaia obshchestvennaia meditsina v period mezhdu dvumia revoliutsiiami, 1907–1917 gg.* Moscow, 1964.

Straus, Kenneth. *Factory and Community in Stalin's Russia: The Making of an Industrial Working Class.* Pittsburgh, 1997.

Takala, I. R. *Veselie Rusi: Istoriia alkogol'noi problemy v Rossii.* St. Petersburg, 2002.

Thorner, Daniel, Basile Kerblay, and R. E. F. Smith, eds. *A. V. Chayanov on the Theory of Peasant Economy.* Homewood, 1996.

White, Stephan. *Russia Goes Dry: Alcohol, State, and Society.* Cambridge, 1996.

Wood, Elizabeth. "The Trial of Lenin: Legitimizing the Revolution Through Political Theater." *Russian Review* 61 (April 2002): 235–48.

INDEX

absenteeism, 26, 68

abstinence. *See* temperance

agitprop plays (agitational propaganda plays), 116–20; *Arapy*, 120; *On a New Path*, 117; *Pautina*, 118–19; *Smychka*, 120–21. See also *agitsudy*; anti-alcohol propaganda

agitsudy (agitation trials), 114–16; *Sud nad p'ianitsei* (Trial of a Drunk), 115–16

alcohol boycotts. *See* liquor boycotts

alcohol consumption, 94, 132, 154–55; among clergy, 18–19, 20, 42, 53; collective, 15–17, 20; deviant, 20; in dining halls, 141–42; modern (urban), 23–26; traditional (rural), 14–21, 43–44; upper-class concerns about, 40; and women, 10, 15; and worker skill level, 132, 133; in workplaces, 26–27, 68, 134–35; and youth, 19, 95. *See also* drinking practices

alcohol monopoly. *See* liquor monopoly

alcoholics: *bytovoi* (habitual), 82, 85, 112; forced treatment of, 61, 110

alcoholism, 7; causes of, 3, 47, 52–53, 56–57, 59, 83–85, 147–48; in the countryside, 20; definitions of, 2–3, 10, 46, 51–52, 56–57, 149; as a medical problem, 52, 55–56; and moral degeneration, 62; and professional discourse, 50–53, 57–65, 64; and the Russian Orthodox Church, 53–55; socialist definitions of, 59–63, 74, 149; and social problems, 62, 68; treatment of, 85–86. *See also* drunkenness

Alexander II, 43

Alexander Nevskii Temperance Society, 53–54

All-Russian Congress for the Struggle against Drunkenness. *See* First All-Russian Congress for the Struggle against Drunkenness

All-Union Council of Anti-Alcohol Societies. *See* VSPO

anti-alcohol campaign, 94–98, 151; assimilative reform, 104, 105, 106; coercive reform, 104, 110–12; and Gorbachev, 155–57; and Khrushchev, 155; and women, 96, 117; working-class participation in, 96–97; and youth, 95. *See also* OBSA; temperance

anti-alcohol education, 58–59

anti-alcohol propaganda, 84–85, 101–22. *See also* agitprop plays, *agitsudy*

Bol'shekov, A. M., 71

Bolshevik Communist Party: and alcohol policy, 93–95, 151–52; anti-alcohol sentiments in, 68–69, 73, 74–75, 98, 104, 109, 149; as colonizing power, 151; and cultural revolution, 127; cultural values, 75, 103, 105, 124, 145, 151; and the liquor monopoly, 72–73, 148–49; and political socialization, 99, 100, 113, 121, 152; and prohibition, 70; and propaganda, 101–2, 106–22; purges of, 111–12; and *samogon*, 76; and social reform, 104–6, 108, 120; and temperance movement, 89–91; and worker categorization, 128–30; working-class opposition to, 109, 137, 139, 142

Bednyi, D., 89, 106, 113

Bekhterev, Dr. V. M., 57

Belliustin, Father I. S., 20

bootlegging, 71–72, 78–80; and grain supplies, 70, 72; penalties for, 78–80; and state liquor revenues, 72; and women, 71–72, 76–80

Borodin, D. N., 57, 64

Brezhnev, L., 154

Bukharin, N. I., 74, 89, 90, 91, 125, 177n114